Indigeneity and Occupational Change

This book is about the presence of the absent – the tribes of Punjab, India, many of them still nomadic, constituting the poorest of the poor in the state. Drawing on exhaustive fieldwork and ethnographic accounts of more than 750 respondents, it explores the occupational change across generations to prove their presence in the state before the Criminal Tribes Act was implemented in 1871. The archival reports reveal the atrocities unleashed by the colonial government on these people. The volume shows how the post-colonial government too has proved no different; it has done little to bring them into the mainstream society by not exploiting their traditional expertise or equipping them with modern skills.

This book will be of great interest to scholars of sociology, social anthropology, social history, public policy, development studies, tribal communities and South Asian studies.

Birinder Pal Singh is Professor of Eminence in the Department of Sociology and Social Anthropology at Punjabi University, Patiala, India, where he joined as lecturer in 1976. He was a Fellow of the Indian Institute of Advanced Study, Shimla (1993–1995). His areas of study include tribal and peasant communities and the sociology of violence. His publications include: *Economy and Society in the Himalayas: Social Formation in Pangi Valley* (1996); *Problems of Violence: Themes in Literature* (1999); *Violence as Political Discourse: Sikh Militancy Confronts the Indian State* (2002); *Punjab Peasantry in Turmoil* (ed.; 2010); *'Criminal' Tribes of Punjab: A Social-Anthropological Inquiry* (ed.; 2010) and *Sikhs in the Deccan and North-East India* (2018). He has about 70 research papers and articles and has worked on seven research projects.

Indigeneity and Occupational Change
The Tribes of Punjab

Birinder Pal Singh

LONDON AND NEW YORK

First published 2020
by Routledge
2 Park Square, Milton Park, Abingdon, Oxon OX14 4RN

and by Routledge
52 Vanderbilt Avenue, New York, NY 10017

Routledge is an imprint of the Taylor & Francis Group, an informa business

© 2020 Birinder Pal Singh

The right of Birinder Pal Singh to be identified as author of this work has been asserted by him in accordance with sections 77 and 78 of the Copyright, Designs and Patents Act 1988.

All rights reserved. No part of this book may be reprinted or reproduced or utilised in any form or by any electronic, mechanical, or other means, now known or hereafter invented, including photocopying and recording, or in any information storage or retrieval system, without permission in writing from the publishers.

Trademark notice: Product or corporate names may be trademarks or registered trademarks, and are used only for identification and explanation without intent to infringe.

British Library Cataloguing-in-Publication Data
A catalogue record for this book is available from the British Library

Library of Congress Cataloging-in-Publication Data
A catalog record for this book has been requested

ISBN: 978-0-367-33586-1(hbk)
ISBN: 978-0-429-32133-7(ebk)

Typeset in Sabon
by Apex CoVantage, LLC

Contents

	List of figures	vi
	List of tables	vii
	Preface	viii
1	Presence of the absent: an introduction	1
2	Punjab and its people	13
3	Tribal communities in the colonial Punjab	26
4	Tribal communities in the post-colonial Punjab	63
5	Socio-economic profile of the tribal communities in Punjab	106
6	Occupations of the tribal communities	138
7	Intergenerational occupational change	149
8	In lieu of conclusion	162
	Glossary	202
	References	207
	Index	215

Figures

4.1	A Bazigar doing *bazi*	70
4.2	Bazigar women engaging the host	71
4.3	Bauria women	73
4.4	Bauria men	74
4.5	A Bangala with snake in *patari*	79
4.6	An old Barad couple	80
4.7	*Jude* and *binne* or *innus*	81
4.8	A Gandhila fisherman	84
4.9	A Sikligar at work	92
4.10	Gaadi Lohar women	94
4.11	A typical *gaadi* (bullock cart)	95
4.12	Instruments of Gaadi Lohars	96
4.13	A Gaadi Lohar at work	97
4.14	A Gujjar man	98
4.15	Kitchen side of a Gujjar dera	99
5.1	A tribal settlement	107
5.2	A *kulli* in making	115
5.3	A *kulli*	115
5.4	A well-built *kulli*	116

Tables

4.1	Population (sex- and area-wise) of 'other communities' of Punjab	65
5.1	Tribes	109
5.2	Family income	110
5.3	Family members	111
5.4	Sex of the respondents	112
5.5	Age of the respondents	112
5.6	House ownership	116
5.7	House type	117
5.8	Number of rooms	118
5.9	Roof type	120
5.10	Floor type	121
5.11	Kitchen	122
5.12	Toilet	122
5.13	Bathroom	123
5.14	Water source	124
5.15	Light source	125
5.16	Cooking source	127
5.17	Stove	128
5.18	Pressure cooker	128
5.19	Fan and cooler	129
5.20	Cot/bed	130
5.21	Television	130
5.22	Landline/mobile phones	131
5.23	Vehicles	132
5.24	Pets	134
5.25	Cattle	135
6.1	Types of occupations of the respondents	142
6.2	Seasonal cycle of work	145
6.3	Number of days of work	146
6.4	Are you satisfied with your present occupation?	147
7.1	Occupation of the respondents' fathers	151
7.2	Occupation of the respondents' mothers	155

Preface

The idea to undertake the present study has its roots in the project – *An ethnographic study of the nomadic, semi-nomadic and denotified tribes of Punjab* (2008a) – given by the Punjab government to the department of Sociology and Social Anthropology at Punjabi University, Patiala, to ascertain the tribal character of some communities contesting for tribal status. Until then, for us too, these tribal communities were absent from the state. Once having worked with them on their ethnography, some interesting aspects of their lives and history came to light that generated more interest in inquiring into their present and the past. The inquisitiveness to look into their history becomes more pronounced when one finds them declared as criminal tribes more than a century and a half ago. How come these people living with bare minimum means of subsistence and roaming around with or without some cattle could disturb the law and order of the land? Why were they perceived as a potential threat to the mighty colonial power? Why did such people thriving in forests for centuries become conspicuous to the foreign regime that declared an aggressive operation to hunt them out from their habitat and subject them to 'civilisational' processes of production and lifestyle? If they were criminals, what sort of crime they were committing and why? These are a few major questions that generated interest to look into the patterns of their livelihood and the occupations they were engaged in to make a living.

Three state universities established well over four decades, each with a department of sociology and the fourth one and the oldest in the region at Panjab University, Chandigarh (union territory), never made these people the subject of their research and study. Two of these universities with their centres for the study of exclusion and inclusive development too focused on the Scheduled Castes and within them on Balmiks (Harijan/Mazhabi) and Ramdasias/Ravidassis (Chamars) and did not bother about the tribal communities as tribes. The Institute for Development and Communication, Chandigarh, however, does include four tribes in its study *Status of Depressed Scheduled Castes in Punjab* (1996) but that too not as tribal communities but one amongst other depressed castes. This is despite the fact that Sher Singh Sher, a sociologist, had produced empirical studies on the Sikligars and the Sansis of the region as early as 1966 and 1965 respectively.

In the absence of social scientific studies of the tribal communities in Punjab, two types of studies are available. One is by the insiders, the members of own community writing largely about the socio-cultural aspects of own people. Darya (1997) writes about the Sansis, Inder Singh Valjot (2009) and Mohan Tyagi (2013) about the Bazigars. The first and the third are university teachers and the second one a practising lawyer. These works are in Punjabi. Other works in the same genre are by Kirpal Kazak on Sikligars (1990) and Gaadi Lohars (2005), and by Bhupinder Kaur on Gujjars (2010a). Chahal's (2007) work on Baurias is also in the same mould but in Hindi.

The present study of occupational change over generations in the tribes has been charted out with an intention to confirm their presence in the state where their very existence is negated. They are no longer acknowledged as tribal people but as a variant of the numerous low castes living on the periphery of the villages or in the slums of the state towns. The detailed interviews with respect to their traditional occupations and especially those of their elders – parents and grandparents – show beyond doubt that the majority of them were nomadic, so much so, that the respondents have returned invariably 'nomadism' as their ancestors' traditional occupation.

This is not at all clear that why such communities, duly identified and numerated in the census of 1881 by Denzil Ibbetson and given ethnographic details subsequently by Rose (1883/1970), have been declared to be absent altogether from the north Indian states of Punjab and Haryana. This is a subject of independent inquiry. A few preliminary attempts in this respect did not yield anything. How do the 'criminal' tribes declared denotified suddenly become the Scheduled Castes? It would be interesting to look into the dynamics of certain agency or agencies of decision-making and non–decision-making à la Bachrach and Baratz (1970) in the then power structure of the state. How have these communities been propelled out of their due listing in the Scheduled Tribes and included in the larger category of the Scheduled Castes whose share in the Punjab population is largest in the country? It is 31.94 per cent in 2011.

To study the occupations of the present generation and the traditional occupations of their ancestors with an eye on extensive interviews especially of the senior respondents, an interview questionnaire is served to the stratified sample of respondents randomly with open and closed questions. The details about their occupation, where opinions matter, are kept open to capture the range of views the respondents could deliver. The research investigators are asked to record such views verbatim and in the language of the respondent, that is, Punjabi. They are also instructed to maintain a field diary giving noteworthy details of each community and their own observations, critical and descriptive, not mentioned in the questionnaire. The research investigators are asked to note down the contact numbers of the well-informed and eloquent respondents who could be approached later for necessary information.

A total of 763 respondents belonging to ten major tribal communities across the state make the substantial sample. Certain communities have been clubbed under the major one since there are communities within communities. For instance, Sansi community comprises of numerous groups like Dehe, Kuch Bann, Chhaj Bann, Sirki Bann, Bhedkutt, Baan Batt, Gadaria etc. This community has 33 sub-groups, and many amongst them assume themselves to be independent ones. Most tribal communities were largely nomadic and semi-nomadic, though many of them are still to quite an extent. Such a size of the sample is sufficiently large given the homogeneity of the population on almost all the parameters of socio-economic indices. Their living conditions are quite similar even if there are income differences relatively. The better ones are few and far between, though they too are less likely to be distinguished from their poor fellow beings except in the ownership of a few extra gadgets or vehicles or a relatively furnished house.

The ethnographic accounts of the select respondents are best obtained by detailed interviews that have been conducted and recorded by the author himself. These are the leaders of the communities, certain heads of households, welfare organisations, institutions and other well-informed persons of the community and outside. The case studies of those well-informed respondents who could not make to the sample have also been included that enriches the quality of qualitative data. The ethnographic details from the senior generation are very useful to know the elements of oral history travelling with them thus far. Such respondents will take away the details of their past with them soon. Here is an attempt to tap such resources for the present study and also for further research. Such valuable ethnographies will be lost in the times changing fast. The younger generation hardly has time to listen to the elders about them and their community's past.

All information from the questionnaire is transferred to the code sheets for computation. The frequency distribution tables are prepared for all questions for various classifying variables. In the columns, the tables give options of the question that have been analysed. In the rows, the tables give various sub-groups of the classifying variable. The Chi square test of independence and the coefficient of contingency (C) based on the same have also been computed but for the tables that are reconstructed. The notations used are: (**) shows significance at 0.01 level while (*) shows significance at 0.05 level. It is easier to make tables of the codified data especially of the closed- or fixed-options type questions but difficult for the open-end types. The latter are handled manually. As a table is self-explanatory, its description is made to bring out certain manifest patterns in the respondents' information only wherever necessary, thus avoiding duplication of details in words and figures. The facility of computation has helped relate all data to income levels of the respondents, but all of these are not necessarily explained to avoid repetition and monotony of description since most of these are self-explanatory. The tables showing necessary and significant patterns have been described to make the discussion interesting and lucid.

Given the problem of clubbing certain occupations in the tabulated data, certain tables have been recast manually, which is why their computation with respect to income variable has not been carried out. It was, in fact, not possible.

The translations in the text are by the author unless specified. An attempt has been made to remain closest to the original meaning, literally, even if it means 'bad' English. It is for the benefit of those who are well versed in Punjabi and the local dialects. The photographs also, unless specified, are by the author.

The University Grants Commission, New Delhi, deserve only half-hearted thanks for the funding of this project. The research fellows who went to the field for the collection of data and later for its tabulation deserve my sincere thanks. Buta Singh, who had the training and experience of my previous study, deserves special thanks for the painstaking efforts he invested in the field to collect rich details. The detailed field notes give insight into the lives and histories of the tribal communities. Dr. Geet Lamba, Gurpreet Mehta and Manpreet Kaur had put in their labour to make this study worthwhile. Manpreet Kaur deserves special thanks for helping me plug holes wherever found during the course of explanation.

Sarah Gande of Leeds University, England, is to be thanked for sharing information that she painstakingly collected from *The Tribune* archives at Chandigarh. The institutional staff at the National Archives, New Delhi, and the Punjab State Archives, Patiala, are to be thanked for their much-needed assistance in accessing the relevant files. The library staffs' assistance at Nehru Memorial Museum and Library, New Delhi, Jawaharlal Nehru University, New Delhi, and Punjabi University, Patiala, is also duly acknowledged.

Baltej Singh Bhathal of the department of Economics is to be thanked for account keeping and related administrative chores. Thanks are due to Jagmal Singh of the department of Sociology and Social Anthropology for ferrying material and information from one place to another.

My wife, Professor Harinder Kaur of Sociology in the department of Distance Education at Punjabi University, assisted this work in so many ways that are difficult to count. Any kind of thanks would be less than what she deserves. Same is true of my son, Himpreet Singh, and his wife, Jasmin, who did everything that I asked them to do for this work besides what a parent may expect from her children. All of them together not only did not disturb me from working on this project but made everything easy and comfortable.

Birinder Pal Singh

1 Presence of the absent
An introduction

Tusin vekhe nahin hone kadi vi ghar darakhtan te
Te na hi vekhiya hona'i kade is dhang da jeevan
Uh ik bori'ch pa ke ghar savere tang jande ne
Te aapi lang jande ne kite bhalan nu majdoori.

Shiv Nath

[You musn't have seen houses atop trees
And neither a life of such sorts
They pack up their house in a sack
And leave it hanging, each morning
looking out for work, anywhere.]

(Author's free translation)

Punjab and Haryana are two states in the north-west India whose respective governments have declared the absence of tribal communities on their territories over the last few decades. They are declared the Scheduled Castes at both places. The census of Punjab, 2001, however, enumerates the tribal people under the category of 'other communities'. But the next census of 2011 lists them under the Scheduled Castes.[1] This list names 39 castes including all the erstwhile criminal tribes now called the denotified tribes or vimukt jatis since August 1952. According to the *Annual Report* (2003–2004) of the Ministry of Tribal Affairs, Government of India, there is no tribal population in the state of Punjab.

It is intriguing since the colonial Punjab had all the tribes, 'criminal' and others, from its north-west frontier to the hill states of the present Himachal Pradesh and Jammu and Kashmir. *A Glossary of the Tribes and Castes of the Punjab and North-West Frontier Province* by H. A. Rose in 1883 based on the census data collected by Sir Denzil Ibbetson in 1881 is a comprehensive three-volume work. Volumes two and three provide rich ethnographic details on the tribal communities and castes of the region. The nomadic tribes were declared criminal by the imperial government under the Criminal Tribes Act (CTA) of 1871, and their presence is very much conspicuous still. All the districts of the present-day 'little' Punjab have their share of tribal population that are nomadic, semi-nomadic and settled. Of all the 'criminal' tribes then, Sansis have been devoted the largest space (pp. 362–79) in the *Glossary* followed by the Bauria (pp. 70–79). All others have been brushed aside virtually providing minor accounts, largely introductory and superficial. Such low-key reporting, however, does not negate their existence. K. Suresh Singh's *People of India* volume on *Punjab* too has limited information on each tribe that has been classified and categorised as the Scheduled Castes in independent India. There too, the information does not go beyond broad general characteristics not exceeding a page and a half or two at the best for a tribe.

Such a vacuum in the ethnography of these communities is partially filled by a recent work, *'Criminal' Tribes of Punjab: A Social-Anthropological Inquiry* edited by Birinder Pal Singh (2010c). Interestingly, this volume is not the result of sociological exploration by the academic sociologists in their departments in the three well-established universities of the state including the fourth and the oldest one, the Panjab University at Chandigarh. The said volume could take shape because the existing tribal (denotified) communities were protesting and mobilising public support for the restoration of their tribal status. The Punjab chapter of the All India Denotified Tribes (Vimukt Jatis) Sewak Sangh established in 1982 was persistently raising this demand at the level of the central and the state governments. Other state-level organisations like All India Tapriwas & Vimukt Jatis Federation, Uttari Bharat Vimukt Jati Sangh, All India Nomadic Tribes Sangh, All India Tribal Communities Dal and Punjab Scheduled Tribes Dal etc. too are contesting the cause of these communities and constantly raising their voice at various levels. As a result of their consistent efforts to pressurise the government, the department of social welfare of the Punjab government asked the department of Sociology and Social Anthropology at Punjabi University, Patiala, to conduct *An ethnographic study of the denotified, nomadic and semi-nomadic tribes of Punjab* (2008a) to ascertain the tribal traits of certain communities. It was then that the presence of tribal communities in the state assumed importance in the eyes of social science academic, who were hitherto unconcerned about them. These communities were 'non-existent' for them too, and insignificant.

The major demand of the tribal communities' mobilisation is to acquire the tribal status to avail the benefits of their right to a separate quota prescribed in the reservation policy of the government of India for the welfare and uplift of the hitherto backward, primitive and marginalised communities in the country. Their main argument is that the colonial government had called them criminal tribes and the post-colonial government too declared them denotified tribes, then suddenly they have been clubbed with the Scheduled Castes by the Punjab, and other governments. Their grouse against the present government is at two levels. One, they have not only been denied their genuine traditional social status of being higher-caste Kshatriyas but degraded them further by clubbing with the lowest Scheduled Castes, from whom they themselves keep social distance. It amounts to adding insult to injury. Two, they have been denied their right to separate quota prescribed in the reservation policy of the country. They lament that since they have been clubbed with the Scheduled Castes, the creamy layer in Punjab – Balmiks and Chamars – takes all the benefits, and hardly any benefit reaches their population.

Each one of the tribal communities has its own mythology of princely lineage and connection with the Rajput royalty. They narrate vividly how they have been rendered poor over time. Most of these people believe themselves to be 'nationalists' and patriots whose ancestors fought against the Mughal ruler (Akbar) to save their territory and their honour and later against the British colonialism. The oral history of majority tribal communities informs that they are the progeny of the kings of Rajputana (land of the Rajputs), most notably Maharaja Rana Pratap of Chittor. They justify their nomadic existence due to the defeat of their ancestors in the battle following which the Mughal army was hunting them out, which is why they dispersed into the forests and became nomadic wandering from one place to another. They not only changed their dress and costumes but also developed a secret language for their safety. They claim that since then they are leading the nomadic life.

Such myths characterise the origin of each tribal community, and each has its own reasons to be adopting a particular way of life, say, for instance, to sleep on the ground and vowing never to use a cot or settle permanently at a place. The respondents inform that their ancestors had taken a vow to use cots only when they had regained their lost empire. The descendant generations are living up to the vow and the tradition of their ancestors.

Each tribal community has its own distinctive traditional occupation for survival that does not come in clash with other community either in terms of appropriation of material resources for purposes of production or for exchange with consumers of fellow communities or the larger society. For instance, if Bangalas explore the forests for collecting snakes and herbs for snake charming and selling medicines, Barads collect the grass for making small brooms and *innus* (cushioned loops). Gandhilas too make the brooms, but from the leaves of a particular tree (*Phoenix sylvestris*). They also collect honey etc. from the forest. The Sansi women too make brooms but not from the above materials like the Bazigar women. These processes of production may be dependent and interdependent but never encroach upon the domain and territory of the other community so as to become an issue for conflict. Thus, there is absence of competition both at the levels of procurement of raw materials and exchange of finished products. Moreover, each tribal community has its own specific area of operation to earn its livelihood (more on this later).

This way the finished products based on the natural raw materials from the forest are exchanged either in kind or in cash with the local people. This also empowers them to buy essential commodities from the bazaar or *haat*. The rise of the market economy holding cash in prominence as medium of exchange has no doubt become dominant, but the earlier mode of transaction in kind is continuing still with certain communities to some extent, be it the products for domestic use produced by the Barad, Bangala or Gaadi Lohar tribes or performances for entertainment by the Bazigar and Nat communities. Even in the thick of market society, some tribal women do exchange new utensils of steel for old clothes, for instance. The Gaadi Lohars still prefer green fodder or wheat chaff (*toori*) for their oxen to cash payment. Thus, the nomadic and semi-nomadic communities settled on the periphery of towns and villages could render service to the settled population and earn their livelihood.

The rise of the market economy and industrialisation and declaring the natural forests as government property by the Indian Forests Act 1865 and subsequent amendments, followed by the declaration of the CTA 1871, had not only drastically affected the lives of these communities but endangered their very existence and survival. Following these Acts, the nomadic and semi-nomadic communities were settled forcibly on the outskirts of the towns and villages, and those declared criminal were interned in the industrial and agricultural reformatories. The tag of criminality was put on numerous tribal communities. However, some other nomadic communities like the Gaadi Lohar and Gujjar, for instance, were not included in this category. The modern machine technology producing cheap and durable products with relatively good finish and stacking the shelves of the shops in the market also made the products of their labour redundant. The market is now a permanent institution, unlike its earlier temporary existence. These developments made the tribal people paupers and coerced them to undertake unskilled wage labour or petty jobs in the towns and cities like picking rags, polishing shoes and selling cheap goods as hawkers.

The present study intends to examine the issue of occupational change in the tribal communities, denotified and others, in the state of Punjab over three generations. The majority respondents (83 per cent) in the sample are born in independent India that itself is seven decades old. The remaining senior generation of old respondents above 70 years is no small proportion (16.91 per cent) of the sample. This generation in its childhood must have assisted their parents in their traditional occupation(s) besides hearing stories about their families and work. The younger generation, that is, the children of the respondents having tasted the fruit of modernisation and development, are not only not following their traditional occupations but keep distance from them. They find these not only insufficiently remunerative to meet their needs but low in prestige and status as well. They prefer to take any petty job than continue with the community's traditional occupation. The hassle of obtaining raw material and poor marketing of their products vis-à-vis cheap industrial products are strong deterrents to them in continuing with their traditional occupations besides the tag of tribal lineage and low social esteem. The percentage of work force in the traditional and non-traditional occupations will be charted out from their distribution in them across three generations.

Besides marking contours of occupational change over three generations, the present study proposes to look into the direction of change and improvement, if any, in their lifestyle and traditional occupational skills. Have these skills been gainfully modernised and updated for better standards of living and income, or have these communities been pushed farther to the margins of the present society? It is the responsibility of the modern state not only to ensure welfare measures but also to empower adequately the weaker sections of the population through modern skills to make them self-dependent.

This study also intends to supplement the previous work by Singh (2010c), whose principal objective was to ascertain the tribal identity of major communities in Punjab after conducting their ethnographic study. This study will supplement the above work in many ways besides adding another dimension of occupation change across three generations. It may also belie the claims of the government at the centre and at the state levels that these hitherto marginalised communities are being brought into the mainstream development society since huge funds are earmarked annually for this purpose. An intergenerational occupational change tends to show the present status of their socio-economic conditions, throwing light on the hitherto marginalised and branded communities. Has there been an improvement in their living conditions? Or have these people been marginalised further and their living and occupational conditions have gone worse?

Another aspect of the study is to ascertain the history of their habitation that is officially believed to be non-existent in Punjab. This study intends to establish continuity with the *Glossary* of Ibbetson and Rose (1883) to validate the existence of these very communities in this very area over the past more than a century. This would belie the claims of the state government with regard to their absence here and question the intentions of the administration in this respect. Why have the present been declared absent? It is in this context that the sub-title of the present study focuses on the 'tribes of Punjab' besides deliberating on their 'intergenerational occupational change'. The latter aspect is meant to validate beyond doubt their physical presence in the state from the days of their ancestors.

Yet another underlying idea of the present study is to record the stories of the senior generation. There are 16.91 per cent respondents above 70 years. No one has heard them ever as Scheduled Tribes, and they are not used to make others hear them. This generation has been closely associated with their tradition, both material and cultural, in every respect and in every aspect of their lives. This is virtually the last surviving generation that can speak for themselves and about themselves and their tradition authentically. They have lived it and heard it from their elders. Recording their narratives in crisp statements is an essential task of this research, and this may be the last chance to do so. They will fade away not long from now. The middle generation under the influence of modernisation and other processes of change has a different notion and interpretation of their tradition. It is a mix of numerous influences. The youngest generation has not lived it but only heard about it from their elders. Of the three generations, they are least conversant with their tradition.

The universe of the present study is the entire state of Punjab delineated in north-west India in 1966 that shares a part of its border with west Punjab in Pakistan, with which it has social and cultural contiguity. It has three socio-culturally distinct tracts called Malwa, Majha and Doaba. An attempt has been made to ensure that the respondents selected randomly duly represent all the communities in all the three cultural tracts.

The latest available count for all the seven denotified tribes or vimukt jatis in Punjab – Bauria, Bazigar Banjara, Bangala, Barad, Gandhila, Nat and Sansi – according to the *Census of Punjab* 2011 stands at 5,12,800 persons. According to Singh (2010c) following the census data of 2001:

> All of these jatis have their areas or districts of concentration though these may be distributed fairly in other parts of the state. But some of these communities do not have a single person at some places. For instance, Baurias have large population all over the state but not a single person in Amritsar district. Barads are also missing from Muktsar and Nats from Nawanshahr and Ropar districts. Gandhilas are an exception in this regard. These people are completely missing from Gurdaspur, Kapurthala, Nawanshahr, Fatehgarh Sahib and Muktsar. They are mainly concentrated in Jalandhar and Ludhiana (Singh 2010c, xl).

There is hardly any change since then.

The tracking of these people and making them respondents is not an easy task for three reasons. One, the tag of criminality still haunts them. The presence of an outsider in their closed community and virtually insulated settlements asking them to give responses to a detailed interview questionnaire intimidates them. They get scared that some police case pending against their ancestors may be opened. Singh notes:

> During the field work we encountered numerous stories and personalized anecdotes from the members of such communities who had been harassed especially by the police over the years. And, they quote this as an evidence of the police terror on their minds till date. An old Bauria man quipped: "*Bauriye hale vi police nu dekh ke seham jande ne.*" That a Bauria person gets scared still at the very sight of a policeman. This is one reason why it is hard to ascertain the true identity of the members of these communities even today. They fear that some old cases might be raked up again.
>
> (2010c, xvii)

The gravity of this fear may be assessed from a similar observation made 53 years ago by Sher: 'The other difficulty is the legacy of their past treatment under the Criminal Tribes Act which has frightened them to such an extent that it is very difficult to get correct information from them. Some of them still view strangers and educated persons with suspicion. So labouring under some past fears, they do not tell the real facts' (1965, xvii). Over this, they are otherwise shy people who would not give information about them without a clear signal from their *pardhan* or local head.

Two, as one approaches them to know their identity they do not disclose their tribal roots in the first place. One, for fear of the criminal tag and two, that the Punjab government has classified them as Scheduled Castes (SC). Thus, they too claim to be so. On further goading and probing, which '*biradari*' you belong to? What is your community's traditional occupation? etc. that one may ascertain their tribal lineage. Three, their presence in the town is so inconspicuous that people of the mainstream society, even in the vicinity of their settlement, are not sure of their identity. An informant would often quip: '*Shayad othhe baithhe ne!*' Probably, that is their settlement. Singh notes:

> Locating the concerned community was not an easy affair as many a times we found out that the local people too were ignorant of the true credentials of a community. For instance, one of our research investigators was sure that Gandhilas are settled since long on the periphery of his home town. Everybody there too believed similarly but when the investigator himself approached them they were found to be Bangalas and Sansis. This story was repeated at numerous places. The people usually characterise a community on the basis of certain traits they are believed to possess, as in this case they might have seen donkeys there hence thought them to be Gandhilas. Else they would identify a community on the basis of their familiarity with some that is numerically large as Sansi or Bauria whose names are often used as an abuse just as *Sansi jeha*, like a Sansi . . . Thus, peoples' information was more impressionistic than authentic just as in Punjab all labour from Uttar Pradesh and Bihar were earlier called Bhaiyas and now Biharis, and all south Indians are labelled as Madrasis.
>
> (2010c, xx–xxi)

Hence, locating their settlements is not so easy, though it is not a problem in the rural areas. Traditionally each community had a distinctive dress pattern and a specific style of their hut, but the easy access and cheap polythene covers have not only homogenised the tribal communities but made them indistinguishable from the settlements of the migrant labour. They are all alike. But we have the advantage of previous study in locating them and in procuring the requisite information from the desired respondents. The research investigators too had the experience of working with them since they had personal rapport with them and their headmen. Thus, data collection was quite a smooth affair this time.

All the erstwhile nomadic and denotified communities are a victim of misrecognition. It has layers to it. Their upper-caste Kshatriya and tribal status has been marred by the government. Over that they are given an identity of the lowly Scheduled Castes from whom they keep social distance. Above all, the stigma of criminality is still not leaving them. The public and the police are one on this issue. There is ever a dilemma with them to disclose their true identity. An investigator approaching them with a performa heightens their ambivalence about themselves. Should they inform about their SC status since some welfare measures due to them may be given? Are they going to get the yellow cards or some other benefit under some scheme? Is the government filling forms for old-age pension? Is such a person from the police or the CID department? The people around them do not know who they are. The police and the people always look at them with suspicion. And they are themselves not sure whom to reply what about their identity.

The loss of their traditional occupations is yet another blow to not only their livelihood but also their social identity. There was skill required in the traditional occupations and they produced objects of use with some sense of art and aesthetics. But their present occupations not only need any skill and aesthetics but are manifestly lowly and of mean nature such as collecting scrap or rags and iron filings from the sewerage drains in the cities. They are living with heaps of humiliations and yet they believe in the will of the god (*rabb di raza*).

The lives and living conditions of such people who have been a part of the older and the present Punjab, but unfortunately if not erased have definitely been eclipsed by the government, must be subjected to an academic study for the benefit of posterity. These people who are living with their lost glory of Rajput royalty and with 'hardships' of the forest nomadic life were branded criminal and later clubbed with the lowest castes. It is desirable that their past and the present be chalked out, howsoever, broadly in this maiden attempt of sociological inquiry. They have stories to narrate, and there are archives of the administrative reports and documents besides the archives of a prominent newspaper of the region. What has been said and recorded about these tribal communities at various levels should be assessed and interpreted to bring out their problems and sufferings over all these decades.

The declaration of the draconian CTA 1871 is a turning point in the lives and histories of the tribal communities. They got branded, captured like wild beasts and interned in reformatories. They lost touch with their traditional occupations that were hit already by the Indian Forest Act 1865. It is a plausible argument that their encounter with the already defamed Punjab police and the treatment given to them in the reformatories made them criminals. The state police are quite infamous for their ruthlessness. It is interesting that there is no significant difference in the mistreatment of these communities in the colonial and the post-colonial Punjab. In some ways, the latter proved more harsh than the former.

The nationalists may disagree in my labelling the post-partition and post-independence state as post-colonial, but it is apt to do so since there is a strong streak of continuity in the attitude of the two state governments and its officers, especially of the police in the discrimination and maltreatment of the tribal people. In a way, all the negative aspects of the colonial regime in dealing with them – criminality, confinement, corruption – have become more intense and cruel in the democratic state. Speaking relatively, the colonial police appear more humane and less ruthless compared to their post-colonial counterpart. The former only tagged the tribal people 'criminal', the latter tattooed them by writing criminal on their foreheads and their women over that. The former seems more disciplined a force that exercised restraint while the post-colonial officers behave like autocrats who are boss unto themselves.

Sundar also argues in the same vein seeking continuity between the colonial and post-colonial regimes:

> Although the history of "development" as a specific idea dates only to the post World War II period, there are specific similarities between the "development regime" and the colonial state. While both couch their policies in terms of public progress, their major contribution is to the development and extension of state power and capitalist market systems. In a place like Bastar, there are further continuities between the colonial and post-colonial regimes in that the individuals who are doing the "developing" continue to see themselves as more "advanced" than the "natives" being "developed", and have retained the language of a civilising mission.
>
> (2007, 251)

Padel also comments on the strong streak of continuity between the two types of governments:

> Adivasis in modern India remain far from free. Tribal communities in present times face displacement and dispossession from their land on a vaster scale than they faced under the colonial rule. Today's movements by tribal people resisting displacement from their land have significant parallels with movements from colonial times, and the pattern of the recent state repression of these movements is remarkably similar to repression during British times.
>
> (2011, 316)

The tribal people have tasted virtually nothing of the nationalist development policy, and over that it is unfortunate that the officers of the people's government think like their colonial mind-setters. They are faithfully carrying on their shoulders the white man's burden. It is instructive to read Sundar in detail what the administrative head of a district, an officer of the elite Indian Administrative Services (IAS) divulged to her in his interview:

> In an interview I had with him apropos the steel plant proposed to be set up in Bastar, the then Collector, Mr. J.P. Vyas, argued that there had never been any precedent for informing the people beforehand about impending displacement: "If the people were consulted beforehand and asked for permission, inherent in this is the possibility that they might refuse. And, then where would the government be?" Where, indeed? In any case, he argued, the people were ignorant and once the experts had decided where a project was going to be located, there was nothing more to be said. He went to offer several other astonishing insights, such as the fact that the government was doing the adivasis a *favour by uprooting them* because long occupation created stagnation and stagnation was a form of death. "Mobility is a sign of progress," he said, "Look at me". As to the demand for shares in the factory to be given to those to be displaced by it: "This is a *very wrong demand* and *totally alien to their culture*. It will create possessiveness as tribals are very selfless people."[2]
>
> (2007, 257–58; emphases added)

Each tribal community has its own niche in nature, drawing upon a huge variety of resources to earn their livelihood and in a distinctly characteristic manner making objects of use by them as well as for the larger society. But there was no competition and conflict between them at any level. Their pauperisation started with the industrial production and the consumer market. From producers, the tribal people became consumers, and from skilled workers they became de-skilled workers. They were coerced to become beggars and lumpen people. The profiling of these people on the scales of socio-economic status presents a dismal account. To claim that they are the poorest of the poor people in the 'developed' state (of Punjab) with no hearth and home still is a brutal reality 70 years after freedom from the British rule. India's freedom for the tribal communities means struggle for their basic rights enshrined in the constitution of the country itself. Their living conditions are worse without civic amenities. It is good to speak about seeing *swachh Bharat* through Mahatma Gandhi's spectacles but the reality on the ground is its converse. And, that too in a 'developed' state like Punjab.

The loss of traditional occupations is manifest across three generations. The tribal heterogeneity in this respect is getting homogenised since they are taking 'modern' occupations like rag-picking, peddling and wage labour cutting across tribes. To make sense of their predicament, it is important to look into the role of the state in general economic development and education amongst other sectors since it is the basic premise to a person's empowerment in a modern society. The development of tribes in the state could take place only if the overall economy of the state is doing well and its educational system is inclusive and working properly. The twin aspects of economy and education contextualise the predicament of the tribal communities here as also elsewhere in independent India.

The above-mentioned issues are discussed cogently in eight chapters. The first one, **Presence of the Absent: An Introduction**, sets the ball rolling by defining the parameters of the study, providing all the necessary preliminaries involved in research and writing.

The socio-economic contours in the course of history experienced by Punjab and Punjabis are broadly delineated in the second chapter, **Punjab and Its People**, so that one is better able to situate the occupational change across generations in the tribal communities in the larger context of social change unleashed by the hegemonic and dominant classes over the years. The state and fate of the marginalised classes and castes depend much upon these factors.

The nature and type of tribes inhabiting the state is discussed in the third chapter, entitled **Tribal Communities in the Colonial Punjab**. It intends to establish continuity with the *Glossary* that so far remains the pioneering and most authentic work since the last quarter of the nineteenth century. No such comprehensive work on tribes is available so far. This chapter also intends to supplement an ethnographic study, *'Criminal' Tribes of Punjab* by Singh (2010c) in some ways more exhaustive than the *Glossary*.

The fourth chapter, **Tribal Communities in the Post-Colonial Punjab**, introduces each tribal community in (independent) Punjab, briefly touching upon its history and the traditional occupations as also their present-day work engagements or 'modern' occupations. A glimpse of their struggles is also provided to show that they are no passive onlookers but fighters in their own right and protesting perpetually for their rights nonviolently.

The fifth chapter describes the **Socio-Economic Profile of the Tribal Communities in Punjab**, providing details on their social and economic indicators. The extent of their poverty becomes more than conspicuous. These people constitute the poorest of the poor in the state.

The nature and types of traditional occupations of the different communities are described in the **Occupations of the Tribal Communities**. It makes the sixth chapter that describes the occupations of the respondents across tribes of the present generation. The seventh chapter explains the **Intergenerational Occupational Change** over three generations, from the respondents' parents to their children. It shows clearly that the traditional occupations of the parents' generation are no longer followed by the children.

The eighth chapter, called **In Lieu of Conclusion**, suggests that the tribal communities are trapped in a quagmire of complexities characteristic of a traditional society (country) treading the path of industrialisation and modernisation without expert drivers on the wheels. The state is a holy cow for the political and the administrative elite to milk. The masses are left high and dry without basic amenities, especially the already marginalised tribal communities. This chapter makes an attempt to contextualise these multiple complexities that are directly and indirectly, intendedly and unintendedly responsible for the marginalisation and ultimate detribalisation of these communities in Punjab.

Notes

1 Table A-10 (appendix) of the *Census Punjab* 2011 provides the total population of the Scheduled Castes, followed by their district-wise population for male and female and in urban and rural areas.
2 Note the insensitive and illogical argument of the Collector. He shows concern for the culture of the tribal people and debunks it simultaneously.

2 Punjab and its people

Punjab *de jammian nu nitt muhimman* (an old saying).
(Those born in Punjab are ever exposed to warring expeditions.)

The present Punjab is a small part of the erstwhile state in north-west India then called Sapt-Sindhu, the land of the Sindhu river, the Indus originating from the Himalayas in the Kashmir region and falling into the Arabian Sea traversing the whole length of the area now called Pakistan. Besides, the 'five rivers', there is now extinct Saraswati too also sometimes called in its present remnant smaller form as Ghaggar. In the epic *Mahabharata*, it is known as Panchnada that means the land of five rivers while its Persianised name currently prevalent is used for the first time in the 14th century. This name of the land of five rivers – Satluj, Beas, Ravi, Chenab and Jhelum – that is, Punjab (earlier written as Panjab), *Panj* (five) + *ab* (water) is continuing still. Paradoxically, the present state is left with only three rivers without Chenab and Jhelum.

Grewal, an authority on Punjab history, writes:

> The literal meaning of the Persian term *panj-ab* is 'five waters'. It was meant to signify the land of five rivers. But it was not meant to be taken literally. When it became current in the reign of Akbar in the late sixteenth century, it was synonymous with the province of Lahore and, therefore, actually smaller than the area lying between the rivers Indus and Satlej. The British Punjab, however, embraced the entire plain between the Jamuna and the Indus. This region had a geographical entity of its own. Its southern boundary was marked by a desert in historical times. The Himalayas stood in its north even before the Punjab plains emerged as a geological entity.
>
> (1990, 1)

More recently Rajmohan Gandhi writes that 'Presenters of Punjab stories often divided the region into its doabs, a doab (or doaba) being the space between two rivers, and pointed out that each doab possessed special physical and linguistic features, often a different agriculture and, at times, a different politics' (2013, 20; no italics). He adds that the Mughal emperor Akbar was the first to use this term and gave each doab its name. So there was (and is)

> the Chej (or Chaj or Jech) doab between the rivers Chenab and Jhelum, the Rachna doab between the Ravi and the Chenab, the Bari doab between the Beas and the Ravi, and the Bist (or Bet) doab between the Beas and the Sutlej. The space between the Jhelum and the Sindhu (Indus), the great continental river which formed the western boundary of Punjab and of which the five Punjabi rivers were tributaries, was (and is) the Sindh Sagar doab.
>
> "Delhi doab" was another name for the large Birun Panchnad (i.e. outside the five rivers) area. In later times, the Sikhs would use the term "Malwa" for much of this area, while the British would think of this space south of Sutlej as "cis-Sutlej" territory.
>
> (ibid, 20; no italics)

If the Mughals thought it appropriate to divide the Punjab territory geographically, naturally in terms of doabs, the British devised their own territorial divisions in terms of administrative suitability. There were six divisions in all namely Rawalpindi, Lahore, Multan, Jullunder (now spelled Jalandhar), Ambala and the independent princely states that were not directly under the British rule. The present states of Punjab, Haryana and Himachal Pradesh and the west Punjab of Pakistan have been carved out from these divisions. The state had a fairly large geographical spread prior to partition of the country surrounded by United Province (now Uttar Pradesh) in the east, Kashmir in the north, Baluchistan, North West Frontier Province in the north-west, Sindh in the west and Rajputana in the south. It extended from Simla and Kangra in north-east to Rawalpindi and Attak in North West and from Gurgaon in South East to Bahawalpur and Dera Gani Khan in South West. Lahore was the capital city (*State of Environment Punjab* 2007, 3).

The range and plurality of each aspect of the earlier Punjab is well sketched by Gandhi:

> Large in area, undivided Punjab was varied in soil, temperature, dryness or dampness, population density, religion, caste and sect. What was common to the area and to almost all its inhabitants was the Punjabi language, which seems to have existed for a thousand years or more, though spoken in several variants and written in more than one script. *Their language seemed to reveal the Punjabis as a distinct people*; not homogeneous by any means, yet distinct.
>
> (2013, 19; emphasis in original)

The range and diversity of natural processes is matched by the plurality and variety of invasions on Punjab. The invaders range from the Mongol Changez Khan to the central Asians, the Turks, the Mughals, the Arabs, the Scythians, the Hun, the Kushan, the Afghan, the Iranian, the Greek, the British etc. and the list does not end there. It is for this reason that it is said that Punjab *de jammian nu nitt muhimman*. That those born in Punjab are ever exposed to warring expeditions. The geophysical location of Punjab, as gateway to Hindustan, exposed its people to frequent and ferocious invasions from the outsiders starting from Alexander (the Great) to Ahmad Shah Abdali. A peasant who is improvident, becomes doubly so in Punjab because of the above mentioned reason. He cannot afford to save and store in the wake of frequent invasions and consequent devastation. That is how he has learnt to live in the present and enjoy life to its full. There is a saying: *Khada-peeta lahe da, baqi Ahmad Shahe da*. That, whatever you consume is yours, the remainder shall be taken away by Ahmad Shah (Abdali).

Mohan Singh (Diwana), a noted Punjabi litterateur, aptly sums up the physical and social aspects of the region responsible for making its literature. He elucidates in his *A History of Punjabi Literature* that is worth quoting in full:

The people that now occupies the Panjab was formed by the fusion of the natives and of several superimposed races.

The full and real history of the Panjab and Panjabis is yet to be written. What extremes meet in its climate and physical configuration, – the beautiful valley of Kashmir, the dense vegetable growth of the Bar, the arid areas of Multan and Bahawalpur, the huge plains and wide and long snow-fed rivers in the centre and the narrow ravines on the west. These extremes of surface and atmosphere have preserved all the regional and, the consequent, social and linguistic differences and prevented the whole of what we know now as the Panjab (inclusive of Delhi, the Hill States and the Frontier Province) from welding into one political and philological unit. The glory-crowned reign of the Sikh Lion of the Panjab, Maharaja Ranjit Singh, was too brief for any real achievement of common coalescence. Thus, the Province has always been an aggregate of *tribal territories* or small factious principalities. With so many neighbouring, jealous units of power there could be little peace and co-operation. On top of that the first foreign blows always fell on the heads of the poor Panjabis, whose whole time and attention were occupied either in defending their homes and hearths against the internal and external foes, or in tilling the land, fighting the soil for material sufficiency. The sword and the lance, and the plough and the Persian wheel have alternated as the weapons of men and the handmill and the spinning-wheel, of women. And it was not a physical scramble alone, to keep their freedom and possessions; it was also, a mental, moral, and spiritual struggle. But could they contend against powerful hordes for long and successfully? They could not and did not. *Continuous assimilation of each new influence*, constant absorbing of more and more blood was the only course of safety for existence. Thus, social toleration and admixture, cultivation of a sort of impassive religion, an agglomerate, and composite language based in Sanskrit ever adding to itself from foreign stock, a heroic attitude towards life and love have ever marked Panjabi culture, mainly ethical in nature.

(1933/2014, 1–2; emphases added)

The above description of the larger undivided Punjab suggesting a blending of enormous range of races, peoples, cultures and languages, and yet giving rise to a composite Punjabi culture and language could only be possible in this part of the sub-continent that fits well into the description given by Jawaharlal Nehru in his oft-quoted 'unity and variety of India'. Let us read him:

Ancient India, like ancient China, was a world itself, a culture and a civilization which gave shape to all things. Foreign influences poured in and often influenced that culture and were absorbed. Disruptive tendencies gave rise immediately to an attempt to find a synthesis. Some kind of a dream of unity has occupied the mind of India since the dawn of civilization. That unity was not conceived as something imposed from outside, a standardization of externals or even of beliefs. It was something deeper and, within its fold, the widest tolerance of belief and custom was practised and every variety acknowledged and even encouraged.

(1961/1977, 62)

Thus, we may liken Punjab to a large cauldron where a whole lot of major races, peoples, cultures and languages were brewing at a low temperature for centuries for a fine blending of all its ingredients. The region witnessed the writing of *Vedas*, *Bhagvad Gita*, *Mahabharata*, *Ramayana* and entrenchment of Buddhism and last but not the least, the rise of Sikh religion and philosophy with the compilation of *Guru Granth Sahib* by the fifth Nanak, Guru Arjan Dev in 1604. It is another documented blending of teachings and preachings of a variety of religious and spiritual streams of thought, of sects and cults, of sufis, bhagats and saints including Islam, the belief and faith of the then-ruling monarchs, the Mughals. It may not be impudent to argue that the philosophical bases of such a religion were conceived by Guru Nanak to fit in a society of multiple cultures and communities whose solidarity need be upheld and cemented firmly. The *Granth Sahib* celebrates unity in variety in the true spirit since the guru proclaims: *Manas ki jaat sabhai eko pehchanbo*, that all human beings are one and the same, cutting across castes and races.

Being the youngest and the most recent religion in an ancient civilisation, it has tremendous influence on the society and culture of Punjab. Belief in one and only one god, the Akalpurakh Waheguru, the omnipotent and omnipresent one must always be remembered (*Naam japo*) while doing labour (*kirat karo*) and sharing the fruit of labour with all (*wand chhako*). It preaches unflinching equality of men, women and races. The last guru Gobind Singh finally created the Khalsa, a brotherhood of five low-caste men from different parts of the country by serving them *amrit*– sweetened water stirred with a double-edged sword (*khanda*) from a common bowl. It signifies the termination of caste hierarchy and a solidarity of all people, especially of the lowly oppressed castes against the ruling classes. These men (*panj piaras*) were given a new name and a new assignment of overseeing the society against exploitation of any kind. Niharranjan Ray, a historian suggests that Guru Nanak was very particular about the socio-temporal, that is, the secular aspect of life. He took it with as much seriousness as the ethical and the spiritual. He argues: 'This emphasis on the material basis of life generated in the community an activistic attitude towards life from the very beginning, unlike any other sect that emerged out of the Bhakti movement' (1975, 107). He continues: 'History therefore taught the Punjab and her people one very important lesson, namely, not to forget or be oblivious of temporal or secular situations of any given time space, howsoever engrossed one might find oneself in matters of mind and spirit' (ibid, 105).

The Jatts[1] of the region came into the fold of this new religion during the period of the sixth guru Hargobind. They impacted the overall culture and society of Punjab in myriad ways. Irfan Habib writes: 'We have seen that in Sind the Jatts had been a large primitive community based on pastoral economy and with an egalitarian or semi-egalitarian social structure. They had "neither rich nor poor", nor "small nor great", in the words of two quite independent accounts' (1976, 95). The historical sources suggest that the pastoral tribe of Sind living on either side of Indus gradually moved to this land of five rivers. Their expansion took place between the 12th and 16th centuries. They settled in this region at the beginning of the later century when they encountered the Persian Wheel. This converted them into cultivators. But socially their status was still lower. According to *Dabistan-i-Mazahib*, Jatts were 'the lowest caste of the Vaishyas even in the middle of the seventeenth century' (ibid, 97).

Why did peasantry (Jatts) in Punjab accept Sikhism? Habib suggests: 'the Jatts received Sikhism at a time when by historical circumstances they were in need of it most' (ibid, 99). More than the problem of sanskritisation was the problem of revenue burden they had to bear in the seventeenth century. This oppression from the ruling classes of the Mughal empire pushed them towards armed violence. Habib concludes: 'This further cemented the historical association between the Jatt peasantry and Sikhism, though the association certainly antedates the agrarian crisis of the Mughal empire' (ibid, 100).

The Jatts not only accepted Sikhism but also joined the Sikh army first organised by the sixth guru Hargobind. This army also consisted of certain anti-social elements and marginal castes and classes as well. Habib argues that shift from Khatris to Jatt leadership within the Sikh movement had already taken place by the middle of seventeenth century. He quotes *Dabistan-i-Mazahib* that although the gurus had been Khatris, 'they have made the Khatris subservient to the Jatts' (ibid, 98). Since then they have remained in the forefront of each and every militant movement launched by the Sikhs against their adversaries, which included the Afghan invaders, the Mughal emperors, the British imperialists, the Indian capitalists and lately the Indian state for the implementation of Anandpur Sahib Resolution[2] and the Sikh militants demanding a federal political system. The Sikh rulers, notably Maharaja Ranjit Singh, did not undermine other castes. The formation of *misls*, confederacies, in the 18th century was an illustration par excellence of equality and fraternity. Many chiefs belonged to castes lower than the Jatts but there was no discrimination against them.

The Sikh religious tradition and administrative control on the enlargement of landholdings together have given rise to a milieu of equality in the rural areas of the present East Punjab in India.[3] The peasants amongst themselves and with their agricultural labour force from lower castes keep much diluted social distance compared to the peasant/rural society elsewhere in India. In her anthropological inquiry of the Jatt Sikhs whom she calls *The Robber Noblemen*, Pettigrew notes: 'The way of life of the Jats (read Jatt) is essentially the same whether they were rich or poor' (1975, 38). 'Moreover, labourers, whether Jat or *Mazhabi*, were treated exactly alike by their Jat employers. The core of the relationship was the same in all these instances and unaffected by caste' (ibid, 45). Banga provides a material basis of this character of Jatt society by suggesting that the most powerful Sikh ruler, Ranjit Singh, is believed to have completely ousted the *ta'alluqdars* (the holders of a superior right over land, largely the descendants of former chiefs, *jagirdars*, *ijaradars* and other officials) from certain parts of his dominions (1978). Baden Powell notes that the proportion of area held by all the big and small *zamindars* in the total cultivated area in the Punjab was 10 per cent, since 'the Sikh rulers encouraged the actual cultivators as against the holders of superior ownership, which "levelled down the differences and compelled an equality of the landlord and inferior"' (Banga 1978, 171).

This elevation of the lower castes in Punjab, the land of the Sikh gurus, has its roots in the period preceding the *misls* (confederacies). In the words of Ganda Singh: 'Banda Singh[4] was a great political leveller and a thorough social uplifter. Wherever he went, he raised the down-trodden to position of authority and social prestige' (1956, 20). He further quotes William Irvine:

> In all the *parganas* occupied by the Sikhs, the reversal of the previous customs was striking and complete. A low scavenger or leather dresser, the lowest of the low in Indian estimation had only to leave home and

join the Guru (meaning Banda Singh) when in a short space of time he would return to his birth-place as its ruler, with his order of appointment in his hand. As soon as he set foot within the boundaries, the well-born and wealthy went out to greet him and escort him home.

(ibid, 20)

Ranjit Singh had consolidated the Sikh empire and expanded the territory of Punjab up to Afghanistan. After his demise, the British made it into a composite unit by defeating the Sikh forces in 1849. The advent of the English empire and colonialism set a different sort of turbulence in Punjab. They were not only racially distinct and culturally different but came with an intention not to be a part of this society or nation like the Mughals but to exploit it. They were here to control these people and administer them to their advantage. They introduced modern Western ways of doing things that helped them in effective administration. This had set in the dialectic of tradition and modernity, of religion and politics, of communalism and secularism etc.

The socio-religious turbulence in the region started in the last quarter of the 19th century when Swami Dayanand started the Arya Samaj movement and the Christian missionaries were trying conversion of some Sikh children. The seeds of polarisation of the two communities were sown then. Bhai Kahn Singh Nabha in his *Hum Hindu Nahin* (we are not Hindus) in 1898 reacted to the Sikh Sanatanists who were proclaiming that the Sikhs are Hindus. This work was later often quoted out of context to plead respective arguments by the Hindu and Sikh leaders. The Singh Sabha movement that took off in 1875 tried to assert the Sikh distinctive traits vis-à-vis the Hindus. Bhai Vir Singh, a noted Punjabi litterateur, wrote novels depicting Sikh characters[5] with distinctive value system and chivalry characteristic of what Richard Fox (1987) would later call the 'martial race'.

The nationalist politics too had its share in the first quarter of the twentieth century. The Marxist approach of Bhagat Singh, liberal radicalism of Lala Lajpat Rai of the Indian National Congress and the revolutionary stance of the Gadari Babas had put Punjab in the political limelight. The Jallianwala Bagh (Amritsar) genocide of innocent people by Reginald Dyer stirred the nation turbulently as never before. The then Lieutenant Governor of Punjab, Michael O'Dwyer was later shot dead in Caxton Hall, London by Udham Singh on 13 March 1940. This incident was followed closely by the Jaito Morcha, a non-violent Sikh struggle to release the gurdwaras from *mahants* (priests) who were stooges of the colonial empire. The massacre of 150 Sikhs was another stirrer in the nationalist politics that was lauded by the 'three leading intellectuals of the country, namely Rabindra Nath Tagore, Mahatma Gandhi and Vishnu Digambar Savarkar'.[6]

The gurdwara reform movement led to the formation of Shiromani Gurdwara Parbandhak Committee (SGPC) in 1925 that was preceded by the organisation of Shiromani Akali Dal, a political party (of the Sikhs) in 1920 with long-term consequences for the regional politics of the region until today. These political developments heated up the nationalist struggle and enhanced people's involvement in the freedom struggle. All communities were engaged in political strife against the colonial rule for independence. The demographic configuration of this region with preponderance of Muslims in the western Punjab, Sikhs and Hindus in the central and eastern sectors, respectively, had its own consequences for the region after independence in 1947. Besides, the transfer of populations between India and Pakistan, never heard before in the history of humankind anywhere in the world, has left permanent scars on the society and culture of the region and Punjab in particular.

The second partition of Punjab took place following the linguistic reorganisation of the Indian states in 1966 when the Hindu Jat dominated east Punjab region was made into Haryana and the hill states with majority Hindu denomination were merged with Himachal Pradesh. This process was not an easy one since it involved protests and fasts, including fast unto death by certain leaders[7] for the formation of Punjabi Suba, a Punjabi-speaking province, as promised by the leaders of the Indian National Congress much before the partition of the country. The Indian National Congress in its session of 1929 at Lahore moved the resolution of *poorna swaraj* or complete self-rule to mobilise people across the country for the nationalist movement. It was a proposition alluding towards their self-determination for the federal structure of free India. The formation of linguistic states was the first step in this direction. Unfortunately, Punjabis had to fight for the realisation of a linguistic state while many states in the south were duly formed on the basis of language. This was a sore point with the Akali Dal that remains ever a case of discrimination by the Hindu-dominated Congress party against the Sikhs. The whole issue of linguistic state formation in Punjab not only attained a communal tinge subsequently but became fiercely so that was not willing to fade out with time. The Hindus subscribing to the Arya Samaj ideology chose to return Hindi as their mother tongue, as the Punjabi suba movement spearheaded by the Akali Dal came to be associated with the Sikhs. The Urdu language taught in the schools was the official language until 1947 that came to be associated with Muslims. With their exodus, Urdu too lost roots in Punjab.

The communalising of language and communities in Punjab was again flamed during the years of Sikh militancy from 1978 to 1993 (Gupta 1985). The Jalandhar group of Hindi press spear headed by Lala Jagat Narain vociferously spoke against Jarnail Singh Bhindranwale, who was allegedly considered the fountainhead of Sikh militancy for the formation of Khalistan, a separate state for the Sikhs. Lala Jagat Narain was shot dead by the militants in broad daylight on the Grant Trunk road in September 1981. He was a Member of Parliament (MP) from Jalandhar constituency, speaking the language of the central government and blaming the Sikh leaders for disintegrating the nation. He was the founder editor of the Hind Samachar group of papers known for communal slant.[8] A wedge raised already was reinforced between the two linguistic and religious communities. Such polarisation was quite manifest in the urban areas. The local Hindi and Punjabi media were opposed to each other (Singh 2002).

The decade-and-a-half period of Sikh militancy (1978–1993) brought forth the contradictions between the rural and the urban, the rich and the poor, the governing elite and the governed, the state and the people, and the state (Punjab) and the centre (Delhi/Indian government), etc. The militants' diktats were quite effective, and in certain years the state government was virtually ineffective and the main leaders of all the political parties were heavily guarded by the police, paramilitary and variety of other forces, including special security by the commandos depending on one's hierarchy in the party and the government. The security forces were more visible in the public places than the people. Dipankar Gupta writes that in the Majha area the militants ruled at night and the government during the day (1992). A consequence of these developments was the weakening of the state government, rise in the numerical strength of the police forces and their relative autonomy from the administrative control indulging in 'fake encounters' or illegal elimination of the militants. People lost complete trust in the police. It became law unto itself. The problem of corruption and illegitimate practices of trying criminals and nexus with the underworld became deep seated. Later, it manifested in the drug pedalling that became a serious problem in the whole of Punjab, cutting cross the rural and urban divide. So much so, this became the election issue in the state assembly elections of 2017.[9]

It was a disturbing turn in the history of Punjab that succeeded the phase of radical Marxism, called the Naxalite movement, in the last half of the sixth decade of the 20th century. This movement based on the Marxist-Leninist ideology or Maoism, in popular parlance, that started in West Bengal was readily picked up by the left leaning youth and students in Punjab. It believed in the physical elimination of the class enemy, that is, the big landlords (and the bourgeoisie) to capture the state power in the interests of small peasantry and the working class. This movement based on violence was suppressed violently by the state power in a short span. The Punjab Students Union (PSU) is a product of this movement that remained quite effective in the student politics of the state. It marginalised the Communist Party of India's All India Students Federation (AISF) and the Communist Party of India's (Marxist) Students Federation of India (SFI) in the student politics quite effectively. The left politics remained dominant until the rise of Sikh militancy (Judge 1992).

The processes of modernisation of society and traditional agriculture with the establishment of Punjab Agricultural University at Ludhiana have gone a long way in determining the future of this state. It was to be made the granary of India with the introduction of hybrid seeds of wheat and rice and new agricultural technology for tilling and pumping water from the ground. The green revolution made the Punjab's Sikh peasant a model for the rest of the peasantry in India. The green revolution undoubtedly brought more riches to the peasantry in the early phase, and more land was brought under cultivation at the cost of forest cover (more details in Chapter 8).

Vandana Shiva locates the Punjab crisis (the violence of the 1980s) in the failure of the green revolution. She provides an explanation of the decade-long violence as a consequence of resource-intensive, politically and economically centralised experiment with food production that created disparities among classes and increased commercialisation of social relations. In her own words: 'The present essay presents the other side of the Green Revolution story – its social and ecological costs hidden and hitherto unnoticed. In doing so, it also offers a different perspective on the multiple roots of ethnic and political violence' (1992, 12). Later she extends her logic to explain social conflicts in the whole of the South Asian region: '[T]he most "successful" experiments in economic growth and development have become in less than two decades, crucibles of violence and civil war' (ibid, 190).

Joyce Pettigrew also provides a similar explanation that is worth quoting in full:

> The story of the rise and fall of the guerrilla movement is essentially and materially a story of what happened to a community of farmers as they experienced the effects of a process of economic change known as the Green Revolution . . . Sant Bhindranwale had wished religious values to be placed at the centre of life in a rapidly changing society . . . His primary objective was to undercut the spread of consumerism in family life. There was no one to whom this appealed more than the small farmers who were struggling hard under the impact of Green Revolution.
>
> (1995, 55)

Punjab is demographically divided into two major religious communities, that is, Sikhs and Hindus. The Census of India (Punjab) 2011 records Sikhs at 57.69 per cent and the Hindus 38.49 per cent. They are further spatially segregated between the rural and the urban areas. The Jatts as Sikh peasants are dominant in the rural areas, though all other castes too are existing in their company, including the Brahmins, whose number may not be large but in certain villages they have significant presence that are engaged in agriculture and keep complete Sikh form. They are *keshadharis* with flowing beards though with names without 'Singh'. It is not surprising to see a Ram Kumar dressed in turban with a flowing beard. The Scheduled Castes (SC), dalits or the Balmiks in the villages subscribe to the Sikh religion and are called Mazhabi Sikhs. Their presence is quite significant whose residential area is usually on the outskirts of the village, on *phirni*, the outer road. Traditionally, these residences were on the southern side of the village. Their number is significantly high in the rural areas of the Malwa region. They make the poorest in the village economy, though still superior to the tribal communities.

Ramdasia or Chamar is another lower caste, the SCs. They are Sikhs and their Hindu counterparts are called Ravidassi, who consider Ravidas their guru. Their preponderance in the Doaba region is conspicuous, and as business people in the skin trade, none excels them. The Boota Mandi at Jalandhar is their citadel. They are also called Ad-dharmis. Their outmigration to the western world has enhanced their socio-economic status significantly. This has heightened their political consciousness as well, and they no longer fight shy of their low caste status, rather take pride in calling themselves '*Putt Chamaran de*', the sons of Chamars, though imitating the Jatt boys who flaunt '*Putt Jattan de*' on their sedans, SUVs and motorcycles. Over the years, the subservience internalised by the SCs is giving way to resistance and assertion. The conflict between the dominant Jatt Sikhs and the Ramdasias/Ravidassis has not only become manifest but took to actual fights (Ram 2010).

I.P. Singh profiling a village in the early 1970s in the Amritsar district writes about the Mazhabis (SC):

> They live on one side of the village, and a long wall of the backs of the houses of the higher caste group separates them from others in the village. About twenty families live a hundred yards away on the land given to them for residence by the father of the Sarpanc on the birth of his first son. Mazhabis work as farm laborers, while their wives clean the courtyards, collect cow dung and make cow dung cakes.
>
> (1975, 279)

Further, they have a separate well and a separate small room as a marriage palace (*janj ghar*) 'in their part of the village' while all other castes use the gurdwara premises for marriages (ibid, 280). Balbir Madhopuri in his autobiography describes an aspect of discrimination in his own village that his own people had been undergoing:

> If an untouchable (*chamar/churah*) boy moves out from home after a bath and combed hair, then someone from the Jutt group (*dhani*) sitting under a tree or *tharah* (platform of bricks) would put sand on his head. If he protested, he was thrashed (*fainta chariah janda*). Similarly an untouchable moving out with a new set of clothes was beaten too on the pretext that he was trying to be like them.
>
> (2004, 13; author's translation)

The situation in the 21st century is not all well. Judge and Bal write about five villages in the district and the city as well:

> [M]azabi respondents of Amritsar district reported caste-based exclusion of religious practices. Many of them said that the upper caste Sikhs

did not allow them to carry the sacred book to their residence for purpose of performing various rituals/ceremonies . . . Similar information was given by the mazabis of Guru Ki Wadali – an erstwhile village that has become a locality of Amritsar city.

(2008, 52)

Judge and Bal note much change over time, yet: 'At the level of the caste system, inequalities and exclusion continue to show their existence, the evidence of which could be ascertained on the basis of data on social ecology, occupation and access to religious places' (ibid, 55). And before them Jodhka too concludes from his survey on untouchability in 51 villages: 'Notwithstanding the changes experienced in almost all spheres of life, the continuities are not yet insignificant. Rural Punjab has not forgotten caste' (2002, 1822).

Bania as traders belonging to the vaishya varna have little presence in the rural areas obviously due to the lack of trading business. With the development of *mandi* (market) towns following the grain production, these people moved there. These small towns were meant to decentralise the urban development and lessen concentration of population in a few cities. The Banias are Hindus and are into all kinds of retail and wholesale trade. The Sikh traders are khatris/Aroras in the urban areas only. The latter people have significant presence in the Amritsar city especially, while those khatri Sikh traders who migrated from west Punjab (Pakistan) in 1947 dominate the Patiala city. They are called *bhapas* in local parlance and are distinctly distinguishable from the Jatt Sikhs. There are cultural differences between them as well.

The artisan and other backward classes (OBCs) are also a part of the regular village community who render various types of services to them. Their socio-economic status is definitely superior to those of the SCs. Not long ago, they were engaged in their respective traditional occupations, most of them have now become obsolete. If the small and marginal peasants are leaving their traditional occupations due to agrarian crisis and fragmentation of landholdings, so are the artisan castes losing their occupations because their services are no longer required in the modern society.

In the present Punjab there are four major cities – Amritsar, Ludhiana, Jalandhar and Patiala – with population over one lakh since India's independence. If one were to name the defining character of these cities it could be religious, industrial, sports, and education, art and culture, respectively. The Patiala *gharana* of north Indian classical music is famous for its style. Patiala *salwar* (trousers) is also very popular besides the *prandas* (braids) and *desi jutis* (traditional shoes of leather). In the cities, Hindu population overshadows the Sikhs, and its converse is true of the rural areas.

Thus, Punjab is a curious mix and blend of castes, classes, communities and religions since millennia. They interacted with one another and confronted the invaders together developing solidarity and animosity simultaneously. In this context Ray notes: 'By far the largest number of foreigners that entered

India, in wave after wave and over a period of about 1500 years, was that of the Central Asian nomadic and pastoral-nomadic peoples' (1972, 12). These people were first to make home here in the agriculturally productive region of the five rivers, which was richly forested with large numbers of water reservoirs, the two prerequisites for the nomadic people to feed their cattle and themselves. The present-day nomadic and semi-nomadic tribal people who claim to originate from Rajasthan about four centuries ago are now settled on the outskirts of the villages and the cities following the CTA 1871. These people make the poorest of the poor in the state without exception. Who are these people? What do they do? How do they make their living? These issues will make the subject of the next chapter.

Notes

1 Jatts in Indian Punjab subscribe to the Sikh religion, while Jats are Hindus in the north-west Indian states.
2 The *Anandpur Sahib Resolution* (ASR) is 'The Draft of the New Policy Programme of the Shiromani Akali Dal' adopted by its Working Committee on 16–17 October 1973 and approved by the General House on 28 August 1977 in the form of 12 Resolutions. For reasons of space, it is not possible to list here all of these, but the first one which goes to speak for itself against the much-maligned propaganda over all these years, about the separatist and disintegrationist character of the ASR. Another feature worth noticing is its thrust on the economic issues rather than religion. Without giving details it would suffice to mention that the 'Economic Policy Resolution No. 3' (pp. 8–11) occupies largest space compared to all the remaining resolutions (pp. 12–15).
3 The west Punjab is in Pakistan after the state's division in 1947.
4 Banda Singh Bahadur, aka Banda Bairagi, was a renunciate who was inspired by Guru Gobind Singh at Nanded (Maharashtra) and brought into the fold of Khalsa Sikhs. He was made to take *amrit* and dispatched to Punjab in 1708 to fight the Mughal oppression on religious minorities.
5 For instance, *Sundari*.
6 Bhagwan Josh's inaugural address to the *50th Punjab History Conference*, Punjabi University, Patiala, 23 February 2018.
7 Sant Fateh Singh of Shiromani Akali Dal sat on fast unto death for the Punjabi suba on 18 December 1960 and broke that on 9 January 1961 on assurance from the central government. The new Punjab was formed on 1 November 1966 excluding Chandigarh. Then agitation started for that. Darshan Singh Pheruman sat on fast unto death. He fulfilled his vow and died after 74 days on 27 October 1969.
8 Jalandhar remains the hub of communally polarised press reporting. Another popular daily in Punjabi, *Ajit* is associated with Akali Dal.
9 The drug issue became the subject of Hindi (*Udta Punjab*) and Punjabi films (*Mr. and Mrs. 420 Return*) amongst others.

3 Tribal communities in the colonial Punjab

> They (Andamanese) must see the superior comforts of the civilization compared to their miserable condition ... we are in reality laying the foundation stone for civilizing a people hitherto living in a perfectly barbarous state, replete with treachery, murder and every other savageness.
>
> Colonel R.C. Tytler (1863)

In the contemporary parlance of modern society, a tribe is a pejorative term, and to call someone a tribal is an abuse. It is a gauge of one's primitiveness and 'other savageness(es)' in the epigraph. In popular perception, a tribe connotes primitive people, isolated from the urbane and civilised society, making a closed community in some remote area. They do not wish to tread the path of 'progress' but rather cling to their age old customs and traditional practices of life and livelihood. They consciously defy the modern means of development, hygiene and sanitation. An official document dwells on the subject:

> hygienic principles were repulsive to these *wild creatures*. The people moreover had a variety of hereditary superstition which proved the formidable obstacles to all attempts at reform. When ordered to bathe on Sundays in May and June, some of the inmates strongly objected on the ground that they were not prisoners and would not offend against their tradition by frequent baths.
>
> (*Report* 1918, 7–8; emphasis added)

This is just an example to make the point how the higher classes and other elite think about the tribal people.[1]

The rise of evolutionary theory in the disciplines of biology and sociology in the second half of the 19th century and the formation of the Salvation Army[2] in the United Kingdom have gone into the making of the CTA 1871. The latter discipline inspired by the former identifies stages in the development of human society and all its institutions to conclude that the tribal people and their society are at the lowest level of civilisational and human development. The Salvation Army believes that people who do not engage in productive work are vagabonds. They indulge in petty crime in the cities for their subsistence. Such work shirkers must be brought to the correction homes and taught skills for productive labour. The ideology of the Army and its agenda for the salvation of tribal people is made clear by one of its commissioners, F. Booth-Tucker:

> The "wont-be-goods" be either transported to some island or settled in remote Himalaya valleys, where they would "soon become absorbed by inter-marriage with hill tribes, many of whom greatly need new blood, while the majority of "would-be-goods" be placed in agricultural reservations like those which had produced the "successful and complete pacification" of 3,000 Red Indians in the United States of America.
> (1923)

The Salvation Army launched the correctional programme in London and moved to India to help the colonial administration in legitimising its civilising agenda and to lighten the 'white man's burden'. The *Report* for the year ending December 1911 mentions its role in Punjab: 'The Salvation Army have been quietly and steadily extending their scheme for the reclamation of criminal tribes. They have, with the assistance of the Local Government, established four settlements for members of these tribes: some success has already attended their efforts, and the prospects of the scheme are decidedly encouraging' (*Report on the Working of the Criminal Tribes Act [Act III of 1911] For the year 1911*. 1912, 6, henceforth *Report*). E. Lee French, the Inspector-General of Police (Punjab) instructs: 'All Police officers concerned are being requested to co-operate cordially with the officers of the Salvation Army in furtherance of the efforts of the latter for the reclamation of criminal tribes; and it is hoped that it will be soon possible to report that good progress has been made' (ibid, 7).

Criminal Tribes Act

The Criminal Tribes Act (Act XXVII of 1871) was passed by the Governor-General of India in Council on 12 October 1871. The main provisions of the CTA may be outlined for a quick reference. The Act had empowered the local government to declare any tribe, gang or class of persons criminal, and the criterion according to section 4 of the Act was their engagement in a 'lawful occupation'. It should be made clear in the report 'whether such occupation is, in the opinion of the Local Government, the real occupation of the tribe, gang or class, or a pretence of the purpose of facilitating the commission of crimes, . . . and the report shall also specify the place of residence in which such wandering tribe, gang or class is to be settled' (Simhadri 1991). The names of such persons were put in a register that was kept under the custody of the District Superintendent of the Police. The limits of residence of such people were laid out by the local government. They were issued passes with conditions inserted in them such as (a) the place where the pass holder could go or reside; (b) the officers before whom he was bound to present himself for attendance; and (c) the time during which he could absent himself from the residence.

The local government would also prescribe the inmates of the settlements' works, number of working hours and the rates of their payment. The violation of the settlement rules was punished with six months' imprisonment, fine or whipping, and the term of imprisonment was doubled and made rigorous with second conviction, with or without other punishments. The village headman and the village watchman were to keep track of the arrival or departure of any member of such tribes, gangs or class that had been declared and notified as criminal. It was to be reported to the nearest police station at the earliest. The failure in this duty was punishable under Indian Penal Code.

The prescriptions of Captain W. H. Sleeman and others connected with the Thuggee and Dacoity operations in the Central India had proved this point to the authorities that such people without a permanent hearth and home were a potential threat to the administration. This led to the enactment of CTA 1871, and the Punjab administration then readily asked for its implementation in the state. The Sansi and Bauria communities were most notorious for their allegedly criminal activities and were the first to be included in the list of the notified criminal tribes in the state. Interestingly, the Punjab police could foresee the provisions of the CTA and started subjecting some tribes to the system of roll call as early as 1856. The police, thus, got a fabulous tool in the Act to oppress the tribes. Taravaskis wrote: 'From time to time attempts were made to check the activities of these gangs but it was only when Sir Michael O'Dwyer became Lieutenant Governor, a thorough investigation was made into their mode of life. He was determined to wean them from their criminal instincts, and his policy was given effect to in the Criminal Tribes Act' (quoted in Sher 1965, 262).

In British India, 99 'criminal tribe' communities were identified and 44 in the Madras Presidency (Radhakrishna 2001, 171–75). In the first decade of the twentieth century there were sixteen criminal tribes in the Punjab (*Report* 1910, 14). The CTA 1871 was amended first in 1911 and then in 1924. After Indian independence in 1947, the CTA 1924 was repealed by the Criminal Tribes Laws (Repeal) Act, 1952 and these were called the denotified tribes or simply DNT. The CTA had identified the following six categories of people belonging to the Criminal Tribes:

I Petty traders that carried their merchandise like salt and forest produce on the back of animals.
II Communities that entertained the public through performing arts like musicians, dancers, singers, storytellers, acrobats, gymnasts, puppeteers and tightrope walkers.

III Communities that entertained the public with the help of performing animals such as bears, monkeys, snakes, owls, birds etc.
IV Pastoral groups and hunting, gathering, shifting cultivator communities within forests that traded not just in forest produce, but in animals as well.
V Artisan communities that worked with bamboo, iron, clay etc. and made and repaired a variety of useful articles, implements and artefacts.
VI Nomadic individuals who subsisted on charity or were paid in kind for 'spiritual' services rendered to traditional Indian society such as sadhus, fakirs, religious mendicants, fortune tellers and genealogists. Some carried medicinal herbs to provide healing services as well (http://nac.nic.in/pdf/final_dnt_recommendations.pdf; cited in Singh 2015).

The CTA laid out rules for identifying and registering the criminal tribes, sending the adults, both male and female, to settlements and their children to the reformatory. The Act defined the authority of different officials and punishment to the criminals for violating the rules. The principal provisions of the Act recorded in the *Proceedings of the Hon'ble Lieutenant-Governor in the Home (Police) Department, Resolution No. 75 dated 4th March 1902* are an amendment to the Criminal Tribes Act (XXVII of 1871) to improve the working of the system:

> Under the law relating to criminal tribes a tribe or part of a tribe may be proclaimed with the previous sanction of the Governor-General in council, and the Local Government may then order the District Magistrate of any district in which it is found to register it in part or in whole. Besides enabling government to deal with proclaimed tribes by settling them in prescribed places and by establishing reformatories for them (Sections 13, 15, 17) under pain of punishment for breach of rules made regarding such settlements and reformatories (Sections 19 (2)), proclamation makes all members of the tribe subject (Section 19 A) to minimum punishment on reconviction for certain offences, and makes it the duty of village officers, and of land-owners occupiers and agents of land, everywhere to report the arrival of persons suspected to belong to criminal tribes, and also to report the departure, from places where they had been residing, of the members of criminal tribes. Registration in addition brings the members of a criminal tribe under the operation of rules requiring their registration, within fixed limits, and attendance at roll-calls, and it makes them liable to arrest without warrant (Section 20) and to severe punishment (Section 19 (1)) for absence without leave from their registered places of residence or for breach of conditions of absence, and to punishment (Section 19 B) if they are found anywhere under suspicious circumstances, while the children of registered members of a tribe may be placed in reformatories (Section 17 A).
> (*Report* 1902, 1)

The framing of the rules under the CTA III of 1911 by the Punjab government in accordance with the requirements in the province sanctioned by the Secretary of State on 3 July 1917 are: (i) placing of all notified tribes, whether settled or wandering, under the full restrictions of section 12 of the Act; (b) the establishment of a Reformatory Settlement and several Industrial and Agricultural Settlements; (iii) removal of the worst characters to the Reformatory Settlement, the transfer of less undesirable people to the Industrial Settlement and the placing of the best behaved and half reformed members in Agricultural Settlement; (iv) the education of children; (v) the gradual training of the inmates of the Reformatory and Industrial Settlements into regular workers earning their livelihood by honest means; and (vi) the supervision of members of criminal tribes outside the settlements with a view to ensure that they have sufficient remunerative occupation and that they are kept out of harm's way. It is important to note that the allocation of a settlement is not based on the basis of traditional occupation of a tribe but on the basis of his worst, bad and good conduct.

It was suggested that the industrial and agricultural settlements are to be run through the agency of philanthropic societies (*Report* 1918, 2). It was under the order of Sir Michael O'Dwyer, the governor of Punjab, that the co-operation of philanthropic societies was sought to support the settlements, and many came forward to comply with the order (ibid, 6). Some of the noted ones other than the Salvation Army were Ahmadiyya Anjuman Ishaat Islam, Anjuman-i-Islamia, Arya Samaj, Chief Khalsa Diwan, Dev Samaj and Hindu Sabha (ibid, 6–7). Many scholars argue that the Imperial authority's criteria of characterising a community as criminal were however lopsided and methodologically flawed; that is why it created more problems than solve the issue. Yang also argues that 'the official descriptions of criminal tribes were also static and ignored the historical dimension' (1985, 116).

'Criminal' tribes

The *Report on the Administration of the Punjab and Its Dependencies for 1908–09* informs: 'There are sixteen criminal tribes in the Punjab proclaimed under the Criminal Tribes Act either throughout the Punjab or in particular districts. The largest of these are the Sansis and the Baurias' (*Report* 1910, 14). These tribes were not only large in numbers then but were the first and the second tribe, respectively, to be notified as criminal in the province. Their registration was not limited to a particular area or district but wherever they might be, throughout the state. A later *Report* of 1911 mentions: 'At the close of the year 1910 the total number of registered members of criminal tribes was 20,523 as compared to 20,444 at the end of the preceding year . . . The finger prints of 17,789 registered members were on record at the end of the year, and the work is being proceeded with' (1911, 3). Later, 'It was proposed, therefore, that all male members of certain tribes – Sansi, Bauria, . . . – over the age of 12 years, should be registered throughout the Province and anthropometrically measured, and that in all cases females should be exempted from registration and restriction' (Kaul and Tomkins 1914, 8). They mention that 21 wandering tribes – Nat, Kuchband, Dhe, Sansi, Bhangali, Barar, Gandhila, Bauria, Bhedkut, Mir Shikari, Kikan, Singhikat – to mention those included in the present study were admittedly criminal and were found in the province at the time of census. Thirteen other wandering tribes including those in the present study, namely Bazigar and Sapela 'though not professedly criminal, are yet not completely free from suspicion of committing theft and other crimes' (ibid, 68).

The colonial administration identified two broad types of criminal tribes, namely, the carriers and the vagrants. In the former were included Banjara/Labana, who ferried goods from one place to other for the people's consumption, while the latter type was split into many types such as grindstone makers, earth and stone workers, knife grinders (Shikligars); mat and cane workers included Buruds (read Barad); hunters and fowlers; jugglers and acrobats (Nats) and the miscellaneous including the Sansis (Baines 1893, 205–6).[3] About two decades later, Kaul and Tomkins made their own elaborate classification of the tribes in Punjab besides reflecting on their criminality:

> Exactly at what period, or in which circumstances, the various tribes became addicted to criminal pursuits is naturally in most cases uncertain, but the extent to which these communities have become hardened in traditions and habits of crime depends upon the length of time during which they have followed criminal pursuits as a profession and the circumstances in which they have been nurtured. The difference in their criminality at the present time is, therefore, one of degree; and the tribes with which we have to deal may be divided broadly into two large classes, viz., (1) the robbers and burglars and (2) the cattle-lifters. The former class is divided into two distinct groups, viz., (a) gypsy tribes which have, from time immemorial, led a wandering life, residing mainly in the jungles as hunters and fowlers, under easily portable cloth, or reed, shelters and availing themselves of all opportunities of thieving, until crime became a hereditary occupation with them; and (b) other settled tribes which, for one reason or another, took to thieving, with or without violence, either from love of adventure or as a lucrative profession. Members of the latter class have usually had a fixed residence, although they have mostly been graziers and have consequently led a more or less nomadic life within a certain area.
>
> (1914, 3–4)

The two authors, H.K. Kaul, an administrator, and L.L. Tomkins, a police officer, continue to deliberate on their methodology of surveying the criminal tribes that they considered was an arduous task:

> With a view to obtain an estimate of the strength of the wandering tribes of criminal propensities, we arranged to take a regular census of all wandering gangs who reside under portable reed, or cloth, shelters

and to collect information regarding their ostensible means of livelihood, to enable us to judge of their criminality. The total number of persons thus enumerated on the evening of 7th February was 1,14,440 but on going through the entries we found that 63,396 of them belonged to tribes undoubtedly harmless. The population of the tribes generally admitted to be notoriously criminal was found to be – males 7,463, females 6,998, total 14,461. At the same time, 36,583 persons (males 19,189, females 17,394) appeared to fall in a doubtful category.

(ibid, 2)[4]

A provision was made by the government of India so that the tribal people could earn a living honestly. According to that, the

Deputy Commissioners should give to the Lambardar of the village in which the gang resides, an order in writing stating the limits beyond which members of the gang, male or female, old or young, are not to go without special leave, and take care that the limit is clearly explained to the gang. It should be extensive enough to enable the gang to go for employment to any neighbouring village within 5 or 6 miles.

(ibid, 6)

The lieutenant-governor of the Punjab takes note of similar issues and suggests that such measures will induce the nomads to settle:

It is represented by the Deputy Commissioner of Hoshiarpur that there are many Sansis in his district who have *no fixed residence*, but the Commissioner, Mr. Melvill, has justly pointed out that there need be no difficulty on this account as the rules provide for Sansis changing their residence with the permission of the District Officers. Such permission should be granted without difficulty. At the same time it is to be hoped that the fact of having to apply to the District Officer for leave to change residence and to state the place of their future residence will in time induce the wandering members *to adopt fixed residences.*

(Kaul and Tomkins 1914, 63; emphases added)

It is not only the case of shifting places with the 'criminal' tribes but also that of shifting identities. The administrators thought that

There is a strong probability that many real Sansis have misled the enumerators into returning them as belonging to other harmless tribes and that others have escaped enumeration altogether. These wandering Sansi gangs are known as a whole among themselves as Bhantus, Bhattus or Chhatus and the tribe is broken up into *gots* or sub-castes known as Harrar, Barrar, Mahla, Biddu, Langali, Mahesh, Kopet, Tettlu, Kalkhar and Chhadi. They may style themselves as anyone of these *got* names or be known as Gandhila, Kanjar, Kikan, Bhedkut, Beria, Arhar, Aheria, Kuchband, Habura, Bhangali, Birtwan, Rehluwala, Gedri, Nat, Mir Shikaris, Behalia, Singikat, Dhe, Singiwala, etc.

(ibid, 68)

C.J. Hallifax, Judicial and General Secretary to Government, Punjab, in his note dated 22 July 1902 also wrote:

> It would appear that those entered (in certain lists) as (a) Sansi, Kanjar, Bhedkut, Kikan, Gedari, Habura or Rehluwala are really Sansis of the tribe known also as Bhantu, Bhattu or Chattu of which the principal sub-divisions are the Harar, Barar, Mahla, Bidu, Langah, Mahesh, Kopet and Tetlu . . . and that some of those entered as (b) Bazigar, Bangali, Changar, Gandhila, Nat, Perna, Jogi and Dumara are also real Sansis. The Sansi tribe appears to be the only one with regard to which action is necessary for the supervision of *deras* and the registration of individuals, and it would probably be sufficient at first to confine proceedings against wandering tribes to wanderers who are Sansis.

(ibid, 65)

It is not a case of concealing identities but having multiple identities simultaneously based sometimes on their birth, lineage, major and minor occupations and sometimes simply as *ull* (nickname). In the premodern society singular identity was not the norm. It was more for use amongst them or the people at large than for purposes of the state administration to make some entry somewhere. A particular identity was invoked given its context and reference. Therefore, these multiple identities appear more a case of misunderstood internal divisions within and between the tribal communities by the administrators, especially of a large one like the Sansis (presently 33 sub-groups), than a deliberate attempt on the part of its members to conceal their identity for purposes of duping the police.[5]

Modus operandi of the 'criminal' tribes

Crime, like any other activity, is a specialist's task that needs a particular type of skill and expertise. It requires training, and there are masters of the art as well. Teku and Panju, the two Bauria men were known thieves. Their reputation reached the palace of the Maharaja of Faridkot who summoned them to his darbar and asked them to show their skill by trying it on his treasury, *toshakhana*. They pleaded pardon but the Maharaja insisted. They were left with no option but to show their skill. Finally, they agreed to give it a try but on one condition: that they would not be executed. The Maharaja agreed. Some days later they carried out their mission successfully despite enhanced security. The Maharaja too kept his promise. He not only forgave them but also granted some land as a reward. Kaul and Tomkins also report the case of Kanjars:

> They had committed burglaries, robberies and dacoities, not one of which had been brought home to them and they were justified in concluding that their ways were perfect. They had dared to commit robberies and burglaries in the Ambala cantonment, and they had stolen things from the railway stations, and still there was no sign of their being held responsible for the crimes. So cleverly did they manage everything that very seldom did any suspicion fall upon them.
>
> (1914, 67)

The case of Mangroo of the Barwal tribe is equally interesting who was never caught by the police (see Chapter VIII, note 52).

The modus operandi of each tribal community is, thus, unique, which is why it is not possible to outline a general theory of their practices. Kaul and Tomkins provide some details of the following precautionary measures, which experience has shown to the Kanjars to be conducive to their business and were strictly observed by them. For instance: (a) No gangs were sent out on moonlight nights. (b) They never molested at night the villages near their *deras* (camps). (c) They would commit thefts and robberies in villages or roadside places that were 5 or 6 miles off. (d) Their *deras* would keep shifting. They would march off the place after each theft. (e) The village once robbed was not visited during the same wanderings. It is elaborated further: 'A village was pounced upon all of a sudden by a gang which committed two or three or sometimes four thefts or robberies, and then the offenders disappeared to be heard of no more for months or years. The village became alarmed by the occurrences, but as they were not repeated, no one thought of taking any active measures to find out who the culprits were' (1914, 66). The *Report* continues elaborating their modus operandi:

> The success and ease with which the Kanjars were able to carry on their depredations were due to their superior organization and training as a criminal class. They always went out in gangs of from five to ten men with sticks in hand, and determined to carry off anything that presented itself. They entered the village during midnight, and would mostly rob houses that were on one side of the village, so that if there was a row, they might be able to get away easily. They did not resort to making breaches in the wall, because that would take time such burglaries would cause much noise and necessitate a report to the *thana* and investigation by the police. They, therefore, took to the easiest and less noisy mode of moving the door from its stand – *chula utarna* – and thus got in or thrust in their hands and unloosen the chain. If they could find houses or huts which had no doors so much the better, but to them the business of *chula utarna* had become a habit, and they did not find any

difficulty in effecting an entrance. Usually only one or two men went in stealthily, the others watching on the outside. If he found that any man or men were sleeping in the house, comrades were called in, who, with sticks ready for use, stood at the cot, so that if the sleeping man wakes he will either be frightened or struck so as to disable him from pursuit. The members of the gang stuck to each other in time of danger, and each knew what part he had to play in the business. The thief had always a match box with him, and he would, in the dark night light a match to see where the property was. If a man, woman or child was fast asleep, a match was lighted to see if he or she had any jewel on. The dexterity with which they were able to take off a *hansli* or *nath or murkis* from the person of the robbed was great, and they were always sure of their booty when once they had it in their grip. They knew their own powers, and though they never unnecessarily used violence, they never scrupled to use force if it was necessary for securing the jewels, or for rescuing one of their party.

(ibid, 66)

A former Inspector-General of Police (Punjab) also informs about the style of another tribe called Jangali and its value system:

Cattle-lifting is their favourite crime and it is literally true that during dark nights they consider the cattle of others as their own. Not long ago, a young lad could not aspire for a wife or a turban unless he had stolen cattle. The chain or "Rassa" with them is a perfect institution and there are cases of stolen cattle being exchanged as far afield as U.P., Bikaner or Sindh. . . . They are generally averse to homicide and garrotting is not in their game.

(*The Tribune*, 3 March 1961)

It is recorded elsewhere for a tribe whose name is not given: 'The mouth of an infant of less than a year's age is stocked with a silver coin tied with a thread. Thus, the child develops a cavity to swallow jewelry and other such articles which are later safely "vomitted out", a technique to initiate the off springs into crime' (Deswal 1993).

The *Report* of 1923 notes that some wandering tribes consider stealing a divine right and resorted to it according to their requirements, just as an honest man would supplement his ordinary resources to meet some special need. It continues reflecting on their modus operandi:

The same is the case with the settled people who, though settled in name, had no settled work to provide them with the necessities of life. These included some of the worst criminals who by associating themselves with other bad characters among whom they lived, got better chances of operating at night upon the very houses at the doors of which they went about begging during the day. They were known as permanent local thieves and the thrifty house-wives propitiated them by liberal offerings of *lassi* (butter milk) and butter when they called at their doors.

(1923, 2)

The organisation of the group and sustenance of solidarity was a norm with these people. The *Report* validates the said viewpoint:

> The socialistic rules for the division of the stolen property and the provision made for the support of widows and families of persons imprisoned gave the organisation a compactness and secrecy which cannot be accounted for otherwise. They had their code of rules, and the *panchayat*, which settled their mutual disputes appears to have ensured to them a sort of autonomy. They never brought their quarrels to a court or to an outsider.
>
> (Kaul and Tomkins 1914, 67)

The authors of the above report further inform that in 1889, as a result of exhaustive inquiries ordered by the government, Turton Smith, the Deputy Inspector-General of Police (Punjab), wrote:

> As to the criminality of Sansis, I conclude from the reports now received by me and from the records to which I have access, that crime by Sansis, registered in our districts, is generally committed at no great distance from the place in which they are settled in their own district, or the districts immediately adjoining. There is an absence of evidence that the Sansis generally go far afield to commit crime. The Bengalis, a sect of Sansis, are constantly on the move in the Kangra district and in the submontane parts of Gurdaspur and Hoshiarpur, where they have at times given much trouble. The Sansiyas of the North-Western (United) Provinces are scarcely to be distinguished from the Sansis and Mr. Warburton proved that they were very dangerous criminals, addicted to violent crime, and that they travelled long distances to commit it. Speaking of the Sansis generally in the Punjab, the crime committed by them is not of a serious type, though they number among them some habitual house-breakers and thieves. * * * . . . The returns show that taking the convictions obtained in the seven districts in which Sansis were registered, there were in all in the nine years only an average of 31 Sansis convicted per year for theft, 12 for house-breaking, $2^{1/3}$ for robbery and dakaiti and 12 annually for other offences under the Penal Code.
>
> (ibid, 8; no italics)

It is noted further: 'These figures indicate the great improvement which has been brought about in the conduct of the registered Sansis during the sixteen years since they were first brought under the operations of the Act' (ibid, 8).

Tribal communities in colonial Punjab 37

The Sansis of certain area are quite troublesome but the Superintendent of Police, Lahore, 'recommends that the Sansis of his district deserve to be entirely exempted' from registration (*Report* 1911, 4).

The above views of the Deputy Inspector General of Police with regard to the distances covered during their expeditions are contested by certain accounts. A former Inspector-General of Police (Punjab) informs: 'A Biloch is seldom found committing crime outside his home district' (*The Tribune*, 3 March 1961). But there are some tribes that go distances from their place of residence. According to one such account, the District Superintendent of Police, Ludhiana, Ludlam, 'obtained information that a large number of absentees were living in Bombay. He went there and succeeded in arresting 38 persons. The Bombay Police were unaware that these persons were members of a criminal tribe' (*Report* 1903, 5). And, 'During the year (1922) only four criminal tribes' members belonging to (the) United Provinces and 15 belonging to the Indian States were convicted for the crimes committed within this province' (*Report* 1923, 4).[6] The District Superintendent of Police, Sailkot, has his own version of their modus operandi and the distances covered to commit a crime. He informs; 'The Pakhiwaras of Kot Mokhal are particularly criminal; the recent investigations ... in connection with some dakaities in the Gurdaspur District show to what distances these people travel to commit crime and how intimate is their connection with the Pakhiwaras of other districts, especially with those of Ferozepore' (*Report* 1903, 7; no italics).

A review report of the Police Administration in Punjab for the year 1925 reveals:

> Among the principal offenders are the Baurias of Muzaffarnagar in the United Provinces, a tribe infesting the low jungles of the Jumna riverain, and from their head quarters at Bidauli accustomed to overrun the adjoining districts of the Punjab. Adopting all sorts of disguises they appear as beggars, medicine-vendors or sadhus according to inclination, but all these devises are but a mask for crime. Next in precedence are the Bettiahs, Bangalis and Sansis whose share of operation covers most of the Central and Eastern Punjab.
>
> (*The Tribune*, 22 September 1926)

On the basis of the above discussion, it is not possible to draw a conclusive inference with regard to the distances from their habitat covered by the 'criminal' tribes during their expeditions. The colonial Punjab was huge in size, spread from Afghanistan to Jammu, to the United Provinces and to the Rajasthan borders, besides the fact that residents of this state were apprehended as far away as Bombay.

The Tribune of 31 August 1932 carries another news item under the head 'Sadhus by day and house-breakers at night' about the style of operation of some tribes. 'The police officials declared that the Sadhus were really members of a criminal tribe known as "Bauriah" hailing from the United Provinces, Rajputana, the Punjab, carrying daggers, axes, hatchets and other dangerous weapons committing house-breaking and other serious crimes and whose womenfolk decoyed prospective victims.' Sharma also writes in *The Tribune*, 20 December 1992 about the dexterity of the Sansis in house-breaking at night when they carve a hole in the wall with a pick axe: 'Invariably the hole was shapely, a monument to the Sansi patience and workmanship. The burglars were seldom caught'. There is another news report of rounding up of 75 persons including women by the Criminal Investigation Department (CID) of Bombay in December 1964. These arrests were made in connection with a series of dacoities in the far-flung suburbs of Bombay. The CID claimed: 'The dacoits are suspected to be "Bawarias", a former criminal tribe of Rajasthan set free from their settlements since Independence . . . these gangs have a "highly developed" system of gathering information' (*The Tribune*, 12 December 1964).

The police, however, do find patterns in the modus operandi of the tribes and from these try to identify the culprits. For instance, *The Tribune* reporting the death of a poultry chowkidar (watchman) and injuries to his wife informs the reaction of local police in attributing that crime to be the handiwork of a criminal tribe since its modus operandi is similar. And the similarities are: (i) Attack took place on a 'dark' night which is preferred by the tribe members. (ii) The gang members eat at the place where they strike, and in this case they had soft drinks. (iii) The location of the strike area is close to the GT (Grand Trunk) Road with the railway line running parallel is also typical of a denotified criminal tribe since it is easy for them to escape. (iv) A particular criminal tribe always defecates at the scene of crime. (v) Also, the criminal tribe members do not prefer to carry weapons (*The Tribune*, 22 June 2001).[7]

Settlements

The idea of settlements comes from the colonial modernist perspective that a person or a group without a permanent hearth and home is bound to be not only mischievous but a criminal since s/he is not engaged in a productive work. To make a living they commit crime since that is the only alternative. This issue was first raised by Lieutenant-Colonel Hutchinson, the Inspector-General of Police, in his letter No. 143, 21 December 1870:

> In the Punjab we have many migratory tribes such as the Gandhilas and many of the Bauria family, who cannot be said to have a *fixed habitation anywhere*. They live near a village whose lambardars consent to harbour them for a short time on payment of a portion of their ill-gotten gains. The place after a while gets too hot for them, and they move to some new locality. I think power should be given to the Local Government to *fix a place of residence* for such people. The only other

alternative is to declare such families or tribes liable to surveillance wherever they go and compel them to report to the Police.

(Kaul and Tomkins 1914, 63; emphases added)

The members of tribal communities notified according to the CTA were to be registered individually and subsequently interned in respective settlements depending on the nature of the tribe and its criminality. For the said purpose, they were literally hunted out for registration. The *Report* of 1918 provides a graphic account of the method deployed by the administration:

> Before daybreak on January 8th, 1917, every gang of the wandering criminal tribes, wherever located, was simultaneously raided in accordance with a prearranged plan and all adult male members thereof were taken to the police station where a registering officer, nominated by the District Magistrate, was present to register them and announced to them the restrictions imposed on them by section 12 of the Criminal Tribes Act. Considering the volatile nature of the people to be dealt with and the magnitude of the operations, the arrangements for registration were successful beyond all expectations. Very few registerable members escaped the net.
>
> (1918, 3)

Singh too notes how these members were subjected to surveillance:

> They were also issued identity cards that were mandatory for them to carry whenever they moved out of their settlement. For instance, the Bauria males were made to carry with them *chittha*, an identity card contained in a metallic pipe. Its absence was an un-bailable offense and one could be arrested then and there without any warrants. These people were roll called thrice a day by the local *chowkidar*, *lambardar* or at the police post. They could move out of their settlement only after furnishing full details of their destination and purpose of movement.
>
> (Singh 2010c, xv)

The tracking of 'criminal' tribes only was not enough, but to make their control effective, the administrative measures too were taken. The lieutenant-governor believed that to sustain the attention of the authorities, it is desirable that the report on the working of CTA be separated from the annual report on the Police administration. A direction was thus issued to that effect in 1901:

> the working of the Criminal Tribes Act shall not in future be dealt with in connexion with the Annual Police Report and shall form the subject of a separate report to be submitted for each calendar year by the District Superintendent of Police to the District Magistrate not later than

the 1st of May of the year after that to which the report relates. This report shall be forwarded by the District Magistrate with his remarks to the Deputy Inspector-General of Police, who after adding such remarks as he thinks desirable shall forward it to the Commissioner to be forwarded with his remarks to the Inspector-General of Police. The Inspector-General of Police shall review and forward all the reports for the Province to the Local Government not later than the 1st October in each year.

(*Report* 1902, 7)

Despite these measures the wandering tribes that had not been brought under control 'were giving a good deal of trouble' to the administration. The lieutenant-governor, thus, constituted a small committee to examine the issue and formulate a policy for the reformation of the criminal tribes. The committee suggested general principles, and the first recommendation was:

(i) A strict and effective, but sympathetic, control over the worst tribes or divisions thereof, where possible through philanthropic bodies, combined with the provision of sufficient opportunity for them to earn an honest living within the area to which they are restricted. (ii) The provision of definite conditions under which members of criminal tribes may, by continued good conduct, individually earn relaxation from restrictions and may thereby contribute towards the ultimate emancipation of the community from the operation of the Act. (iii) Provision for the education of children so as to wean them from their hereditary criminal traditions and open to them fresh fields of thought and occupation.

(*Report* 1918, 2–3)

It was normal and natural for the tribal people to escape registration since that meant not only surveillance but incarceration in a settlement. This confinement and police-controlled discipline imposed on the nomadic people could not be to their liking, which is why they would create problems there, misbehave with the authorities and attempt to escape. The *Report* 1914 informs:

When the registration took place in 1873, the more restless and wily of the gangs appeared to have escaped notice and they have been wandering ever since, driven about, on the one hand, by the fear of being registered, settled and *deprived of the only means of livelihood they understand*, and pursued by the notice-to-quit policy which has been evolved by the police under the guise of surveillance, on the other. Indeed, it would appear that the working of the Act, while tending to settle those who have been registered, has at the same time operated to a large extent to prevent wanderers from adopting fixed habitations by keeping them ever on the move, the officers in charge of police stations passing them on from one jurisdiction to another and hustling their movements to get rid of the nuisance with the least possible delay . . . Why, when they are so caught, they are not immediately registered, is not clear.

(Kaul and Tomkins 1914, 64; emphasis added)

The registered members of tribes notified as criminal by the government were interned in the industrial and agricultural settlements, where 'they should be provided work and *compelled to work for their living*' (Punjab Government n.d., 122; emphasis added). The special features of these settlements were:

(i) There was one Reformatory Settlement at Amritsar where hardened criminals of these tribes were detained for a period of five to ten years. It was practically a jail.
(ii) Industrial settlements were meant for criminals of lesser degree. The members of criminal tribes were provided work either in forests, factories or railway workshops.
(iii) In agricultural settlements, at various places, ten acres of government land was allotted free of cost to each member of the criminal tribe who had not been convicted of a non-bailable offence or absence during the last ten consecutive years.
(iv) The members of criminal tribes were also given land on a *batai* (share-cropping) system, and the government share was collected in the form of produce.

In the Reformatory School at Amritsar, children of these tribes between the ages of 9 and 18 years were removed for imparting education and industrial training (ibid, 122–23). This half-century-old reformatory, housing 232 members of the criminal tribes was wound up in September 1952, and all its inmates were 'freed from all restrictions' following the repeal of the CTA (*The Tribune*, 4 September 1952).

The tribal people brought to the reformatory or settlements were not detained there for life. The taming and training of these people was closely supervised by the settlement's officers and wardens. Their quotidian life was scrutinised minutely with respect to their productive labour, their learning of a skill for an occupation, general discipline, and overall behaviour towards the authorities and other inmates. Their release depended on the good report by the officers. According to the *Report* 1927:

After detention for five years in case of a member of a settled, and of ten years in the case of member of a wandering tribe the question of release is considered in consultation with the local officers, and the person concerned is released on two years' probation if he can find a paying occupation and a house to live in . . . The cases of others who wish to stay on are considered for grant of land if they are found fit for agricultural work. Final discharge is allowed if the conditions for release are fulfilled and conduct is well reported on by the local police.

(1927, 7)[8]

The inmates of settlements who were decent enough in the eyes of the officers were evaluated positively and rewarded duly. Some of them were made a part of the police force as well. The *Report*1912 confirms: 'The Superintendent of Police, Ludhiana, proposes to enrol in the Police some 30 members of the Sansi tribe who have behaved well. There are already one or two men of the same tribe in the force in the Ludhiana and Gurdaspur districts who are doing good work' (1912, 4). A later *Report* attests to the decent behaviour of another tribe: 'The Baurias are the next important tribe. They are said to have behaved well on the whole . . . In Ferozepore they have come forward in large numbers as recruits and their entry into military service should be a turning point in their means of livelihood' (1918, 18). It may be noted that the above-mentioned tribes were at the top of the list of tribes notified under the CTA.

The colonial administration believed that 'The criminal tribes' settlements are by far the best media for reformation of the criminal tribes. Close supervision, proper restraint and sympathetic guidance go a long way to reform the habitual criminals, and steady improvement is visible all round. Growing aptitude for work, increasing contentment under irksome restrictions, domestic responsibility and thrifty habits augur well for the future' (*Report* 1927, 5). The *Report* continues:

> The wandering criminal tribes and even some settled ones come to the settlements with hardly any idea of religion or any faith in the religions which they nominally profess. Their *moral is despicable* and their *old customs and rites repellent*. Under the guidance of the staff in charge and special preachers appointed everywhere for this purpose they have begun to understand their religions, and have to a considerable extent freed themselves from superstitions and degrading rites. Except for a few cases of immorality the general tone has vastly improved. Many of them can now sing songs and Bhajans . . .
>
> (1927, 8; emphases added)

A previous *Report* of 1923 also notes:

> The economical, social, moral, as well as physical improvement effected among the tribes settled in the agricultural settlements provides a convincing proof that settlement on land is the best solution for the homeless wanderers still to be dealt with and the future allotment on the Sutlej Canal is therefore awaited anxiously with a view to provide for such expectant inmates of the industrial settlements.
>
> (1923, 7)

Subsequently, the *Report* lauds the congenial atmosphere of the forest settlements as well: 'The atmosphere of these settlements is particularly congenial to the wanderers who though accommodated in well built quarters find themselves for the greater part of the day amidst the environments to which they are used already' (ibid, 10). The inmates' view of these settlements and conditions, however, was in direct contrast to the official version.[9]

There is much gap in the theory and practice of the settlements. In practice, the tribal people could be interned on flimsy grounds. Sher quotes from Raghavaiah:

> They were sent to the criminal settlements for not paying a fine of one rupee. In this punishment we also find, "I have seen persons rotting in settlements from birth to death. Even in regard to this matter the courts have no rights to intervene. Known principles of jurisprudence and enlightened sections of criminal justice have always required that punishment should be proportional to the offence committed."
>
> (1965, 247)

The administration, however, was quite aware of the hard conditions prevailing in certain settlements. For instance, 'Some difficulty in filling the Changa Manga settlement has been experienced, due to the nature of work which has hitherto been the sole occupation of the settlers, viz., woodcutting, which involves hard and uncongenial toil. But the Salvation Army are now introducing silk-worm breeding and silk-reeling, and this measure should ensure the popularity of the settlement' (*Report* 1912, 7). The laborious work and the suffocating atmosphere of the settlement especially industrial did not go well with the nomadic people, which got reflected in their behaviour. An *Annual Report* informs:

> On the whole it may be stated that the inmates of some of the Industrial Settlements have not behaved well and this is obviously due to hard conditions of life obtaining there . . ., whereas the inmates of the Agricultural Settlements have generally given a good account of themselves. This fact indicates that as soon as suitable provision is made for the comfort of these people, they normally behave well.
>
> (*Report* 1938, 6)

There were apprehensions in certain quarters of the police administration that provision for land etc. to the criminal tribes' people was no solution to their remedy but effective punishment to those who violate the rules. They advocated strongly that no leniency should be shown towards such criminals. C. Brown, the Inspector-General of Police (Punjab), writes:

> I agree generally with the remarks expressed by Mr. Tollintont whether sufficient land has been given to the criminal tribes in Sialkot District to enable them to earn an honest livelihood I cannot say, but there is little

doubt that these tribes are *averse to hard work* and *prefer to beg and steal*, at the risk of punishment, to settling down as cultivators. Whether the efforts now being made to keep these hereditary criminals under proper control will have any effect must depend on the punishments awarded for the breaches of rules. Undue *leniency* for absence without leave will merely encourage vagabondism, which it is our endeavour to suppress. The object in view is to protect the law-abiding community from the depredations of *these pests*.

(*Report* 1903, 9; emphases added)

The 'congenial' atmosphere of the settlements claimed by the authorities becomes doubtful given the structure of the reformatory, for instance, as at Amritsar that was established in a disused jail in April 1917, which

is the most important settlement. It is meant for the worst class of men who require stringent control. Its population at the close of the year under report amounted to 1,018 souls including 433 men, 218 women and 367 children. Men are admitted either direct from the jail on the expiry of their sentence or on the recommendation of the District Officer... Men of the worst class are kept in a separate ward and placed under strict supervision. Desperate men who cannot be trusted or men who owing to their having no families with them cannot be relied upon, are made to work in the settlement factory on piece-work system. The rest are under proper supervision employed in the city at different places where paying work is available. Shoe-making, carpentry, and tailoring classes are maintained for youths under suitable instructors and at the close of the year 52 youths were under training. Seventeen trained carpenters, two tailors and 11 shoe-makers are working in the city and earning from Re. 0–8–0 to Re. 1–8–0 a day. The average earning per family per mensem during the year comes to Rs. 11–8–0.

(*Report* 1923, 8)[10]

An earlier *Report* for the year 1917, when the Amritsar Reformatory was established, informs that the inmates were

engaged on rope-twisting, niwar-making, durrie-weaving, carpentry, chick-making, caning chairs. Since the close of the year cloth-weaving and munj mat-making have also been introduced at the factory. The total earnings during the 9 months, April to December 1917, amounted to Rs. 15,852–10–1 against a total strength of 59,024 workers, giving a daily average per head, including men, women and children, of Re. 0–4–3. In the earlier days, possession of ill-begotten money and the aversion of the people to work kept down their earnings, but they gradually settled down to hard work... Nevertheless individual workers often earned as much as 14 annas or Re. 1 a day and ordinarily men seldom got less than 8 annas a day. A family of five, containing three working members, viz., a man, a woman and a child usually earn from Rs. 20 to Rs. 25 a month. Since the close of the year there has been an all-round improvement and the development of the factory at the Settlement has provided an excellent means of employment for some 100 to 200 workers, several of whom are learning skilled work.

(*Report* 1918, 8; no italics)

The administration was aware of the difficulties in managing the tribal people in the settlements. 'The most practical difficulty however lay in inducing the inmates to earn a regular and honest living. The majority of male members had never done a stroke of honest work in their life and being accustomed to live on other peoples' money, took time to understand the meaning of 'self-help"' (ibid, 8). The *Report* provides details on the problems of the administration:

The task undertaken at the Reformatory was beset with numerous difficulties in the earlier stages of the work. To begin with it was extremely difficult to reconcile the wandering section of criminal tribes to residents in a walled enclosure particularly under the restrictions imposed by rules relating to settlements. The very idea of being tied down to one place and to have their liberty, to follow their hereditary pursuit of thieving, restricted, was repugnant to them. A brief account of the attitude of the first gang of the wandering criminal tribes which was drafted into the Reformatory Settlement will illustrate my meaning. It was a typical Bhedkut gang consisting of a score of desperate ruffians who, on arrival at the Reformatory Settlement with their families under Police escort, squatted down on an open piece of ground in front of the Settlement and adopted an attitude of stubborn resistance against entering it. Men and women alike indulged in a continuous shower of threats and curses. The prospects of this first attempt at the reclaiming the wandering criminal tribe were by no means hopeful, but perseverance and tact bore fruit and a series of meetings of their panchayats coupled with explanation by the staff broke down the opposition and eventually the gang made up its mind to accept the inevitable and enter the Settlement. The members, however, made a last suspicious pause at the main gateway and, as ill luck would have it, they saw *looming large on one side the gallows* which the procrastination of the local Public Works Department subordinate had kept in existence in spite of repeated requests for its removal. This served as a red rag to a bull. And all members of the gang swore that they would much rather be shot than be hung at convenient on those gallows. Prolonged explanation follows and it was not till my General Assistant had exhausted his eloquence and power of persuasion that the gang streamed into the settlement, although it took the more obstinate characters another two days to get into the room. The ice having been broken the gangs that followed were easier to tackle but *none entered the Settlement without an outburst of temper*. Most of the gangs were, on arrival, found to be intolerably unclean, addicted to eating carrion and other unwholesome articles of food, while many indulged in intoxicants of all kinds. More laws were known only in their crudest form and even the simplest hygienic principles were repulsive to these *wild creatures*. The people moreover had a variety hereditary superstition which proved the formidable obstacles to all attempts at reform.

(ibid, 7–8; emphases added)

The problem of managing the tribes people in the settlements and in running the organisation was not something new but beset from the very beginning, as brought forth in a report written four years prior to the above mentioned one:

But the whole history of these settlements since their inception in 1856 is a record of trouble and difficulty. In the first instance, when placed in the settlements, the Sansis knew nothing of cultivation and were without the necessary capital and knowledge to develop the land and, later on when they acquired or were given the necessary implements and took to the land, their numbers increased far beyond the capacity of the land to support them.

(Kaul and Tomkins 1914, 9)

One problem that was reported was the lack of land allotted to each inmate of the settlement sufficient enough to make a comfortable living out of that. With increasing severity in the implementation of the CTA and lauding the efficiency of the police in apprehending the criminal tribes' people, the number of inmates in the settlements was rising. Following the Punjab Government Resolution No. 75 dated 4 March 1902, the number of registered persons in Sansi *kots* (settlements) rose from 391 to 550. This reduced the per-capita land. Kaul and Tomkins report: 'the average quantity of land in the hands of every male Sansi came to something like 15 kanals, which was insufficient for the maintenance of himself and his family' (ibid, 9). The Deputy Commissioner of a certain district also mentions in this regard:

It appears to me, therefore, that the whole system is radically unsound, and I think that the idea of dumping down a lot of Pariahs on land which they are not habituated to cultivate, and which if cultivated would admittedly be insufficient for their maintenance, and then calling it a reformatory, discloses a misnomer the equal of which it would be difficult to find.

(ibid, 9)

In an earlier report for the year 1902, this issue was raised by Tollintont, who expressed concern over the insufficient land provided to the criminal tribes in the district of Sialkot that could enable them to earn an honest livelihood (*Report* 1903, 9).

It was not the economic problem that was worrisome, but the issue of religious conversion too plagued these settlements. The inmates of these settlements were targeted by the philanthropic agencies to convert them to their faith since they were expected to follow no organised religion of the civilised society. According to a report: 'These tribes do not belong to any particular religion. Sometimes the head of the family is a Hindu, his wife a Muslim, someone a Christian and another a Sikh' (*The Tribune*, 20 December 1951). Weaning them away from their primitive religion would grant them salvation, so believed the reformers. It would increase the numerical strength of that particular religion (Christianity). The settlements thus became the contesting space for altering the religious affiliation of its inmates. There are numerous reports in the newspapers then that brought this aspect of the reformatories to public view. Some communities were charging the authorities of certain settlements for forcing the tribal people to convert to Christianity especially those that were assisted by the Salvation Army.

A.S. Satyarthi of the Punjab Dalit Sewa Mission (Lahore) scripted the grievances of the Sansis of a settlement at Kot Adian, which was with the Salvation Army. He writes in his letter to the Editor of *The Tribune*:

> There is a universal complaint amongst the poor Sansi Hindus of the settlement that they are being harassed by certain persons and asked to quit their faith . . . There is definite provision in the CTA that the superintending agencies will observe strict neutrality and impartiality in the matter of religious concession and shall abstain from any sort of coercion.
>
> They are so sick with the present condition that they would prefer direct Government management to the present Christian settlement.
> (*The Tribune*, 6 June 1931)

There is yet another case of a serious dimension in which Abdul Karim levels charges against the Criminal Tribes Department in the High Court at Lahore under Habeas Corpus. He alleged that his wife 'Gauri and 13 months old daughter were illegally detained in the Reformatory Settlement, Amritsar under straightened circumstances and were being deprived of all help and assistance with a view to induce the woman by prolonged indigence and hunger to renounce her religion' (*The Tribune*, 16 December 1934).

At other places, a minority is labelling charges on the administration to be partisan with the majority community. For instance,

> The Ahmadiyya Anjuman Ishaat-i-Islam, Lahore at a meeting recently protested against the action of the Superintendent incharge in obstructing

certain Sansi inmates of the criminal tribes settlement 19/9 Eastern Kachakhuh, from declaring themselves as Muslims (sic) converts and against the attempts made to make them renounce Islam under pressure brought to bear on them by Arya Samaj preachers imported into the settlement. They have asked the Government to intervene.

(*The Tribune*, 20 April 1934)

Such issues plagued not only the settlements in Punjab but in other parts of the country. The Bombay Presidency was equally affected, and many organisations there raised their voices against religious interference on the part of the administration. The government of Bombay constituted an Enquiry Committee to look into these problems and made useful recommendations:

With regard to the administration, conduct and management of the various settlements the Committee has recommended that the Government itself should undertake the work instead of delegating it to voluntary agencies. The report says there are definite disadvantages in handing over the management of such settlements to agencies belonging to religion other than those of the settlers concerned and adds that there is a definite disadvantage in handing over management to Christian missionary societies.

(*The Tribune*, 8 August 1939)[11]

The partition of the country in 1947 and migration of populations including the criminal tribes added its own woes to the administration of the settlements. The *Report* for the year ending 1949 notes:

The location of the refugee members of the Criminal Tribes gangs and parts of tribes is very essential in the interests of the Criminal Administration of the State.

It is very difficult to watch their activities unless they are located and settled at a proper place. If they settle permanently, they will call (to their place of permanent settlements) their un-traced relatives and associates as well and the Police will be able to take notice of their activities. It is suggested that their previous record may be called (secured) from West Punjab and special staff (equipped with their previous record) be deputed to trace them so that new permanent record may be formed after a thorough search of the Criminal Tribes' persons.

(1952, 7)

It was also reported in the press:

After the carnage in West Punjab, a large number of non-Muslim members of criminal tribes migrated to East Punjab. 8043 acres of land in the Ludhiana district on the banks of Sutlej have been secured for them on temporary allotment basis. Settlers on these 8043 acres of land are also being encouraged to supplant their income by preparing "Murhas", baskets and brooms and working as labourers on the Railway Track.

According to the scheme of the Rehabilitation Department regarding allotment of land, some Criminal Tribes land-holders of West Punjab have also been settled on land in the districts of Ferozepore, Hissar, Karnal and Jullundur.

(*The Tribune*, 15 August 1948)

In the month of May, some 4,000 members of the Bazigar community crossed from the West Punjab into the East Punjab. The authorities announced that they would be settled at labour colonies near Bhakhra and Nangal (*The Tribune*, 10 May 1948).

Education

The education of children was considered important to wean them from their traditional occupations and to inculcate in them values of the modern society. They were to be equipped with modern skills for earning their livelihood through modern occupations. The education of children of all criminal tribes between the ages of 6 and 12 years whether living in settlements or villages was made compulsory via Punjab Government Notification dated 11 August 1920. For the education of tribal children, the *Report* 1923 mentions:

> At the close of the year 19 boys and 13 girls schools were working in the settlements and were attended by 730 boys and 339 girls respectively. A considerable difficulty has been experienced in securing suitable staff for these schools . . . Owing to this dearth of suitable female teachers girls' schools have not yet been started in some of the settlements. Similar difficulty is being experienced in the four schools made over to District Boards.
>
> (1923, 11)[12]

Four years later,

> Twenty-four Boys' and 22 Girls' Schools in settlements were attended by 1,167 boys and 580 girls at the close of the year 1926, as compared with 950 boys and 547 girls at the close of the preceding year . . . With a view to providing facilities for higher education a Co-operative Anglo-Vernacular Middle School has been established in Kachakhuh, which was attended by 56 boys at the end of December last.
>
> (1927, 8)[13]

50   *Tribal communities in colonial Punjab*

The above-mentioned *Report* lauds the efforts of the Special Officers, whose efforts have increased the number of boys from 1,100 to 1,701, though the number left out of schools is still very large (ibid, 9).

The administration was aware of the dearth of staff in the schools of the settlements and its reasons. The problem of suitable staff despite increased salary lies not only in the isolated location of these schools but also 'the unpleasant society with which they have to deal there' (ibid, 11). The authorities announced scholarships to the deserving students for their adequate motivation. The tribal children who were above average in intelligence were given scholarships of 2 Rupees each. The administration patted own back and recorded in the report: 'The sight of these well clad, smart, and intelligent children at some of the well managed schools is most refreshing when one remembers their starved and half clad appearance when first imported to settlements . . . The effects of education on the impressionable minds of these children are most salutary and indicate a very hopeful future' (ibid, 12).

A popular daily of the region with head quarters at Lahore, *The Tribune* also lauded the education programme for the tribal children:

> The education of the children of criminal tribes showed an all round improvement during the year. The number of pupils attending the schools for the criminal tribes rose from 2,242 to 2,351 of which there were 740 girls. Six hundred and twelve adults attended the night schools as against 532 last year . . . raising the number of Primary passed boys and girls to 487 and 118 respectively.
>
> (28 May 1932)[14]

The situation way back in 1915 was not good as reported in the news under the head, 'Criminal and Wandering Tribes in the Punjab'. It reads: 'Meanwhile Sansi villages were well reported and it was suggested to the District Boards to open schools for Sansi boys. But unfortunately the scheme was never acted upon, though so far back as in 1882 the suggestion was made by His Honour the Lieutenant-Governor' (*The Tribune*, 16 January 1915).[15]

Police and the tribes

The police, as part of repressive state apparatus, deal directly with people considered deviant by the powers that be. In this case, when the tribal communities were declared criminal, the police confronted them directly for their apprehension and registration. The colonial power used this force for multiple jobs like nabbing the criminals, the rebels, the revolutionaries, the nationalists and for the security of their officers, their families and institutions of the government. The Punjab police, however, is known more for its rough and ruthless behaviour than being a sophisticated and civilised force. The critics argue that this is a legacy of its colonial past. The tribal people even today fear the police most. Whether the police is an accomplice of the powerful or not, these people have strong lamentation that it does not let them live honestly. And this complaint is not a recent one but transcends the barriers of colonial and post-colonial times.

A former Director General of Police (Punjab), K.S. Dhillon, writes that the Indian Police Act of 1861 'retains in totality the traditional police role of subservience and commitment to the rulers rather than service and support to the people' (1996, 3). He refers to the twin legacies – servility and oppression – of police, servility to the ruler and oppression of the masses. He traces the roots of this culture to the chaotic conditions in Punjab just after its annexation in 1849. He argues: 'So from the very beginning the Punjab police had a task which was more medieval than modern' (ibid, 4). It is this medieval task which manifests not only in its rude behaviour with the public but also in the torture for which the Punjab police is quite infamous. The *Third Punjab Report* of 1854 comments on the use of torture:

> The attention of the Panjab Authorities has been earnestly directed to the prevention of torture by the police. It was rash to assert, perhaps vain to hope that the practice may not be occasionally resorted to in a mitigated form, it is to be borne in mind that this practice has been resorted to for ages and having actually become an integral part of native institutions, is now difficult to extirpate.
>
> (ibid, 4–5)

The police as an internal security force was never free from such weaknesses. The New Police Commission appointed by Lord Curzon in 1902 to look into its functioning reported: 'The police is far from efficient; it is defective in training and organisation; it is inadequately supervised; it is generally regarded as corrupt and oppressive; and it has utterly failed to secure the confidence and cordial cooperation of the people' (Bayley 1976, 47). Much water has flowed down the five rivers since then. The moral condition of society and its police have deteriorated further. The findings of a survey conducted in the 1970s well apply to the Punjab police. Bayley says: 'The survey data reveal a profound public distrust of the police, especially with respect to their honesty and their impartiality. The familiar observations of public officials, scholars and policemen themselves that the police are suspected of many kinds of improprieties is clearly borne out' (ibid, 218).

It is surprising that despite changes in the governments and socio-economic and political milieu, the negative traits of the police in Punjab have remained in place over the last more than a century and a half. The story of fake encounters in the second half of the last century, earlier of the Naxalites and later of the Sikh militants, had earned this force much notoriety. There were gross violations of the human and the civil rights of the people. The tribal communities are no exception to the police's brutalities. The police in their bid to cover up such gross irregularities and violations of the rights was either blaming the criminal tribes or the judiciary for being lenient in punishing the culprits. The latter issue was raised to such levels that the lieutenant-governor of Punjab had to take note of the 'undue leniency in punishing members of the criminal tribes' in a meeting of the Home (Police) Department in December 1902. He recommended an increase in the severity of the lighter punishments (*Report* 1903, 3). A.B. Kettlewell, judicial and general secretary to the Punjab government, wrote:

> For breaches of other rules, however, small fines are not generally appropriate, and His Honour would like to know what justification there is for fines such as that of one anna only inflicted on a Sansi convicted in Hoshiarpur or of one or two rupees imposed in several cases and notably in Jullundur where 4 previously convicted Harnis were fined Re. 1 each . . . His Honour thinks it very necessary that persons found guilty of breaches of the rules should be dealt with more severely than is often the case at present.
>
> (ibid, 4)

The copies of these proceedings were ordered to be forwarded to all Inspector-Generals of Police, the Commissioners and the Deputy Commissioners in the Punjab. The order seems to have been effective. E. Lee French, the Inspector-General of Police (Punjab) who had also raised the issue of leniency towards the criminal tribes' people, reports:

> It is satisfactory to note that there have been few cases in which inadequate punishments were inflicted . . . In an Amritsar case the District Magistrate made a reference to the Chief Court, but the punishment was not enhanced. In the Jullundur case a Sansi who had been absent since 1905 and had been living under an assumed name and caste was arrested and sentenced to only one day's simple punishment.
>
> (*Report* 1912, 6)

But the Deputy Inspector-General of Police (Ludhiana) was not relenting and insisted on the severity of the punishment. He was complaining against the judiciary while referring to the cases of absence of inmates from the settlements:

> There is reason to believe that in awarding sentences for absence Magistrates overlook the fact that prolonged absence is usually for the purpose of committing crime. It is also feared that the provisions of Section 23 of the Criminal Tribes Act, under which a registered member of a criminal tribe may not be awarded a lighter sentence than that prescribed by that section on second and third convictions for certain offences, is lost sight of.
>
> (*Report* 1917, 8)

This tension between the police and the judiciary is perennial and continuing still. The top brass of the Punjab police was not only critical of the judiciary but also their lower staff down the line. They expressed worry at the indifference of the deputy inspectors. Kaul and Tomkins report:

> The Deputy Inspectors really not knew how to deal with these wily criminals; stolen property was not forthcoming and theft could not be proved... No one cared to bother his head with their doings, more especially as no complainants came forward to charge them with offences. Laterally, the Kanjars had become very bold; they had seen that the law could not catch them and the police were apathetic.
> (1914, 67)

The cruelty of the police, however, was not receding. They were devising ways and means to achieve the purpose. In order to keep check on the long or short movements of the tribal people, the police used the method of periodic attendance or roll call at the police post or the police station or with the village headman of that tribe's area of residence. The plight of the Sansis of Dida *basti* (district Gurdaspur) is graphically explained by Sunder Singh, the Member of Legislative Assembly (M.L.A.) and Parliamentary Secretary of the Public Works, Punjab, in his letter to the Editor of *The Tribune*:

> But it pained me to see that even at night they were not allowed to have sound sleep. Every male member of this Basti is required to answer the roll call twice at night. It is alleged that during the day time they are required to attend the police station, Dinanagar, twice which is at a distance of about 2 miles from their Basti, that is, they have to cover eight miles a day in coming and going to the police station hardly leaves any time for their earning livelihood. It is also alleged that they have to remain confined within the four walls of this Basti... if they just crossed the wall of their house *even by an inch*, they were liable to be arrested by the police on the ground that they transgressed the boundary line prescribed by the police.
> (18 November 1946; emphasis added)

Such harassment by the police was not peculiar to Punjab but was a pan-Indian phenomenon. The fate of Koravas and other nomadic tribes in the Madras Presidency was similar. Radhakrishna narrates the plight of these people, citing government records of 1931–32:

> [T]he notified people could be called to the police station even at midnight. A large number of CT members were required to report to the police at least once a day, frequently more often. Distance of reporting centres was deliberately made so long, that a CT member could be made to walk 14 miles a day in order to record his attendance. This meant

that if he had to report more than once a day, he could not go home between the intervals at all. Sometimes, it was alleged, they had to walk many miles in the night to appear at the police station and wait there till day break.

(2001, 60)

It was not a case of useless detention of the tribal people, but they were subjected to *begaar*, unpaid labour in the houses of officers and other elite. It is reported:

> In the Punjab, many members of the ex-criminal tribes died in life-long servitude to the village headmen. Sometimes the regular reporting to the police twice or thrice a day lasted for 10 to 15 years, with at night for several out any actual offence having been committed . . . As a result, many people were heavily punished and imprisoned. The times, 11.00 p.m. and 3.00 a.m., for reporting were such as to compel some persons to sleep at the police station and some deaths also took place due to excessive cold. But on the other hand, there were actual criminals who used to be marked present in spite of being absent at night even for several days together, because they shared their booty with the village headman or the police. Thus the innocent was made a criminal by the callous and unjust behavior of the authorities immediately over them, while the real criminals were encouraged to commit more thefts, out of greed.

(Sher 1965, 247)

It was no hearsay. It is stated by Ravi Shankar Vyas before the Bombay Government's Enquiry Committee of 1939:

> If a policeman or a Patel wants people to bring fodder for cattle, he registers a few young Dharalas (A tribe of Kaira district) who would become his servants. If an innocent Dharala goes about the village with a hukka in his hand, it is registered as an impertinence and an insult to the Patel, who gets him registered under the Act.

(ibid, 246; no italics)

It was not the case of illegal extraction of labour power of the tribal people but a legitimate policy of the colonial government. Booth-Tucker (1923) of the Salvation Army had already mooted the idea of sending these people to the Himalayas. *The Tribune* of 3 July 1940 carries a news item titled 'Bhantus Reclaimed: Success of Andaman's Experiment':

> In 1924, the U.P. Government submitted a scheme to send some Bhantus, a criminal tribe to Andamans not as convicts but on probation. 50 convicts were to be taken by the Chief Commissioner, Andamans. The

U.P. Government persuaded their families to accompany them. During 1926, 259 persons arrived. They were given land for agriculture and established a village called Ferozganj Colony. In March 1932, the Bhantu population was 450 persons that rose to 504 in March 1939.[16]

The transfer of power in 1947 seems to have made no difference to the police. Surprisingly, the police became more ruthless and enacted such acts as to put the whole force to shame. So much so, that the brutality of the colonial times stands belittled. Even that force did not indulge in acts such as the notorious case of tattooing *jeb-katri* ('pickpocket') on the foreheads of four Sansi women at the police station in Amritsar. The 65 years old victim, Parmeshwari Devi confesses on hearing the judgement of the CBI (Central Bureau of Investigation) court indicting the defendants in 2016:

> SP Chhina (now retired) did the tattooing to revenge thrashing of some cops when they had raided our bootlegging business. Then posted at Sangrur, Chhina and his men used to take "hafta" (literally, 'weekly' bribe) to let us run the illicit liquor trade. However, despite this, his men raided us and thrashed even women and children. At this we thrashed the police.
>
> (*Hindustan Times*, 9 October 2016)

Mohinder Kaur, another victim of 64 years, tells what happened then: 'I am still in trauma. The case haunts me. I am reminded of how my hands were tied with a chair and four policemen held me in place as a man with a machine used to write on steel utensils wrote those words on my forehead' (ibid).

The labelled community and the branding of women made life hell for them as well as their children. Mohinder Kaur regrets: 'Due to that tattoo, conductors used to force me off buses' (ibid). Her son, Pappu Singh, now 33 years old recalls: 'If any student found things missing from his bag, the teachers questioned me first, because everyone knew me as the son of "jeb katri"' (ibid). According to Parmeshwari Devi,

> This "jeb katri" branding spoiled my family life. I have three daughters and a son. The two daughters who were married before the case, were divorced because of social stigma. The third didn't get any marriage proposal. My son too died of depression as the police slapped many cases on all of us *to pressurise us to not give statement in court.*
>
> (ibid; emphasis added; no italics)

There is much truth in these statements. The Sansis do confess bootlegging since they have nothing else to do. The police too finds in them easy culprits. Whenever there is a theft of chain or purse at the bus stand or elsewhere, the Sansi women are invariably apprehended for interrogation. According to a senior respondent, '*Asin tan sadharan jindagi jeoni chaunde haan par pulaswale ni jeon dende. Sanu jhuthhe cesan vich phad lende ne'*. Literally, we wish to settle and lead a normal life but the (Punjab) police invariably indicts us in false cases (Kirandeep Kaur 2016). In the Malwa region, these women are allegedly more involved in chain-snatching, pickpocketing and assisting men in drug peddling, especially poppy husk (*bhukki*). When enquired about their involvement in such crimes, a common grouse as articulated by an elderly respondent is: '*Ji pulas vale ee ni tikan dainde, aseen tan izzat dee roti kamauna chahunde han.*' Sir, we want to lead a normal life with dignity but the police do not let us do so. A lady respondent blames the system for their alleged involvement: '*Jad badnami saadi hundi hi rehndi hai pher asin vi kyon na paisa kamaiye*'. When we are given to bad reputation then why should we not make easy money?

Such instances are not isolated. Therefore, it is very likely that the Sansis must have been dragged into the business of distillation by the liquor traders when these people were forced to settle down and registered. Once inducted into the circuit, it must have been difficult for them to move out, as is true of all underworld activities. It is very plausible that the police and the liquor traders' nexus that has grown strong over the years since the colonial times must have imposed distillation on the Sansis and inducted more and more of their people into the trade by slapping false cases on them. Once branded and afraid of false implication again in future, one tends to make easy money till one becomes a hardened professional. The Bhils have also been victim of similar circumstances. Hardiman writes: 'Landlords, usurers and liquor dealers who were protected by the colonial and princely states ruthlessly exploited those who became settled' (2011, 295).

It is also alleged by a social worker, N.R. Dardi of Ropar: 'They (CTs) were not being allowed to settle down as responsible citizens. In the event of a crime taking place anywhere, they were illegally taken away from their colonies by the police and subjected to torture' (*The Tribune*, 10 May 1959). Freitag also observes that police often frame the reformed people whenever there was some crime (1991, 254). These charges against the police were not the whims of the tribal people or their sympathisers but also reverberated by the Home Minister of India, Lal Bahadur Shastri, in his address to a three-day seminar on the *Problems of the Denotified Tribes* held at Delhi in 1963: '[I]n helping these tribes many factors had to be considered. The first was education . . . The second was the *tendency among police to swoop on the former criminal tribes* whether they committed an offence or not. The police should radically change their attitude to these communities' (*The Tribune*, 1 April 1963; emphasis added). The seminar was inaugurated by the Prime Minister Jawahar Lal Nehru.

The colonial police are responsible for building and perpetuating a distorted image(s) of these people. The upper classes have their own share in such misinformation. The bases of some beliefs other than criminality are incredibly ambiguous, such as the one reported in *The Tribune* of 1932. A first-class magistrate at Gurdaspur fixed Rs. 25 on a charge of having assaulted a Sansi woman. 'The youth's defence was that he had embraced the complainant, because he was suffering from malaria fever and there is a widespread belief in this part of the country that a man suffering from malaria can cure himself by embracing a Sahnsi (Sansi) woman' (17 August 1932).

The police had developed such notions about their demeanour and movements that the poor tribal people were often apprehended without substantial ground. The following case is an instance in this regard:

> The District Court (Lahore) compound was packed up with members of the nomadic tribe when about 72 persons belonging to the criminal tribes including a bridegroom were brought to the Court in handcuffs. Their relations who were waiting at a distance included the bride in tears. These persons were arrested by the police under section 109, Criminal Procedure Code on vagrancy charge following a raid in Model Town on the information that *they were likely to commit some crime*. A marriage was being performed at the time of the raid. The arrested persons were produced in Court and released.
> (*The Tribune*, 10 February 1945; emphasis added)

There is no change in the perception of independent India's police about the criminality of the nomadic tribes. Jayaraman writes about the fate of fortune-telling nomadic tribes of Tamil Nadu:

> A few months ago, a piece of jewelry went missing in a Chettiar home in Madurai, says Sangeetha, one of the Boomboommarakarars in Saimangalam colony. The police were called and told that the nomads had passed along the route a couple of hours earlier . . . They were arrested, searched, and let off as innocent. In another area, it was the accusation of stealing children for their entourage. They were beaten up, arrested, roughed up, acquitted again.
> (2018)[17]

The colonial police was so 'adept' in reading the minds of the tribal people that they could preempt their actions such as 'they were likely to commit some crime' or Sansis 'as a class they have very little power of resisting their craving for crime' (*Report* 1940, 11) etc. yet the crime could not be checked. The police often indulge in making sweeping statements without basis like 'The Baurias are elusive criminals and the statistics relating to them are not a true index of their criminality. They are responsible for much untraced crime' (ibid, 12). Interestingly, the tribal people are held responsible for such criminal activities that remain untraced. If not prejudice, then what it is? The police as a state apparatus always had a negative opinion of the tribal communities, which is why they invited animosity from the tribal people.

58 Tribal communities in colonial Punjab

This attitude is not peculiar to Punjab but to the tribes everywhere. Prasad notes in Bastar:

> All symbols of exploitation were targeted by the Marias. The focus was on the police and forest officials. The police and the forest guards were the most apparent forms of exploitation and symbols of the Raja's (read the state) misuse of his customary power. The protest was sparked by the establishment of a police station at the centre of the marh. The arrival of the police in one village symbolised the arrival of the 'alien' government.
>
> (2011, 219)

Thus, we find that the police perception of the tribal communities made during the colonial era to meet the requirements of the administration then continues unabashedly in the post-colonial times in dealing with the people of a free country. In some ways the 'nationalist' police rather became more ruthless and brutal, whether it is the case of fake encounters of the naxalites/Maoists or the Sikh militants or the alleged jihadis in Kashmir or tattooing the Sansi women inside the police station with utter disregard for the human rights.

Appearance and morality

It was not only the nomadic trait of the tribal communities that bothered the colonial administration but their general physical appearance and moral values too. Racially they were considered inferior and morally despicable. The latter issue made a ground for the administration to incarcerate them in reformatories. The racial characterisation of the criminals was in tune with the 19th century theory of criminology.[18] Ibbetson and Rose quote from *A Handbook of the Criminal Tribes of the Punjab* about the largest criminal tribe in Punjab, the Sansis:

> Sansi males are generally dark in complexion with bright sparkling eyes, while the females are more often fair. Their faces are cast in the aboriginal mould and are very "foxy" in expression . . . The fairness of complexion which a great number of the Sansis undoubtedly possess is to be attributed to admixture of blood due to the kidnapping of children of higher castes, the introduction of outside elements, and the illicit connections made by the Sansi with persons of decent status. The fleetness and agility of the males has always been noticed, as has the Amazon-like nature of their women-folk. But the Sansi though wiry, active and no mean-athlete is not big-boned or exceptionally powerful. Sansis, it is said, can always be detected by their smell which is described as a combination of musk-rat and rancid grease.
>
> (Ibbetson and Rose 1970, 378)

Major too quotes from *A Handbook*: 'they often eating of vermin, . . . and their religion, mostly a form of Hinduism,' was 'of very primitive, mixed and debased nature' (1999, 671). *The Tribune* of 31 August 1932 carries a news item 'Sadhus by day and house-breakers at night'. It gives the description of the Bauriah people by the prosecution witness before the city magistrate as 'tall stalwart men with ruddy eyes, sun burnt faces and hardened appearance.' *The Rajputana Gazetteer* also makes similar comments on the Bhils: 'They are a dirty race. The men wear their hair long, and hanging in uncombed masses over their shoulders. The women are small and ugly' (Hardiman 2011, 299).

Ibbetson and Rose also record about them that they survive by: '*either alms or theft* . . . The Sansi is still in the *suckling stage of human progress*, . . . To ask a Sansi to work and labour for his daily necessaries is as much an anomaly as to ask an infant at the breast to earn the nourishment it receives by personal effort' (1970, 378; emphases added). The tribal people living in nature are believed to be a dirty and filthy people with no regard for the sanitation and hygiene characteristic of the modern lifestyle besides other problems. The *Report* of 1918 also notes: 'When ordered to bathe on Sundays in May and June, some of the inmates strongly objected on the ground that they were not prisoners and would not offend against their tradition by frequent baths' (1918, 7–8). Thus, there is need to intern them in settlements. But such beliefs are dispelled by Sunder Singh, the M.L.A. (Member Legislative Assembly) and Parliamentary Secretary of the Public Works, Punjab, in 1946:

> A few days ago I paid a visit to Dida Doaba a Basti of Sansis in the District of Gurdaspur. I was pleased to dine and pass a night with them. These Sansis constitute a small group of hardy people mainly living on cultivating surrounding lands. I was surprised to see their *clean mode of life* which might serve a model to several so-called high caste families of Lahore.
> (*The Tribune*, 18 November 1946; emphasis added)

Radhakrishna also lists accusations of the colonial masters against the Koravas, a nomadic tribe of the Madras Presidency, that they have an *insatiable lust for wandering aimlessly*. They are a *lazy and idle* people whose *women have loose character*, and last but not least they are criminal' (2001, 12–13; emphases added). Such characterisation of these people is universal. Grann notes about the Osages of Oklahoma (USA): 'The Indians, in general, are lazy, pathetic, cowardly, dissipated' (2017, 117). He continues: 'A prominent member of the Osage tribe put the matter more bluntly: "It is a question in my mind whether this jury is considering a murder case or not. The question for them to decide is whether a white man killing an Osage is murder – or merely cruelty to animals"' (ibid, 215).

The colonial characterisation of these people has become almost a norm with the larger society to take these people like that – inferior, sub-human, animal-like, unhygienic, immoral and criminal.[19] As late as 1993, the oldest newspaper of the state, *The Tribune*, carries an essay 'Ex-Criminal Tribes: Born Criminals?' by Deswal that describes isolated but interconnected incidents featuring the criminal tendencies and immoral character of these people. For instance, 'A woman resisted the arrest of her husband by catching the legs of her six-month old infant, and swing the child like a club at the policeman who was trying to arrest her husband. The child died' (2 January 1993). Another incident not only describes the incredible cruelty of a human being and a mother over that, featured as a proverbial witch, *dyan* (witch): 'During a raid, a woman set her cottage a fire, and threw her two children in it. She then raised a hue and cry and said it was the handiwork of police' (ibid). Yet another case: 'When the police raided a habitation, the accused scaled a 20-foot brick wall like a lizard, and escaped arrest' (ibid). In this description the tribal person is not 'lizard like' but intended to be a lizard itself, if it is seen in the light of above characterisation of the criminal tribes. A colonial administrator writes about them in 1903: 'The object in view is to protect the law-abiding community from the depredations of *these pests*' (*Report* 1903, 9; emphasis added). Yet another *Report* (1918) refers to them as 'wild creatures'. The animals do not have morals and neither do the tribal people. It is believed in Punjab that a female snake eats its own eggs. So do the tribal mothers.

Notes

1 For instance, in the Pangi valley of Himachal Pradesh, toilets were built by the government in the villages that people dismantled. In Malana (Kullu (H.P.)), often called the oldest democracy in the world, the people dismantled the dispensary and the post office set up there.
2 The Salvation Army is an international charitable organisation founded by William Booth in 1865 in London. It seeks to bring salvation to the poor and the destitute. The Army's purposes are 'the advancement of the Christian religion . . . of education, the relief of poverty, and other charitable objects beneficial to society or the community of mankind as a whole.' It is a hierarchical organization, and the titles of clergy are named after the military ranks. The head of the organisation is called general, followed by the chief of staff. Rachel J. Tolen concludes: 'Yet the criminal caste reformatory was part of the more far-reaching dream of imperial rule. For within this confined, enclosed, and highly controlled circle of barbed wire it was possible to establish the relation between the colonizer and the colonized in concentrated form to maximum effect. The Salvation Army was acknowledged to act as an agent in the establishment of this relation within the reformatory' (Tolen in Jennifer Terry and Jacqueline Urla (eds.), *Deviant Bodies: Critical Perspectives on Difference in Science and Popular Culture*. Bloomington and Indianapolis: Indiana University Press, 1995, pp. 101–02).
3 It is surprising that the largest and the most notorious Sansis, and the first to be notified as a criminal tribe under the CTA, are included in the miscellaneous category.

Tribal communities in colonial Punjab 61

4 Kaul and Tomkins provide more details on the methodology: 'In this report, we have dealt separately with the settled and wandering sections of the criminal tribes. The annual reports on the working of the Criminal Tribes Act contain statistics of adult male members of criminal tribes registered under the Act, but there was no record of the total population of each tribe or section of a tribe declared to be criminal. On the other hand, nothing whatever was known as to the strength of the wandering tribes. We obtained from each district a statement giving details of the population of criminal tribes in villages containing more than 20 male members. These statements, which involved little trouble in preparation, show that the adult males over 12 years of age represent about one-third of the total population. This enables us to form a rough idea of the total population of the settled tribes with reference to the number registered under the Act; and, calculating in this manner, the figure may be assumed to have been (21,215 x 3 =) 63,645 in 1912' (Kaul and Tomkins 1914, 2).

5 For instance, there are 33 sub-groups of the Sansis, and each one has specific claims to its own identity. The department of Sociology and Social Anthropology, Punjabi University, Patiala, was assigned a project by the Punjab Government to ascertain the tribal characteristics of numerous communities including the Sansis. Many of the 33 sub-groups approached the department, complaining that the study did not include them. They had been left out of their chances of acquiring Scheduled Tribes status. It was hard to convince them that all of them had been considered under Sansis, and if the latter had been declared tribal, so were they. They were not relenting still. They wanted their name in the list.

6 The above persons are escapees from the settlements and not leading a normal routine life in their places. Their presence at distant Bombay should not be taken as an index of their inclination or attitude to carry operations at places far off from home.

7 One can only laugh at the similarities between the criminals and a particular criminal tribe suggested by the police to trace the murderers. Eating and defecating simultaneously at the site of murder is intriguing. It is surprising that despite identifying similarities of these criminals with the modus operandi of a certain criminal tribe, the police was not able to understand, why did they attack a poor couple?

8 'Thirty-eight men were sent out on probation during the year (i.e., 1926) and 25 were finally discharged. One hundred and thirty seven men are at present on probation in the districts and their behaviour is being watched. Fifteen of those on probation were recalled during the year owing to unsatisfactory behaviour or failure to comply with the conditions of release. Except in a few cases no complaints were received against those on probation' (*Report* 1927, 7).

9 They would escape from there. They were hunted and brought back. It made a permanent column in the *Annual Reports* on the working of criminal tribes and the police forces. The *Report* 1912 for the year 1911, for instance, records: 'The total number of absentees arrested during the year was 368, of whom 138 belonged to the Eastern Range, 210 to the Central Range and 28 to the Western Range . . . A sum of Rs. 787 was paid during the year 1911 for the capture of absentee members of criminal tribes, against Rs. 911 during the year 1910' (*Report on the Working of the Criminal Tribes Act (Act III of 1911) For the Year 1911*, Punjab Government Branch Press, Simla, 1912, p. 3). It was reported six years later: 'The vigorous enforcement of the Criminal Tribes Act was bound to increase, for a time, the number of absentees. So the number rose from 583 in 1916 to 841 in 1917, but 386 of them were arrested during the year against 189 in the preceding year . . . Rupees 937 were paid from the districts as rewards to persons who led to the arrest of absconders, besides rewards paid in special cases

from my office or by the Criminal Investigation Department' (*Report on the Administration of Criminal Tribes in the Punjab For the Year Ending December 1917*. Superintendent Government Printing, Punjab, Lahore, 1918, p. 17).

10 In then prevalent monetary system, one rupee had 16 annas and each anna had four paisa. In the present system, one rupee has 100 paisa only. The figures given for per day earnings amount to half a rupee (i.e. 8 annas or 50 paisa) to a rupee and a half.

11 This shows that the problem of religious conversion was neither a prejudicial construction of the tribal people and their sympathisers nor fake.

12 The problem of suitable staff despite increased salary lies not only in the isolated location of these schools but also 'the unpleasant society with which they have to deal there' (Report 1927, 11).

13 'Eighty-four boys and 17 girls passed the First Primary Examination and 4 boys secured District Board Scholarships. Sixty-two scholarships have been provided for children who though keen on obtaining education cannot afford the cost of books' (*Report on the Administration of Criminal Tribes in the Punjab For the Year Ending December 1926*. Superintendent Government Printing, Punjab, Lahore, 1927, p. 8).

14 It seems Primary (class V) was the highest level that most students could reach. At the subsequent levels of education, the number of successful students had shown sharp decline. Only 11 pupils passed the Middle examination (class VIII) and seven, the High school, that is, class ten (*The Tribune*, 28 May 1932).

15 Ajay Saini writes: 'The British attempt to inculcate a taste for settled life in the Andamanese by weaning away children from families, forcibly confining them to a home, teaching them English, numerals, crafts, cultivation, and domestic service was an abject failure. The youngsters longed to return home; they ran away; they were brought back; parents were persuaded to part with them using heavy inducements and gifts' ('The Stolen Generations', *The Hindu Magazine*, 28 October 2018).

16 At the end of March 1939, 37 Bhantus were working in the Forest Department; 45 in temporary employment in constructing embankments (*The Tribune*, 3 July 1940).

17 This is a fortune-telling tribe whose members keep a bull for the purpose.

18 With the ascendance of Biology in the 19th century, facial features were made to infer the criminality of a criminal. Cesare Lombroso and his successors believed that criminals are born with detectable inferior physiological differences. There are similarities between primitive human beings and apes like that of receding foreheads, size and shape of the head etc. He believed in the theory of 'born criminals'.

19 Three girl students from the middle class approached me to supervise their research on topics of my choice. I asked them to work on the tribes in Punjab. They agreed. But later expressed inability to continue since their parents did not want them to work on these people because 'they are dangerous' (*khatarnak lok ne*). The students of sociology and social anthropology could not convince their parents. One of them was a graduate from the US.

4 Tribal communities in the post-colonial Punjab

> I suppose I should be ashamed to say that I take the Western view of the Indian. I don't go so far to think that the only good Indians are the dead Indians, but I believe nine out of every ten are, and I shouldn't like to inquire too closely into the case of the tenth. The *most vicious cowboy has more moral principle than the average Indian* (emphasis added).
>
> Theodore Roosevelt in his speech 'Hunting Trips of a Ranchman' (January 1886) (cited in B.D. Sharma 2010)

> And you substitute in the above discourse the terms (i) 'West' by 'Tribal Territory', (ii) 'Indian' by 'tribal' and (iii) 'Theodore Roosevelt' by any one of the members of the Augustian Oligarchy of the Great Indian Democratic Republic, the real content and intent of Green Hunt – Elimination of tribals and Capital's Command over Resources at any cost – will be crystal clear.
>
> B.D. Sharma (2010)

The Punjab government that does not recognise the presence of tribes in the state seems much under the spell of an erroneous definition of a tribe provided by its central and superior counterpart. The Commissioner for the Scheduled Castes and Scheduled Tribes in 1952 defines tribe in a manner that seems more imaginary than realistic. It certainly does not apply to Punjab:

1. They live away from the civilised world in the inaccessible parts lying in the forests and hills.
2. They belong to either one or three stocks – Negritos, Australoids or Mongoloids.
3. They speak the same tribal dialect.
4. Profess primitive religion known as animism in which the worship of ghosts and spirits is the most important element.
5. Follow primitive occupations such as gleaning, hunting, and gathering of forest product.
6. They are largely carnivorous or flesh and meat eaters.
7. They live either naked or semi-naked using tree barks and leaves for clothing.
8. They have nomadic habits and love for drink and dance.

Mathur's comments are apt: 'Personally, I feel it is a typical case of fiction-creation by the government officers. Perhaps in romantic mood, exotic aspects of tribal culture were magnified and sought to be perpetuated, thus defeating the very objective of the Constitution in providing the safeguards' (1972, 460). It seems that to the Punjab government this state does not fit into the above definition, hence the declaration of it being free of tribes. More recently, Damodaran notes: 'Similarly, while the argument for isolation is also not borne out by much of the nineteenth century literature there is little doubt that distinctive cultures and ontologies were practised on the plateau. Many of these showed evidence of complex cultural exchanges from an early historical period distinguished by reciprocity' (2011, 65). 'What is clear from these histories, many of them conjunctural, is that the communities in Singhbhum and elsewhere were not in any sense "isolated" but were constantly interacting with other groups from the north' (ibid, 65).[1]

It is a fact that the present state of Indian Punjab is a miniscule part of the erstwhile state that spread from Afghanistan to Uttar Pradesh (U.P.) and from Jammu and Kashmir to Rajasthan. Despite shrinkage in territory and hence population, first in 1947 and then in 1966, the fundamental plurality and diversity of its people is still intact to a large extent, though in reduced proportions, and this includes the tribal communities as well, even if the government refuses to acknowledge their presence. Almost all the major tribal communities of the larger colonial Punjab register their presence in the shrunken post-colonial state. Ibbetson and Rose (1883) and more than a century later Singh (2010c) provide rich ethnographic details on many of the communities included in this study. The present chapter enriches certain ethnographic details of the tribes in the above works besides describing those that are not included in Singh (2010c) like the Gaadi Lohars, Gujjars and Sikligars. This is to avoid duplication and repetition.

The Punjab government classifies these tribal communities as the Scheduled Castes. The *Census of India (Punjab)*, too, does not recognise their presence as a tribe and enumerates them under a separate column – 'other communities' in 2001 and under the Scheduled Castes in 2011. In 2011, the population of denotified tribes or *vimukt jatis* stands at 520,948 persons. The Bazigars have the highest population (241,125) followed by Baurias (125,259) and Sansis (122,201). The three major communities and Gandhilas are preponderantly rural inhabitants, while the remaining ones are largely urban based. The Nat (3902) and Gandhila (3513) have the lowest population. The Sikligars are 11,807 persons, while Barad and Bangala tribes have 8451 and 4690 persons, respectively. All *vimukt jatis* (denotified tribes) have their areas or districts of concentration, though these may be distributed fairly well in other parts of the state.[2] But some of these communities do not have a single person at certain places. Besides the denotified communities, other nomadic tribes like the Gaadi Lohars and Gujjars are also present in Punjab.

Indian independence was not a smooth and pleasant affair but involved the partition of the country on the basis of transfer of population hitherto unheard off in the history of humankind. The tribal communities too were

Table 4.1 Population (sex- and area-wise) of 'other communities' of Punjab

Tribes	Males	Females	Total Population	Rural	Urban	Total Population
Bazigar	1,24,033	1,17,092	2,41,125	1,90,325	50,800	2,41,125
Bangala	2,436	2,254	4,690	933	3,757	4,690
Barar	4,417	4,034	8,451	1,277	7,174	8,451
Bauria	65,107	60,152	1,25,259	1,11,710	13,549	1,25,259
Gandhila	1,825	1,688	3,513	2,151	1,362	3,513
Nat	2,032	1,870	3,902	821	3,081	3,902
Sansi	62,889	59,312	1,22,201	89,244	32,967	1,22,201
Sikligar	6,219	5,588	11,807	2,859	8,948	11,807

Source: *Census of India (Punjab)* 2011

affected. The Minister of State for Home Affairs, Punjab, reported to the governor:

> At the time of partition of the Punjab, the total population of these criminal tribes was about 1,50,000. Some of these residing in West Pakistan came over as refugees. The present population of these tribes in the East Punjab is 1,01,000. Out of these actual number of persons under restrictions is 2,372 out of a total male population of the tribes of 24,318.
>
> (*The Tribune*, 20 December 1951)

According to a press release by the Punjab government sometimes later:

> The total population of the erstwhile criminal tribes (now known as STs (sic) after the repeal of the CTA in August 1952) in the State is 74,734 according to the Welfare Officer, Mr. P.L. Ohri . . . They are generally found in the rural areas engaged as agricultural labourers or carrying on indigenous industries such as rope and "chhaj" making. For their economic and social uplift, the Punjab Government has approved schemes (a) for establishment of 13 schools, (b) creation of 343 stipends amounting to Rs. 27,060 for education of their children from the primary to M.A. classes and also for training in technical institutions. Nine schools have since been started and four will be opened.
>
> (*The Tribune*, 7 July 1954)

History

Most of the denotified tribes (DNTs) believe themselves to be the descendants of Jaimal and Phatta of Chittorgarh in Rajasthan, while some others trace their lineage to Maharana Partap and his kin. All of them claim to be Kshatriyas of Rajput descent. Those who are not direct descendants claim to be associated with them in one way or another. These communities believe in their 'marshallness', of 'their being indigenous people and fighting against the invaders for their sovereignty and honour of the country' (Singh 2010c). They are not a part of the caste system but their claim for high caste status is a post-settlement phenomenon when they were to situate themselves vis-à-vis others in villages and towns. Singh writes about this practice in them:

> The tribes have generally remained outside the varna system. Therefore, only 11.8 percent of them recognize their place in it . . . When it comes to the self-perception of a tribal community in the regional hierarchy we find that 171 tribes, that is, 26.9 percent see themselves as being of a high status, while 298 tribes (46.9 percent) perceive themselves as being in the middle position. About 25.3 percent, that is, 161 tribes see themselves as being of low status.
>
> (1994/2001, 7)

Therefore, glorification of their Kshatriya past seems reasonable and plausible. The problem of criminality may be attributed to the pricking of this glorified self. What was the nature of their crime? What did they steal? Were they Robin Hooding? Else were these the 'primitive rebels' of Hobsbawm? (for details see Singh 2010c, xlix–lv).

The oral history informs that these people had become nomadic since their ancestors lost battles to Akbar or some other Mughal emperor. The popular legend goes that Jaimal and Phatta, the two brothers, were chiefs of their respective feudatories in Rajputana, who were also the commanders in Akbar's army. It is believed that Akbar 'wanted the hand of' (to marry) Jaimal's beautiful daughter, Sandali. The emperor's proposal was rejected out rightly by her father and uncle. Thus, they were put behind bars. One day, their well wisher advised them to agree to the emperor's proposal; otherwise they would simply perish there. It was the only way to escape. They listened to the advice and sent a message to the emperor agreeing to marry Sandali to him but on a condition that they be freed so that they could go to Chittorgarh to arrange the royal marriage. On a given day, Akbar reached there with all pomp and show. To his utter surprise, he was challenged by the two brothers for a battle. There started the fierce battle that continued for numerous days. The Mughal army had a tough time but ultimately came out victorious. Both Jaimal and Phatta lost their lives, while Sandali committed *jauhar*, jumping into the funeral pyre. The remaining soldiers ran for their lives and hid themselves in the forests. As the Mughal army was hunting them out, they disguised themselves as tribals or *van jati*, the forest dwellers, and developed a secret language for their safety. According to Majumdar: 'some of the tribes like the Bauria are skilled linguists and can speak fluently half a dozen languages or patois to cover their identity if need be' (1965, 378). They have been nomadic since then and had taken a vow to lead a simple life until they recover their kingdom. Some had also taken a vow not to sleep on the cot until then.

There are numerous tribes with their groups and sub-groups on the soil of Punjab. The following discussion is about the major tribes who had been present here for many generations. An attempt is made to introduce each tribal community, briefly touching upon its history to spell out the specificities of its people. Very often their legends of origin and emergence speak about their lifestyle and occupations. Some times their names too suggest their occupations: for instance, the Bazigars perform *bazi*, Nat perform acrobatics, Bauria make *baur*, a trap to capture an animal, Gaadi lohars do blacksmithery and Sikligars do *saiqal* (polishing) etc. The ethnographic details are given for those tribes that are not covered in Singh (2010c) else supplement those already there.

Bazigar Banjara

As a matter of fact, Bazigar and Banjara are two terms with separate meanings and two separate communities, but in Punjab the two go together as Bazigar Banjara. They are popularly known as Banjara in certain areas and Labana elsewhere. Probably, their occupation of *bazi pauna*, display of acrobatics on the ground as distinct from the Nats who do it on rope etc., is more accepted by the Punjabis, hence Bazigar. A *bazi* in Persian means 'play', but it also includes jumps of various types and of increasing complexity and difficulty, reflecting the skill of the performer and thrilling the spectators. According to Ibbetson and Rose: 'The Bazigar is usually a Muhammadan, the Nat a Hindu. Among the Bazigar both sexes perform, but among Nats only the males. Some say the Bazigar is a tumbler and the Nat, a rope-dancer, others that the former is a juggler and also an acrobat, the latter an acrobat only' (1970, 79). They write elsewhere:

> [A]nd it is possible that those who reach the higher ranks of the profession may call themselves by the Persian name: others again say that among the Nats the males only, but among the Bazigars both sexes perform; and this latter distinction is reported from several Districts. On the whole it is perhaps more probable that the Nat is the caste (sic) to which both classes belong, and Bazigar an occupational term. But even Muhammadan who dance and posture are called Natnis or more often Kabutris.
>
> (ibid, 163–64)[3]

The word Banjara stands for a trader, one who does *vanaj* or business. They had a pack of bullock carts that moved together in a caravan called *tanda* carrying trading material. Their camp is also known as *tanda*. Colonel Todd writes:

> The *tanda* or caravan, consisting of four thousand bullocks, has been kept up amidst all the evils which have beset this land through Mughal and Maratha tyranny . . . and they were too strong to be pillaged by

any petty marauder, as anyone who has seen a Banjara encampment will be convinced. They encamp in a square, and their grain-bags piled over each other breast-high, with interstices left for their matchlocks, make no contemptible fortification.

(Encyclopaedia of Indian Tribes and Castes,
Vol. 2: 360)[4]

The Punjabi–English dictionary mentions that the Banjara are traders or peddlers who sell bangles. This community had monopolised the transportation business during the Middle Ages and is still engaged in small trade and peddling especially selling bangles and trinkets. Colonel Todd considers Charans and Banjaras as the same just as Ibbetson and Rose do so for Banjaras and the Labanas of Punjab. The latter duo writes:

> This (Banjara) and the Labana caste are generally said to be identical, being called Banjara in the eastern districts and Labana in the Punjab proper. But Banjara, derived from *banij*, "a trader", or perhaps from *banji* "a pedlar's pack", is used in the west of the Punjab as a generic term for "pedlar". Wanjara (q.v.) is doubtless only another form of the name.
>
> (1970, 62)

They continue: 'the Banjara carriers from Rajputana are principally Hindus. The Musalman Banjaras are probably all pedlars. The headman of Banjara parties are called *naik* (. . . chief) and Banjaras in general are not uncommonly known by that name' (ibid, 63). They write further explaining their relation with other identities: 'The term Labana appears to be derived from *lun* (salt) and *bana* (trade), and the Lubana, Lobana, Labana or Libana was doubtless the great salt-carrying and salt-trading caste, as the Banjara was the general carrier, in former times. Indeed the Labana is occasionally called a Banjara' (ibid, 63). *Mahan Kosh* too subscribes to the Labana identity of being a salt trader, whose leader, called *naik*, would receive a rupee each from a house where a marriage or other celebration is held (Nabha 1995).

In different parts of India, they are called by different names, but in Punjab they are known as Bazigar Banjara, though invariably they are known popularly by the first name, that is, Bazigar. The Banjara term has numerous variations such as 'Brinjara, Lambadi, Lamane, Wanjara, Gohar Herkeri (Carnatic) who are primarily grain and salt carriers, cattle-breeders and cattle dealers, found all over the Dominions... They have no settled homes, but lead a wandering life in bands' (*Encyclopaedia of Indian Tribes and Castes Vol. 2*). Some respondents argue that all these communities are basically Banjaras, but their names are different in different states of the country. For instance, in Rajasthan they are called Guar Rajput, in Punjab Bazigars, in Uttar Pradesh (U.P.) and Madhya Pradesh (C.P.) as Banjara, in Bengal and Maharashtra as Gual Banjara, in Assam and Karnataka as Barjatian and so on.

The general report of the *Census of India*, 1891, by Baines informs that Banjara, also known as Brinjari and Wanjara, are traceable to the forest grazing lands at the foothills of Shivalik range in the Punjab. Their origin is unknown, but they appear in the tenth-century literature. Baines writes:

> Their name is said to be the same as that of the Kanarese castes of traders, Banjiga, from the Sanskrit Banijia-kara, merchant. All over Hindustan and Rajputana they carry loads on their bullocks to and from the coast. In the North Deccan they have settled down as agriculturists, though here this caste denies its connection with the wanderers. In the Panjab the caste most prevalent is that of the Labani, which is probably only a subdivision of the Banjara. The same term is used throughout the South Deccan and the central portions of Madras . . . There is a further distinction between the Labani and Banjara of the north and the same caste in the south, namely, that the former are either settled residents or well-behaved characters, whilst the latter are of very evil repute, and constantly on the move to avoid intimacy with the local police.
>
> (1893, 205)

These beliefs and assumptions about the origin of this community leave everything uncertain about it. But it makes certain at least one thing: that these are the people of great antiquity. Varady concludes:

> Any attempt at defining Banjaras, then, must be at least partly inadequate. Can so many groups with divergent characteristics be referred to under a single heading? What, if anything, sets them apart from other nomads? With nomadism as a point of departure, there are three key features which can serve as identifying criteria. First, Banjaras generally speak a language akin to Marwari, and there is agreement concerning their Rajasthan ancestry. Secondly, virtually all chroniclers of these peoples have noted their connections with oxen. And, finally, a common factor extending well into the nineteenth century was their institutional role as teamsters and transporters.
>
> (1979, 2)

But why are Banjaras called Bazigar Banjaras in Punjab? Singh explains:

> It is quite likely that there is preponderance of the descendents of Mola who was an ace acrobat. And those among the Banjaras who settled here specialized in acrobatics too to make a living especially when the Banjaras were coerced to leave their traditional occupation of trading on bullock-packs with the onset of railways by the British in the second half of the nineteenth century.
>
> (2010b, 29)

The majority of Bazigar Banjara of Punjab trace their origin to the Rajput kings/warriors called Jaimal and Phatta. A few respondents, however, deny this ancestry that they have anything to do with royalty except that they were their *praja* (public). According to Ibbetson and Rose, 'The Bazigars are in fact only an occupational group' (1970, 79). However, they say nothing about the relation between the two – Bazigar and Banjara.

The Bazigars also adopted the Sikh religion in the last quarter of the 19th century. Jaggi writes: 'Some Bazigars took to the Sikh religion under the influence of the Singh Sabha movement. At the time of the census in 1911 A.D., 10 per cent of all the population of Bazigars in Punjab had become Sikhs. Despite adopting Sikhism they are practising their old customs and rites' (2005, 1248).

Economic activities[5]

Bazigars are expert in *bazis* of many sorts, which are a treat to the spectators.[6] Certain *bazis* are extremely difficult and risk the life of the performer. A performing troupe in earlier days had a specific area of operation. They used to camp outside a village and announce the day of their show at the beat of a drum *(dhol)*. The neighbouring villages too were informed. After the show, they would collect whatever was given to them by the villagers, invariably some grain, wheat flour or *gur* (jaggery) etc., and then the band would move to the next place.

They also reared sheep, goats, cows, oxen and camels, especially female, hence known as *botianwale* Bazigar. The Guar Banjaras keep a cart and two

Figure 4.1 A Bazigar doing *bazi*
Source: Author

Tribal communities: post-colonial Punjab 71

oxen. One pulls the cart and the other follows behind. They had been trading since ancient times (*adi kaal ton*). They practised a barter system. Lakhi Shah Banjara and Makhan Shah Labana, whose names are significant in the Sikh religious history, were prominent traders of this community in their times. Goats are also very dear to the community. It is virtually a norm even now that each household must have a goat. Their goats are often of high quality and are kept like a newly wed bride (*navin viahi bahu vang*). Valjot, an insider narrates the traditional occupation of Bazigar men:

> The youth of the Guar Bazigar society (*samaj*) were engaged in either the display of *bazi* (*bazi paun da kumm*) or sale-purchase of cattle depending on the region. It was common to keep sheep, goats and buffaloes in the Doaba region. They would trade in buffaloes and camels in Malwa and buffaloes in Majha. Those members of the community who migrated from Pakistan also traded in scrap (*kabad*) besides the cattle that proved beneficial to them.
>
> (2009, 62)

Bazigar women were rather more engaged in economically productive activities. They used to sell brooms, needles – small (*suian*) and large (*gadhuian or kadhuian*) for long stitches on quilts – and bangles etc. They are still doing this occupation to some extent. They move out, keeping goods on their heads for sale, make melodious calls for drawing people's attention. They have a clear prominent voice and keep repeating at high pitch: '*Koi suian, gadhuian layo bhaine; koi damkade, bhamirian le lo; koi bhamirian bachiyan layi; koi vangan charah lo; koi surkhi lo; le lo bhaine*'(O'sisters

Figure 4.2 Bazigar women engaging the host
Source: Author

you may take needles – small or large. You may take toys for the kids. You may have bangles or lipsticks. Take it o' sisters; Singh 2010b: 44). According to Valjot: 'Guar Rajput/Bazigar are engaged in business since ages. About 25 to 30 years ago, the women of this community would supply all items of use by the domestic women (*gharelu aurtan de vartanwala sara sman*) in the rural households. They would obtain grain in return' (2009: 62). Tyagi (2013) too agrees with Valjot in this respect. He also includes agricultural labour as their traditional occupation besides singing and dancing. The *Sammi* form of folk dance is their favourite.

The Bazigar women are good at dance and go to houses where some celebration is being held like the marriage or birth of a son to congratulate the family (*vadhayian den layi*). They are given some money and/or jewellery now while earlier they used to get some grain or *gur* (jaggery) etc. in return. This happened when they left the nomadic existence and got settled in villages. This practice of women is continuing still, rather this is one of their primary activities now (Manvir Kaur 2014b).

Singh notes:

> In the words of an old respondent: "*Is kabile da loon-tel toran vich bazigar aurtan da bahut vadda yogdaan si.*" That is, the women of our tribe had great role in running their households. It is true even now. According to another respondent: "*Sara din pindan diyan galian napdian, Bazigarna sham tak apne tokre khali karke, dane-phake naal bhar ke hi murdian ne. Mardan nalon vi kayi vaar vadh kma lendian ne.*" Literally, the Bazigar women return home with basketful of grain etc. in the evening after selling their goods from village to village. Many a times they earn more than their husbands.
>
> (Singh 2010b: 42–43)

Bauria

All respondents claim to be the descendants of Jaimal and Phatta of Chittorgarh (Rajasthan). It is believed by them that there was a small water reservoir (*baoli*) near the fort whose water was not only sweet (*mittha*) but also sacred (*sucha/pavittar*). During their battle with Akbar, the injured were brought there and made to take water, which would not only heal their injuries but made them fit again for fighting. The Mughal army was upset and puzzled over the rejuvenation of the enemy's forces. Then a Bauria person informed them about the secret of the Rajput warriors. The emperor was advised to defile the sacred reservoir. Subsequently, some pieces of flesh were thrown there that resulted in the loss of its sacredness and its prowess of healing and rejuvenation. The valiant fighters finally lost to the royal army. Both the brothers were killed, and Sandali lost her life by committing *jauhar*. It is believed that from *baoli* they are called Baolias or Bawalias (Ibbetson and Rose 1970, 73). The ethnographic study informs that the person who revealed the secret to the enemy belonged to the Bhatti gotra, which is why his descendants are still

Figure 4.3 Bauria women
Source: Author

considered outcasts. The Baurias of other gotras do not give their daughters to them in marriage. Some other respondents believe that their community got its name from *baur*, the trap they lay to hunt animals.

The Bauria are otherwise widely distributed in the whole of India, especially in the north-western states where they are known as Bawaria. The *Encyclopaedia of Indian Tribes and Castes* has no entry on Bauria but two entries on Bawaria and Bawariya. The former are described as

> a hunting tribe who take their name from *bawar* or noose with which they snare wild animal . . . the Mahatam's nooses are made of *munj* rope while the Bawaria nooses are made of leather. They are a vagrant tribe whose proper home appears to be Mewar, Ajmer and Jodhpur; in the Punjab they are chiefly found among the middle Satluj valley in Sirsa, Firozpur, Faridkot, Lahore and Patiala though in smaller numbers in Hisar, Rohtak and Gurgaon, all on the Rajputana border.
>
> (*Encyclopaedia*)

Williams, the district superintendent of the police, conducted a special study of this tribe in Punjab. It is worth quoting his firsthand account in detail:

> These people in common with several other outcaste tribes who claim Rajput origin, . . . Nats, Gari Lohars and others, trace their social downfall to some great catastrophe which occurred to the Rajput power at Chictamgarh some centuries ago and which may, I think, be safely

Figure 4.4 Bauria men
Source: Author

assumed to have been the sack of that fortress by Ala-ud-din Khilji in the year 1305 A.D.

The clan names which survive of the Baurias are synonymous with those of the Rajput tribes and, although the Baurias ascribe their degradation to the hardships undergone in their wandering after the fall of Chitaur, which compelled them to feed on unclean jackals and vermin, it is fairly clear, from their own account, that they stood in the relation of vassals and not equals to the Rajput rulers of this country. In the same manner the Ghari Lohars pride themselves on having been swordmen, the Bauriahs are said to have been the bowmen in the Rajput forces. After

Tribal communities: post-colonial Punjab 75

their banishment, it is said, they converted their bowstrings into thong nooses, with which they snare antelope and other wild animals. Hence the name. Some Bauriahs still wear the Rajput Kara on the right ankle.

There are nine divisions, or castes, (sic) among the Bauriah, ... These names have territorial or occupational significance.

(*Report* 1903, 3; no italics)

The *Annual Report* for the year 1938 informs about the criminal aspect of this community: 'The Baurias are elusive criminals and the statistics relating to them are not a true index of their criminality. They are responsible for much untraced crime' (1940, 12). An incident is recorded: 'A gang of 5 Baurias broke into the house of the Tahsildar, Shahpur, and forcibly removed a pair of gold ear-rings off the person of his wife. During the investigation of the case it transpired that this gang was responsible for a number of burglaries in the jurisdiction of different Police stations' (ibid, 12–13).

It is also written about their criminality: 'From these figures it appears that the Bawarias are registered as professional criminals only in Firozpur and Ludhiana, ... Even where they are criminal they usually confine themselves to petty theft, seldom employing violence' (*Encyclopaedia*: 448). The Inspector-General of Police, H.T. Dennys, has also gone on record:

> The general behaviour of the Bauriahs, both in the Eastern and Central Ranges is reported to have been less satisfactory than last year. A large number of them are said to have taken to honest livelihood, but it is feared that they combine honest work with theft and that their camps become the centres for excursions into distant parts for the commission of crime. This feature of the Bauriah methods makes their control somewhat difficult.
>
> (*Report* 1917, 4)

The *Report on the Administration of Criminal and Wandering Tribes* (1914) also labels them as 'hunter by profession' since they use *wanwar*, a rope net for hunting, hence their name. They claim to be different from Sansis,

> But their separate origin appears very doubtful ... late Sir Denzil Ibbetson considered the Kanjars of the eastern Punjab to be Bauria, and it is now well recognized that Kanjars are Sansis ... The obvious reference is that the Baurias, Kanjars and Sansis are really one people, descended from a common ancestor. It is probable that Baurias form an off-shoot which separated from the Sansis at a very early date, apparently before the famous sack of Chittour and crystallized into a separate caste with customs and practices somewhat different to those of the Sansis. In more recent years they have, moreover, largely adopted the Sikh religion 6002 out of a total of 32,856 having been found at the Census of 1911 to be Sikhs.
>
> (Kaul and Tomkins 1914, 12)

The *Report* continues:

> Largely nomad in the beginning and scattered about the Province in small bodies, they were arrested by the application of the Act and pinned down, mostly in small isolated communities greatly inferior in numbers to the various other people amongst whom they found themselves ... The Baurias of Dewatwal and Lilan in Ludhiana, for instance, have been amongst the worst behaved communities in the past and, so late as 1911, those of the former village were strongly suspected in a dakaiti case.
>
> (ibid, 14)

In their nomadic life, the Bauria used to make *sirkis* or huts for residential purposes with the help of split bamboos erected in ground in a circle and covered with elephant grass (*sirkanda*). It was so well interlaced that not a drop of water could enter it. The mud was also raised around the bamboos. The entrance was closed with the help of a door made of the interlaced reeds (*kanian*). The whole family used to live there.

Economic activities

As they were nomadic forest dwellers, hunting and gathering was their source of livelihood. Presently, they work as agricultural labour and may take some land on *theka* (contract) for cropping. The Bauria men were very good at imitating the calls of animals, which endeared them to the rulers of the erstwhile states, who engaged them in their hunting expeditions. They were experts in recognising the footprints of the animals, which is why their men made excellent *khojis* or tracers. The princely states sought their services for tracing the thieves, as did the colonial police. The members of this community, thus, got a name *khura-khoj labbanwale*, the tracers. A *Report on the Working of Criminal Tribes* attests: 'The men of this tribe have been very useful in tracing criminals, but on account of their criminal propensities it is not considered advisable to enlist them in the Police at present' (1911, 5). The annual report of the ensuing year, 1911, also notes while commenting on the general good behaviour of these people: 'In the Ferozepore district they have been very useful as trackers and have on various occasions rendered useful assistance to the Police. At horse and cattle fairs they have made excellent chaukidars' (*Report* 1912, 3–4).

Bangala

A nomadic tribe whose main traditional occupation is snake charming by playing melodious tunes on *been*, a musical instrument made of the gourd pipe, and selling herbal (*desi*) medicines. In *People of India*, Singh refers to them as Bangali, Sapera, Sapela, Sipado or Jogi, a community of nomadic people (2003, 66). In a separate entry under Sapela, they are called a landless community 'engaged primarily as snake-catchers and snake-charmers and also collect wild roots and tubers for medicinal purposes ... They visit different villages while playing their *bin* (gourd pipe), they visit households of various villages and collect *atta* (flour)' (ibid, 399). Ibbetson and Rose also note about this community:

> (1) a native of Bengal; (2) a vagrant tribe, probably akin to the Sansis (with whom they certainly intermarry) and found chiefly in Kangra whither they were probably driven from Hoshiarpur by the passing of the Criminal Tribes Act.
>
> The Bangalis are a small group but are in constant communication with the Sapehras and other criminal tribes of the plains. They live by begging, exhibiting snakes, hunting and pilfering, but are probably not addicted to serious crime. Their camps are said to contain never less than 7 and more than 15 male adults. They make reed huts ... travelling with donkeys as pack-animals. Dogs are kept for hunting, and the Bangali will eat any wild animal, even a hyena but he eschews beef and pork ... Their women are prostitutes, as well as dancers and singers. ... (3) The term Bangali is applied to Kanjar in some districts and in others to any Sapada or snake-charmer in the plains. There is no evidence that (2) and (3) have any connection with Bengal.
>
> (1970, 56–57)

Singh too writes quoting Ibbetson:

> In the Punjab ... none of these people have been returned in our census tables as Bangali by caste ... that in the Delhi division Bangalis have been included with Sansi ... The Bangalis have very probably been included with Jogis in the returns. These are a vagrant tribe of immigrants from Bangal. They keep dogs and donkeys and exhibit snakes, and have a dialect of their own ... The name is also applied generally to Muslim jugglers.
>
> (2003, 66)

Harinder Kaur also writes about them on the basis of her fieldwork in Punjab:

> Bangalas do not lead a settled life. They think that Gugga Pir has cursed them that is why they lead a nomadic life. Even if few of them have their *pucca* houses still they go out for months together in search of snakes and livelihood. They believe that if they tried to lead a settled life and stop begging, then they would suffer from leprosy.
>
> (Kaur 2010b, 73)

Kaur continues:

> These people know nothing about their history but one thing they are sure about is that they are the Rajputs ... Gandhila Chohan once ruled

Delhi who was murdered by the Muslim invaders from Iran. These Muslims then defeated Maharana Pratap, hence started the miseries of Chohan Rajputs . . . They took a vow, then, neither to live in *pucca* (concrete) houses nor to sleep on the cot till they regain their lost kingdom. This is how destiny made these people wear a yogi's dress (saffron robes) with a *been* in one hand and a sling bag (*jholi*) on their shoulder.
(ibid, 52–53)

They are nomadic also for reasons of collecting snakes and herbs. A snake once captured has to be released after six months. This is the word that they give to the snake that has been kept in captivity for making a living. A snake is given in dowry whose prestige depends on the strength of its venom.

Economic activities

There is hardly any change in the number and types of herbal medicines they are preparing now compared to their previous generation. In that sense there is no change in their traditional occupation but for snake charming that is hardly practised for various reasons. One among others is the legal ban on animal shows due to alleged cruelty on them and also for the protection of wildlife. Not so long ago they were often seen in the cities displaying snake charming. At a crowded place they sit down playing *been*, whose melodious tune has been immortalised in the Bollywood film *Nagin*, to gather the crowd. From the *jholi* (sling bag) is taken out a *patari* (cane basket). As its lid is removed, a hooded cobra raises its head and starts playing to the tune of *been*. The show has begun. At the end, the show master moves around the crowd with *patari* cover in hand collecting money. In the villages it is usually some grain or jaggery.

The herbal medicines prepared by them are more in demand in the rural areas and in the colonies of the poor in cities. But the rich people too seek them for their life-enhancing and 'potency' drugs. Kaur writes: 'It is expensive and sold at a very high price which varies from five to ten thousand rupees per ten grams. It is made of various rare herbs obtained from the Himalayas. They . . . are experts in curing skin ailments like *chambal*, *phulvehri*, leucoderma and psoriasis. They also claim to restore masculinity (*mardana taqat*) with medicines' (ibid, 67). The collected herbs are dried, powdered and made into tablets at home, in which women of the house also play a role. They make medicines for a good range of ailments and disorders.[7] Kaur (2010b) notes that they sell certain esoteric elements like *billi di jer* (cat's placenta), *billi da panja* (cat's paw) and *giddar singhi*, with *sindhoor* (vermillion) having mysterious powers. It is believed their possession fulfils all desires. They charge a high price for this material. The snake venom used in various Ayurvedic medicines and tortoise carcass fetch them good money. They are aware that this activity is illegal, but poverty compels indulgence.

Figure 4.5 A Bangala with snake in *patari*
Source: Author

Barad

The people of this community are timid and shy but social. They live in *kullis* (huts) made of *kanis* (reed) and *kahi* (Saccharum spontaneum) covered with tarpaulin or polythene. They trace their origin to Kashi (Banaras) as it is also the birth place of Adharmis, the followers of Ravidas. The respondents inform that they were engaged in similar occupation as Adharmis. They were considered untouchable and atrocities were committed on them, which is why they left Kashi. They came to the Kangra hills in search of a new life. Other respondents defy this belief. Harinder Kaur notes: 'They call it a myth because, as put by a respondent: "Nobody has ever seen any *math* or *dera* of our ancestors in Kashi. Neither any one of us goes there to worship our ancestors nor our elders had any knowledge of it"' (2010c, 76). From Kangra, then in Punjab, they moved down to the Shivalik foothills in the Doaba region of Jalandhar and Hoshiarpur, presently the area of their concentration. The respondents inform that the male members of their community settled in Himachal Pradesh specialise in making *chhaj* (winnowing pan), while they make *kanghis* only. Manpreet Kaur (2018) also suggests similar distinction between the two populations of the Barads.

Ibbetson and Rose call, 'Barar, fem. Barri, a low caste given to begging and roguery. In Jullundur, the Barars make winnowing fans (*chhaj*), baskets

80 *Tribal communities: post-colonial Punjab*

Figure 4.6 An old Barad couple
Source: Author

and sieves (*chhanra*) of reed. They also hunt with dogs. Their observances resemble those of the Chuhras' (1970, 64). Singh also mentions:

> Barar, Burar and Berar are recognized as Scheduled Castes in Punjab. They are an occupational group engaged in making *kanghi* (comb), which are used by the weavers ... The Barars of Banga (district Hoshiarpur) migrated from the district of Kangra (Himachal Pradesh) about one hundred and fifty years ago or six generations back.
>
> (2003, 78)

Kaur too notes:

> It is believed that they migrated from the district Kangra (old Punjab) now in Himachal Paradesh to Punjab nearly 150 to 200 years back that is almost seven generations before ... This community is engaged in making *kanghis* (combs) which are used by *julahas* (weavers) to weave *khadar* (coarse cotton sheet) ... This community is also engaged in making *chhaj* (winnowing fans) and *chhabrian* (baskets for chapattis) for long time but this business has also declined over time.
>
> (2010c, 75)

Economic activities

The main occupation of this tribe was making *kanghis* from reed available from the river banks and sold to Adharmi *julahas* (weavers) to weave *khadar* (coarse cloth) on *hath-khaddis*, the handlooms. With change in technology, the handlooms got outdated and with them the Barads lost their traditional occupation of making *kanghis*. Their women are engaged in the making of household items like *jude/maanje*, *binne/innus* and *charmakhan takle dian* that are sold by women. *Jude* (small) and *manje* (large) brooms are used to clean the floor, whereas *innus* are used to carry load on the head. Some also make *chhaj* (winnowing fans) for the grain and *chhabrian* (baskets). The modernisation of agricultural technology in Punjab has reduced the demand for these items. They also made *murhe* (sitting stools of reed) and *saf* (mattress).

The loss of traditional occupation has affected both men and women. Men are into unskilled jobs, wage labour etc. The women are now concentrating on selling bangles, *mehndi* (hinnah) and hairpins etc. in the towns and villages, which was not their main occupation earlier. The young males are making shutters and repairing scooters and cars while some are barbers and masons. Singh provides the details of the working population as per the census of 1981:

> 27.39 percent are workers (47.35 percent males and 4.14 percent females). Of them, 30.75 percent are engaged in manufacturing and

Figure 4.7 *Jude* and *binne* or *innus*
Source: Author

processing, etc. (17.71 percent in the household industry and 13.04 percent in other-than-household industry) which is probably indicative of their persisting involvement with their traditional occupation; 18.79 percent of the workers are returned as agricultural labourers; and 5.60 percent as cultivators; the balance 44.86 percent are returned under various other services.

(1999, 148)

Gandhila

There is a small entry on this tribe in the *Glossary* by Ibbetson and Rose:

> The Gandhilas are a low vagrant tribe, said by Elliott to be "a few degrees more respectable than the Bawarias", though in the Punjab their positions are perhaps reversed. They wander about bare-headed and bare-footed, beg, work in grass and straw, catch quails, clean and sharpen knives and swords, cut wood and generally do odd jobs. They are said to eat tortoises and vermin. They also keep donkeys, and even engage in trade in a small way.
>
> (1970, 278)

Singh notes in the *People of India* that 'the Gandhila is a small nomadic community who are under a vow to be barefooted and bareheaded . . . According to the *Census of India*' (1981), the total population of Gandhila in the state of Punjab is 1,869 individuals, with 1,000 males and 869 females. The Gandhilas mostly live in Jalandhar and Patiala' (2003, 194). The story of their name goes that their ancestors were Chauhan rulers of Delhi who were defeated by Babur. Subsequently, they escaped to the jungles where they met the Bangala people who advised them to keep donkeys instead of horses since they are deserters. When the Mughal forces encountered them on their search mission to locate the soldiers of the enemy, they informed them to be *gadhewalas* (who keep donkeys), and since then they are known as Gadhela or Gandhilas (ibid).

On the other hand, Malkit Kaur reports that they are settled in Punjab at three places, viz. Banur, the surrounding villages of Patran and Shatrana and in the village Mubarakpur (near Zirakpur), all in the old district of Patiala. Those settled in the villages of Patran and Shatrana mentioned that earlier they were called Bauria (2010d, 93). They too consider themselves Rajputs whose ancestor Kesar Mal Gandhila, hence their name, died fighting the army of Akbar to save the honour of two girls of the community from abduction. Ibbetson and Rose also note that they are under a vow not to wear shoes or turban till their possessions are restored to them (1970).

Economic activities

Their principal occupation was hunting and fishing. Only men used to go hunting, which was a collective venture. If a person fell sick, his share was given out of the hunt, and a widow was given the double share. They specialise in making and selling of brooms from the leaves of date palm (Phoenix Sylvestris) that was also their traditional occupation. The women make the brooms that were earlier taken by men on donkeys for sale and now on bicycles. It is due to this association with *gadha* (donkey) that people called them Gandhila. The goat rearing is also quite dear to them. Singh (2003) notes that they derive their name from their practice of trading in donkeys. Begging is their old 'occupation' but they also make toys from reed and paper.

With the loss of traditional occupation they now work as hawkers selling bedsheets and cloth. Some are working in the marriage band parties while women work as domestic help. Kaur informs: 'They do wage labour but do not work as *seeri* . . . They prefer working with more freedom as labourers than as permanent workers with farmers. They do all kinds of labour . . . they go to work wherever they find employment and even travel long distances. They are considered a hard working people' (2010d, 100).

Nat

This community is traditionally associated with public performance of acrobatics and drama (*natya*) for their livelihood that they are continuing still. They are spread over in many parts of the central and northern India, though their presence in Punjab is scarce and scattered at present. Their settlements are located at Ludhiana, Jalandhar, Phagwara and Khanna. Almost all Nats have migrated mainly from Kathiawar in Gujrat and Saharanpur in Uttar Pradesh. They consider themselves descendants of a warrior community of Gujrat, the Gour-Thakurs. They trace their origin to Amar Singh Rathod, a warrior king of Kathiawar. Their migration to Punjab is a recent phenomenon not stretching beyond the 1930s (Kumar 2010). Those who migrated from Gujrat quote earthquake as the reason for their displacement, while those coming from Uttar Pradesh cite employment and economic factors. They have settled in the urban areas of Punjab, living in shanties built on vacant plots or along the railway tracks.

The *Report*1914 informs that Nat are not a separate tribe. In fact, these are Sansis. It also suggests about their presence in Punjab in contrast to Kumar (2010). The Appendix I of the *Report* listing the 'Wandering tribes admittedly criminal' has put Nats at the top with 4,897 persons in the state as per census of 1911. It has 2,490 males and 2,407 females. These numbers are split further into two categories, 'over 12' years and '12 or under', with 1,542 and 948 males, respectively. The corresponding numbers of females are 1,444 and 963 respectively (Kaul and Tomkins 1914). The *Report* reiterates: 'It has been explained already that, with the exception of Pakhiwaras, . . . and the Harnis the designations given in the margin are merely functional or local names by which the more undisciplined and wandering sections of the Sansi fraternity are variously known' (ibid: 68).

Singh (2003) notes that in 1931, their total population was 3,80,657 persons with 2,07,245 males and 1,73,412 females. The Hindus among them

Figure 4.8 A Gandhila fisherman
Source: Author

were 1,02,358, Sikhs 41,820 and Muslims 2,36,304. The partition of the country had a drastic effect on their population in the state leaving behind 1,887 Hindu and merely 95 Sikh members of the community in 1961. Their population dwindled further to 43 persons in 1971 but rose again to 466 persons in 1981. In the last census (2011) their total number is 3,902.

Ibbetson and Rose tell a different version of their presence in Punjab. It is a typical gipsy caste of the Punjab that is divided into two classes; those whose males only perform as acrobats and those whose women, called Kabutri (lit. female pigeon) perform and prostitute themselves. 'They very generally trace their origin from Mewar; and they are found all over the Punjab, but not in the Frontier Province, where they are apparently almost unknown' (1970, 164). They refer to a curious legend about their connection with the Sirmaur state, now in Himachal Pradesh: 'Its Raja had promised a Natni (female Nat) half his kingdom if she crossed and recrossed the Giri river on a tight rope. She had crossed and was nearly back again when the Raja had the rope cut to evade his promise. The Giri in order to avenge her death in its waters rose and swept away the Raja's capital' (ibid, 165). This proves the point that ropewalking had been associated with this community since early times.

Economic activities

The traditional occupation of the community is performing acrobatic feats and earning a livelihood by holding such performances at various places. The rope walking is, of course, a spectacular event. The performing band consists of boys and girls from 6 to 14 or 15 years whose bodies are so supple and flexible that it is hard to belief them as people with bones and flesh. It is a treat to see a small girl holding a long bamboo in her hands and walking comfortably over a rope tied between two posts raised about ten feet from the ground. The band is usually a joint or an extended family, with the male head of the household as the master. He conducts the show, with a boy controlling the tunes of the Hindi songs during the performance. This is a recent development. Earlier the beat of the *dhol* (drum) created the pleasant milieu. It was played at a loud pitch to pull the crowd before the show. An elderly lady of the family is the master trainer who remains behind the show. Ibbetson and Rose inform about their traditional occupation as well:

> In addition to practising acrobatic feats and conjuring of low class, they make articles of grass, straw, and reeds for sale; and in the centre of the Punjab are said to act as mimics, like the Bhand, and as Mirasis, though this is perhaps doubtful. They often practise surgery and physic in a small way, and are not free from the suspicion of sorcery. Some are herbalists, and other musicians, but the drum is the only instrument they can play.
>
> (ibid, 164)

The number of people in the community pursuing their traditional occupation has declined considerably over the years. Their presence is now confined more to cultural fairs and festivals that are held in the name of conserving heritage than at public places. Besides doing wage labour they also join the marriage band parties. Singh writes: 'At present they are mainly engaged as unskilled labourers in urban areas. For social and economic reasons the traditional occupation of rope-dancing . . . has been discontinued as it is considered degrading by other communities because unmarried girls had to display dance on ropes in fairs and festivals publicly' (2003, 336–37).[8]

Sansis

They are settled in the villages and towns of Punjab. Though large-scale changes have taken place since the times of Ibbetson and Rose, some essential characteristics are still there which demarcate them from others. In the words of a senior respondent: 'We are as old as the legendary *rishi* (saint) Parshu Ram. Our ancestor, Sansar Bau had fought with Parshu Ram but could not defeat him. Thus, he was compelled to retreat to the forests. It is his progeny that has become nomadic.' The first written account of the Sansis is available in the *Glossary* by Ibbetson and Rose (pp. 362–79). It is one community that has the longest entry. It notes:

> The Sansis are the vagrants of the centre of the Punjab, . . . They are most numerous in the Districts around Lahore and Amritsar and are also found in considerable numbers in Ludhiana, Karnal and Gujrat. They trace their origin from Marwar and Ajmer, where they are still very numerous. They are essentially a wandering tribe, seldom or never settling for long in any one place. They are great hunters, catching and eating all sorts of wild animals, both clean and unclean, and eating carrion. They keep sheep, goats, pigs, and donkeys, work in grass and straw and reeds, and beg; and their women very commonly dance and sing and prostitute themselves. They have some curious connection with the Jat tribes of the Central Punjab, to most of whom they are the hereditary genealogists or bards; and even in Rajputana they commonly call themselves *bhart* or 'bards'.
>
> (1970, 362)

The religious composition of the Sansis is also given:

> About 11 per cent are returned as Mussalmans and a very few as Sikhs. The rest are Hindus, but they are of course outcasts. They trace their descent from one Sans Mal of Bharatpur whom they still revere as their Guru . . . They are divided into two great tribes, Kalka and Malka, which do not intermarry. They have a dialect peculiar to themselves.
>
> (ibid, 362)

Jaggi too suggests their link with Bharatpur and Sans Mal but also adds that there is another version that advocates these people to be Aryans or else they are the progeny of the soldiers of Alexander's army that remained here (2005, 221). These are found adhering to all the three major religions of the state. The Sikh Sansis, however, have not abandoned their traditional beliefs and practices despite adopting Sikhism. According to Sher there were 98 Sikh Sansis in 1921 (1965, 150).

There is also a reference to their Aryan connection in the *Encyclopaedia of Sikhism*: 'They claim descent from one of the Aryan tribes entering India centuries ago. Some of the immigrants settled in Rajasthan and parts of the Punjab while others continued in their wandering state like their original Aryan forefathers. The number of the latter increased as those settled in Rajasthan kept joining them under the pressure of Mughal influx' (1998, 46). It is also mentioned that their settlements are on the fringes of the villages but never on their southern side or near a cremation ground or the tomb of a Muslim saint.

Ibbetson and Rose also dwell on the official records: 'The Sansis are the most criminal class in the Punjab; and they are registered under the Criminal Tribes Act in nine districts. Still, though the whole caste is probably open to suspicion of petty pilfering, they are by no means always professional thieves' (1970, 363). They quote what the Punjab government wrote in 1881:

> Their habits vary greatly in different localities. A generation ago they were not considered a criminal class at Lahore, where they kept up the genealogies of the Jat land-holders and worked as agricultural labourers. In Gurdaspur, on the other hand, they are notorious as the worst of criminals.
>
> Where they are professional criminals they are determined and fearless, and commit burglary and highway robbery, though their gangs are seldom large. The thieving Sansis are said to admit any caste to their fraternity on payment, except Dheds and Mihngs; and the man so admitted becomes to all intents and purposes a Sansi.
>
> (ibid, 363)

The *Report* by Kaul and Tomkins also validates the above perception of the community: 'The Sansis constitute by far the most comprehensive and formidable hereditary criminal tribe we have to deal with. They are known by various names such as Sansi, Habura, Bheria, Bhantu, Bhedkut, Kikan, Kanjar and assume, at their convenience, titles like Nat, Perna, Bazigar, in order to conceal their identity, or to make it pretence of an ostensible means of livelihood' (1914, 4). The *Report* continues:

> The Sansis have always headed the list as the chief of the criminal tribes of the Punjab and they contributed very largely, in 1870, to furnishing the objects and reasons for the passing of Act XXVII the following year. Indeed long before then they had, with the Baurias, Harnis, Pakhiwaras and Biloches, been placed under surveillance and restrictions, in accordance with an executive Circular No. 18 of 1856, issued by the Judicial Commissioner. The restrictions over these tribes were increased

in 1865, when the Judicial Commissioner announced the circular to have the force of law, but in November 1867 the Chief court declared it to be illegal.

(ibid, 5)

In 1872, the Sansis were described as ' "well known as criminal" and "as a wandering tribe who do not possess any land. They are addicted to theft, cattle-stealing and house-breaking"' (ibid, 6). It was reiterated in 1873: 'The Sansis . . . and Baurias so far back as 1856 were proclaimed by the Government as criminals. Of their character it may be truly said that it has always, everywhere, and by all persons, been declared highly criminal' (ibid, 6). 'In December 1873, the Government of India selected the Sansi tribe as the worst of the six recommended and authorised the Local Government to declare it a criminal tribe. This was accordingly done in March 1874 in the Karnal, Ludhiana, Jullundur, Hoshiarpur . . . Districts, where members were known to reside' (ibid, 7).[9]'The Sansi men were restricted to a circle with a radius of 5 miles from their village, but women and children under 12 are free to move at will and go out begging, and have the reputation of stealing as well' (ibid, 10). And 'the Sansis are skilful thieves, that their depredations are mostly of a petty nature and that they are seldom caught' (ibid, 11).

Sher claims that Sher-i-Punjab Maharaja Ranjit Singh belonged to the Sansi community. He contests: 'the history of the Sansis of the Punjab would remain incomplete without an account of the life and ancestry of the great Maharaja . . . His real ancestry has been camouflaged by the Jats. The Sansis consider it an historical injustice to them' (1965, 13). Ibbetson and Rose have deliberated on this aspect in the following account:

> A Hindu Jat clan (agricultural) found in Montgomery and Amritsar. In the latter District Raja Sansi a village 7 miles from Amritsar is the ancestral home of the Sindhanwalia family which claims Rajput descent and belongs to this *got*. They are also found in Gujranwala. In Gujranwala they are described as an off shoot of the Bhatti clan and they take their name from one Sansi, whose great-grandson, Udrat, came from Bhatner in Hindustan 18 generations ago, and adopted a pastoral life in that district.

(1970, 362)

Jaggi has a different take on this issue. He says: 'There is Sanhsi caste among Jatts in Punjab. But this word is derived from the Sanskrit's "sahsi", that means courageous (himmatwala), one with guts (juratwala). This has no relation with the Sansi" caste. Maharaja Ranjit Singh belonged to this Jatt *got*' (2005, 221; no italics). Sher (1965) informs, the population of Sansis in Punjab according to 1951 census was 18,114 (Punjab: 15,000, PEPSU (Patiala and East Punjab States Union): 3,114). In 1981 their number rose to 61,986, rural 54,727 and urban 7,259.

Economic activities

They practice numerous occupations like keeping genealogies of Jatt patrons, entertainment by singing, hunting and begging. All these were allegedly going well with petty crime. Ibbetson and Rose draw their own inference in the last quarter of the 19th century:

> It is only recently that the Sansis have settled down in fixed homes and abodes. Their own statements show that up to the last thirty or thirty-five years ago, they used to wander indefinitely about the district living in *pakhis* or temporary shelters of straw matting or thatch. During this life their sole means of existence must necessarily have been either alms or theft and the thirty or thirty-five years which have elapsed since their settlement in various villages have been insufficient for them to fully recognize the fact that society does not permit its members to obey the promptings of nature, by which a man is naturally inclined to utilize anything and everything for his own sustenance, regardless of ownership. The Sansi is still in the suckling stage of human progress, where he expects to receive the means of sustaining life direct from the parent nature. To ask a Sansi to work and labour for his daily necessaries is as much an anomaly as to ask an infant at the breast to earn the nourishment it receives by personal effort . . . His brief acquaintanceship with a domiciliary civilisation has not been sufficient to impress him with the fact that the same liberty cannot be extended to his neighbour's cattle and crops.
>
> (1970, 378)

Darya, an insider, writes that when the Sansis were made to settle down in villages, they distributed about 12 or 15 villages to each group. Then they prepared the genealogies of the families and remembered these by heart. They started laudatory recital of the pedigrees (*kalan*). They would obtain as gift coarse cotton cloth (*khadar*), one rupee and a piece of jaggery (*gur*) (1997, 114). Sher also considers this a hereditary calling of the community, and they are addressed to as *daadas*, a term that literally means grandfather simply because they unfold the history of grandfathers. He provides details:

> At every harvest a Sansi family receives a *bhari* (a bundle of wheat corn) from every house of Jats. It may be remembered that a Jat family is allotted to a certain family . . . a Sansi gets his share of *riri* or *phakka* from the last threshing floor (*pir*) of Jats. Generally he gets eight seers of grain. Sometimes from well-to-do and liberal Jats, he receives riri up to 20 to 30 seers of grain. Sometimes, he is given grain instead of *bhari* also, in addition to his proper share, *riri*.
>
> Then comes the half-yearly *kalaan* of the Sansis. A Sansi goes to his Jat *jajmans* after every six months and recites their genealogy

(*shajra-i-nasab* or *peehri*). Every family gives him two or three seers of grain, and, at times, some rich and generous families, at the recitation of their genealogy, give him clothes and even money. The Sansis also go to the villages of the in-laws of the married girls of the Jats ... the Sansi women and young girls add to the family income by picking cotton in its season or gleaning ears of wheat (*sila*) at the time of harvest.

(1965, 131–32)

The Sansi community is also associated with country made liquor since when they were made to settle down in villages and peripheries of towns. A community elder from Gurdaspur narrates an anecdote that highlights the skills of these people in distillery.

Once some *goras* (lit. white men) came to Dida village and asked for liquor. They were served the local brew, a speciality of our people. They liked the drink and asked for the brand ... Our men were puzzled, since there is no name given to *daru* (liquor). When they insisted on the brand name, then someone said "Dida. It is Dida." Later, they wrote to their government that *Dida* liquor should be imported from Punjab.

Sharma, a native of Dida, writes about the change in the activities of the Sansis: 'Now instead of making holes in the walls they dig holes for matkas (pitchers) of liquor' (*The Tribune*, 20 December 1992).

The running of illicit distillation is not the creed of all people all the time. Like other tribal communities they are also engaged in odd jobs of the unskilled type like wage labour, scrap (*kabad*) collection, shoe polishing and peddling. But their women are often associated with petty crime like chain snatching etc. Singh notes: 'Sansis work as agriculturists, *behrupia*, shoe shiners, collectors of iron dust near the various factories, or work as casual labourers' (2003, 396).

Sikligar

Baines (1893) in his general report based on the *Census of India*, 1891, classifies Sikligars in the 'class' of vagrants and in the 'group' of knife grinders whose total population was recorded as 18,980. The Sikligars spelled Shikligar alone were counted at 16,781 then. Ibbetson and Rose spell it Siqligar and note that this word 'is the name of a pure occupation, and denotes an armourer or burnisher of metal. They are shown chiefly for the large towns and cantonments in Census tables; but many of them probably return themselves as Lohars' (1970, 427). The Sikligars are originally tribal nomadic people manufacturing and polishing swords for the Rajput kings in Rajputana. *Saiqal*, an Arabic word, means to polish, hence *saiqalgar* or colloquially Sikligar. The ancestors of present-day Sikh Sikligars have been converted to this religion by the sixth Nanak, Guru Hargobind (1595–1644) following the martyrdom of his father, Guru Arjan Dev. He donned two swords of *miri* (temporal) and *piri* (spiritual) and organised an army of Sikhs for the first time in their history to fight the mighty Mughals. Jaggi writes: 'They came in contact (*sampark*) with the Sikh religion then when Guru Hargobind Sahib started arming his followers. They were required to clean the weapons' (2005, 247). Subsequently, they were brought into the fold of khalsa brotherhood by Guru Gobind Singh. Sher notes the meeting of Ram Singh, one of their ancestors, with the Guru at Anandpur Sahib (Punjab):

> We have come from Marwar. We are armourers and since generations we have a high reputation for making arms of the best quality. Binjoli and Salamboor are our native places in Marwar. We are Rajput Sikligars. We had seen Guru Tegh Bahadur when he went to Assam and Raja Bishan Singh won victory; we used to make arms for the army of that Raja. We were saved by the grace of the Guru, otherwise we would have been washed away in the river . . . and have come to you on knowing that you succeeded him and you have a great love for the arms.
> (1966, 12)

The Sikligars were made to take *amrit* (nector) to become (*amritdhari*) khalsa Sikhs. The legendary Bachittar Singh, a short-statured man who repulsed the intoxicated armed elephant at the gates of the Lohgarh Fort (Punjab), was a Sikligar (Sikh) (ibid, 69).[10] Subsequently, some of them travelled with the Guru to Nanded in Maharashtra. They were Mohan Singh and Badan Singh. When the Guru despatched a jatha from there to Punjab under the leadership of Banda Bahadur, it included two Sikligars – Sundar Singh and Bhagat Singh (Sher 1966, 16). The Sikligars gradually scattered all over the southern states. In the Deccan, particularly Hyderabad, they have significant presence and are very particular of their Sikh form and identity. They are *amritdharis* invariably. The *pardhan* (president) of the Sikh Sikligar Samaj, Bahadur Singh says with authority that in case of head injury even we do not allow shaving of hair, stitching or no stitching (*tanke lagen ya na*) (Singh 2018).

Kazak mentions three types of Sikligars in the present Indian Punjab. These are (i) *basniye*, that is, permanently settled in cities engaged in manufacturing weapons and in small-scale industry; (ii) *ladniye*, those inclined to settle in cities and small towns in shanties (*jhuggi-numa bastian*) who make knives, locks and keys etc. and multipronged pitchforks (*tangli*); and (iii) *utthaniye*, the nomadic ones who repair shallow iron pans (*tasle*), iron cages and iron containers – large (*tokre*) for kitchen utensils and small (*chhiku*) for vegetables etc. (1990, 36–37).

Sher considers them a gypsy tribe related to the Banjaras. He writes:

> [W]ith the passage of time the Banjara lohars ramified into two sections (1) The Gadi lohars who even now make several articles of iron for sale and mend iron utensils, and other domestic articles, like the tinkers and keep moving from place to place.

92 *Tribal communities: post-colonial Punjab*

Figure 4.9 A Sikligar at work
Source: Author

(2) The Sikligars who used to prepare arms including guns, put them in a cart and move from place to place in order to sell them. The Rajas of the native states were their greatest patrons because they had to supply arms to their state-troops.

(1966, 6)

They also sharpen the weapons on hone (*saan*) for which they used to get 12 paisas for a knife, scissors, or a stab and 50 paisas for sharpening a sword. In the hilly areas of the Punjab, some people call them 'Badhi' as the edge of an arm is called "badh" (*dhaar*).

(ibid, 239)

Sher describes in detail the division of labour amongst Sikligars and their earnings per piece per day in the early 1960s:

The Sikligars divide the making of their iron wares into two types. (1) The thanda (unheated) work. In this type the iron of old and broken articles is beaten without heating it, and the desired shape of the article is given to it by simply flattening, thinning and lengthening by hammering. The thanda work is mostly done by the women. (2) Garam kam (heated-iron work). In this type of work one has to beat the red hot iron at the anvil, with a heavy hammer. This is done by the men. . . . One man can make six sieves in a day. One sieve is sold for 50 paisas. He can make 20 ponis (small sieves) used for straining tea etc. of wire and one poni is sold for 12 paisas. In this way he can earn three or four rupees a day . . . In the past they did not allow their women folk to go out of their encampments . . . But now their old restrictions on the movements of their women have relaxed and the children and women go and sell their iron articles. The main market of their articles is in the rural areas. Besides money they accept gladly the price of their iron wares in kind.

(ibid, 242; no italics)

Kazak writes that in earlier times the Sikligars used to make a special kind of secure lock called *kadi-jindra*. According to the ethics of this community, no Sikligar was allowed to make a duplicate key or even go to a non-Sikligar house to open the lock. Once, a person of this community called Mangal made a lock for the treasury of a king and gave its duplicate key to a thief. He got rich from his share in the treasury loot and settled at Ropar in Punjab. He started making a variety of locks, and his business flourished. Later on, he was caught, and the king punished him by letting loose the hungry dogs on him. Since then, the Sikligar community has excommunicated all those engaged in making locks and keys, as their member brought a bad name to the community (1990, 33–34).

Economic activities

This is one community that is continuing with their traditional occupation to a large extent. This is true of them in the Deccan even (Singh 2018). The scrap is collected from the junkyards where metal equipment is dismantled. Usually, the whole family works on it. Each member, young and old, male and female is engaged in this occupation at different levels of work. The large metal sheets are made into smaller pieces that are beaten and grated to render a piece, the shape of a knife or a vegetable-cutter or an iron pan. No polishing is required on the kitchen items they make. Once the product is ready for marketing, the male head of the household or the son(s) load these on their bicycles and move around, selling them and also repairing or mending the used items. One may encounter them often on a bicycle fitted with a hone for sharpening knives etc. In the cities of Punjab, one may notice them calling for sharpening the knives and fixing new keys to the locks etc. – '*Chaku-chhurian lavalo; chabi lavalo.*' According to Singh:

> Traditionally, the Sikligars are engaged in making swords, knives, daggers, baskets of steel (locally called *tokra*), *taslas* (it is used to carry

soil) and buckets (*balti*). They also replace the decayed bottoms of the buckets and *taslas*. Apart from this, they also manufacture other iron implements such as chisels. The articles or implements prepared by the Sikligars are of daily use for the rural people.

(2003, 413)

Gaadi Lohar

They claim Rajput descent belonging to Rajasthan, where they were manufacturing weapons for the kings. Their exodus from their habitat made them nomadic. They now move in bands of varying sizes that are primarily family units, joint or extended. The total luggage of the household is packed on a bullock cart driven by a single ox. The cart is beautifully decorated with metallic items of different shapes and sizes. Ibbetson and Rose note: 'the Gadiya Lohar, a class of wandering blacksmiths not uncommon throughout the east and south-east of the Province, who come up from Rajputana and the United Provinces and travel about with their families and implements in carts from village to village, doing the finer sorts of iron work which are beyond the capacity of the village artisan' (1970, 37).

Singh notes that 'The Lohars consider the Sikligar, Gadaliya Lohar and Nalband much inferior in status' (2003, 303).[11] This being a nomadic tribe,

Figure 4.10 Gaadi Lohar women
Source: Author

Figure 4.11 A typical *gaadi* (bullock cart)
Source: Amanjot Kaur

it remains on the move, circuiting definite routes. The area a band traverses on a route depends on the size of the band that may vary from 5 to 35 members or may be large. A band may comprise a nuclear family or the joint and extended family. A son-in-law may also be a part of the band as the head's wife's sister (Kaur 2014a). The present times are not supporting nomadism, which is why they are trying to settle down. This settlement becomes their headquarters. They start their nomadic circuit from there and return after four months or may be later.

Their stay at each place depends on the amount of work available there, the size of the band and length of the nomadic circuit. They camp on the outskirts of a village at some open plot and do not usually interact with the local villagers but for the work.[12] The senior generation does believe in the vows their ancestors had taken on losing the battle and adopting a nomadic lifestyle.[13]

Economic activities

There is, as a matter of fact, one major occupation that all Gaadi Lohars carry out till today whether they are in Punjab, Haryana or Rajasthan, and

Figure 4.12 Instruments of Gaadi Lohars
Source: Author

that is to make and repair the iron implements for use in agriculture such as spade, shallow iron pans (*bathhal/tasla*), axes etc. and utensils for domestic use like iron pans, frying pans (*kadahiyan*), tongs (*chimte*), and buckets (*baltian*) to name a few items. These are commonly used in the agricultural households in the villages. The women Gaadi Lohars are actively engaged in collecting and delivering these utensils and implements from the village households that are always repaired by their men. The unmarried girls are forbidden from collecting utensils. At the time of delivering the repaired items, they collect in kind either grain or flour for themselves and *chara* (green fodder) or *toori* (wheat chaff) for their ox(en). Sometimes, when these are not given, they are handed out cash. Kazak mentions three types of traditional occupations of this community that they had been following over a long period of time. These are (i) sale and purchase of oxen from Nagaur[14] and (ii) manufacturing/making of iron implements (*loh-sandan*) used in agriculture[15] and (iii) making and repairing of iron-items (*loh-vastuan*) of domestic use[16](Kazak 2005, 156).

Figure 4.13 A Gaadi Lohar at work
Source: Amanjot Kaur

Gujjar

This name, according to Munshi, 'is the spoken form of the Sanskrit word *gurjara*, the original name of the tract of land in western India where Gujjars had a very powerful and extensive kingdom called Gurjaradesa during the medieval age' (Singh 2003, 210). It is believed they travelled from Gujrat to the plains of Punjab and the lower hills of Himachal and Jammu and Kashmir. Singh (2003) includes Hindu and Muslims Gujjars in the *People of India* volume on Punjab, but there are Sikh followers too settled in the villages of Punjab that find no mention. The Hindu Gujjars are more along the Shivalik range and the Muslims along the Jammu border, where they have high concentration.

The Gujjar community is nomadic, semi-nomadic and permanently settled, who specialise in keeping buffaloes. According to Singh the Hindu Gujjars of Punjab, Haryana, western Uttar Pradesh and Rajasthan are agriculturists and pastoralists (ibid, 210), while the Muslim Gujjars of the sub-mountain region in Punjab and hills are pastoralists and nomadic (ibid, 216). Singh continues: 'By occupation the Gujjars are pastoral. They were once settled agriculturists but as they incurred great losses in agriculture, they disposed of their agricultural land. They keep buffaloes whose milk

98 *Tribal communities: post-colonial Punjab*

is transported to Saharanpur, Ambala, Khanna, Chandigarh, Amritsar and Hoshiarpur' (ibid, 217). Talking about the Hindu Gujjars, Singh notes: 'The land holdings per household varies (sic) from 5 to 50 *bighas* depending upon the size of the household. Each household has four to ten or more buffaloes' (ibid, 213).

Bhupinder Kaur writes about the Gujjars of Beet in the district of Hoshiarpur along the Shivalik foothills, who inhabit 22 villages. Each household owns one to ten acres of the rocky land. Given the terrain and water streams, these fields are fragmented. However, their major occupation is keeping the milch cattle. She writes: 'These Gujjars are different from others. Firstly,

Figure 4.14 A Gujjar man
Source: Author

they are not nomadic and secondly, they do not sell *ghee* (butter oil) like others. It is like selling own son' (Kaur 2010a, 22).

Economic activities

It is clear from the above discussion that whatever may be the type of Gujjar community, its members invariably keep buffaloes for producing milk and its products to earn their livelihood. The increasing demand for milk in the cities that are growing fast is sustaining this community. The households with land, use it for producing fodder besides some wheat etc. for domestic consumption, while the nomadic ones buy these items from the market. Singh notes: 'Buffalo milk is the main source of income which is disposed of in markets of the nearby towns' (2003, 213).

The ethnographic account above of the major tribes in the study shows a continuity of these with those in the colonial times as per the administrative *Reports*, the *Glossary* and *The Tribune* archives. No doubt, the regimes have changed, the powers have been transferred, the colonialists have been expunged and the patriotic nationalists have taken over reins of the free nation-state in their hands, but the plight of the nomadic tribes turned 'criminal' tribes turned denotified tribes has remained constantly dismal over the last more than a century and a half. They have suffered loss of respect, freedom, culture, hearth and home and their occupations at the hands of the game changers, though with some exceptions. They have been rendered de-skilled and coerced to undertake unskilled menial jobs in independent India. Their occupational diversity has disappeared. Baviskar too laments:

> Over the centuries, adivasis have constantly fought an unequal battle against outside oppressors – the state and the market. Although power

Figure 4.15 Kitchen side of a Gujjar dera
Source: Author

changed hands over time, being wrested from the Maratha by the Mughals, from the Mughals by the British, and from the British to the Indian nationalists, the adivasis only experienced a steady erosion of their material base and their cultural autonomy. National independence and the new project of development did not significantly alter this process; the universalising claims of development's benefits were meaningless to people who did not identify with the concept of "India" or "Our Independent State".

(2004, 230)

Xaxa also argues: 'Despite the attempts at absorption through administrative practices at both the central and state levels over the last fifty years, the attainment of constitutional objectives is still an elusive goal, and is going to become more elusive in the future' (2008, 82).

With growing poverty and heightened sense of relative deprivation, the de-skilled tribal communities are getting conscious of their rights and privileges granted to them by the constitution of India, which is why they are trying to raise their voice through their associations at appropriate levels of the political and administrative decision-making centres. The decision of the Punjab and Haryana High Court in favour of their Scheduled Tribes status has given them additional strength in this respect.[17] One thing that goes to their credit is that despite the apathy of the political and the administrative systems, they are struggling relentlessly to awaken the deaf authorities as also to raise the level of political consciousness of their own people. The account below provides a glimpse of their protests and demonstrations over the last few decades in the post-colonial Punjab, whose authorities are no less indifferent to their cause.

Relentless struggle

In the modern parlance, the tribes were first struggling against the vagaries of nature and now with the police and the general administration. It won't be an exaggeration to state that theirs is a life of relentless struggles. Their organisations had been spearheading their protests without missing an opportunity and any forum to impress upon the political leaders the genuineness of their demands. All leaders had been giving them assurances but to no avail. Once, the chief minister of Punjab, Parkash Singh Badal, promised them to do the needful at Gurdwara Muktsar Sahib in December 1977 but took no action. Later, 51 members of the vimukt jatis (DNTs) staged dharna near the MLA's Hostel, Chandigarh, in continuation of a dharna given by a panel of five members from each tribe on 26 January 1979.[18] There were a number of demands, but the main ones were a separate ST corporation in the state, reservation in jobs and that one-third of land allotted to the SCs be given to them (*The Tribune*, 4 February 1979).

In the same year, Gurcharan Singh Bauriya, a 28-year-old member of the All India Tapriwas and Vimukt Jatis Federation (AITVJF), died on 1 October 1979, who had been sitting on hunger strike to press the demands. The AITVJF urged the Punjab government in March 1980 to grant Rs. 5,000 to Mrs. Tej Kaur, the widow of Gurcharan Singh, and to create a trust in the name of Shaheed Gurcharan Singh with a grant of Rs. one lakh from the government. The meeting attended by the representatives from Rajasthan, Uttar Pradesh, Punjab and Haryana also impressed upon the government to start an 'ashram type school' in the name of Gurcharan Singh (*The Tribune*, 3 October 1980).

The AITVJF also submitted a memorandum to a Member Parliament from Punjab and speaker of the Lok Sabha, Balram Jakhar, seeking their inclusion in the list of Scheduled Tribes and also asking 'for a separate column in the Census for those belonging to their castes (sic) to help determine their exact population' (*The Tribune*, 30 November 1980). The denotified tribes have been carrying on their struggle relentlessly without much effect on the authorities. Thus, the Federation decided to sit on a 24-hour relay fast by its two members from 5 January 1980 in support of their demands such as a separate corporation to look into their affairs, reservation in jobs and of course inclusion in the list of STs.

When their stir did not create any ripples over the year, the AITVJF decided to celebrate the Republic Day in a unique way. The president declared: 'since the living conditions of members of these former criminal tribes had worsened after Independence and the Government had paid no heed to their worsening lot, men and women of these tribes accompanied by 40 monkeys, 12 snakes, seven bears and four mangooses will join the January 26 procession and submit a memorandum to Mr. Sarao' (chief commissioner) (*The Tribune*, 25 January 1981). After this novel demonstration, it was decided that two office bearers would sit on an indefinite fast from 5 February 1981. The Federation also decided to organise a rally with buffaloes, cows, mares, pigs, sheep, goats, monkeys and bears in the state capital (Chandigarh) on 24 February in support of their members sitting on fast whose health was deteriorating each day. They also demanded ten marla[19] houses to all the members of the vimukt jatis (DNTs) (*The Tribune*, 23 February 1981).

The president of the Federation also led a delegation to the Union Home Minister at Delhi, who assured them to introduce a bill in the Monsoon Session of the Parliament 'to ameliorate their lot.' When nothing happened, six members of the Federation sat on a fast at the Boat Club, New Delhi. They broke their 19-day-old fast on 10 April 1984 following a written assurance from the Union Home Minister that a bill would be introduced in the current session of the Parliament to include the Rai Sikhs, Gadarias, Saperas, Sansis and 193 other denotified tribes in the list of the STs, in the light of the judgement of Punjab and Haryana High Court (*The Tribune*, 11 April 1984). Another fast was organised at the Boat Club the next year in

May 1985, accusing the 'centre' (Union government) of dilly-dallying with their demands and ignoring the judgement of the High Court as well (*The Tribune*, 12 May 1985).

Interestingly, in Indian democracy the political game of protests and assurances continues unabashedly without delivering anything on the ground. The leaders of the Federation sitting on an indefinite fast called off their agitation after 20 days following a written assurance from the Punjab Minister of Labour and Welfare in September 1996. The hunger strike was threatened to be resumed from 26 November 1996 if the bill was not introduced in the Parliament. The Federation once again announced to withdraw the indefinite fast and their decision to observe 26 January (1997) as a 'black day' following an assurance from the Union government but decided to continue the relay fast at Jantar Mantar, New Delhi, till their demands were met.

Inaction on the part of the government is a perennial problem with regard to their demands simply because these communities do not make a cohesive vote bank. The political leaders, thus, keep on shilly-shallying with their protests, demands and memoranda without taking them seriously. Consequently, a member of the AITVJF, Swaran Bhagat, who had sat on a fast for 32 days in 1982, again decided to go on an indefinite fast from Wednesday, 5 January 1983, outside the Directorate of Social Welfare, Chandigarh, where their former member Gurcharan Singh Bauria had died on 1 October 1979 (*The Tribune*, 2 January 1983). Once again, no action on the part of the government forced the Federation to undertake a chain fast in the beginning of March 1983. The fast was broken after ten days, once again on an assurance from the Labour and Welfare Minister that 'their members will be nominated to the Boards of various government and semi-government organisations . . . the Director General of Police has agreed to recruit 100 members of these tribes as constables if they fulfilled the eligibility requirement' (*The Tribune*, 13 March 1983).

As usual, nothing happened. The AITVJF again issued a threat that if their demands were not met by 15 February 1987, they would resort to protest. Yet nothing materialised over all these years. Indifference on the part of the government made the general secretary of the Federation, Raunki Ram, sit on an indefinite fast on 26 January 1996. He was forcibly taken into police custody on 20th February on grounds of deteriorating health. To keep the fast going, another prominent member, Malak Chand, replaced him. Once again on assurance from the government, the fast unto death was suspended but with a threat to resume that on the coming Wednesday if the demands were not met. Besides the fast, a worker had also decided to commit self-immolation on the same day (*The Tribune*, 28 February 1996).

The above description of protests by the denotified tribes and assurances and promises made by the political elite and the government are a sample of the routine politico-administrative game in the country to the utter disadvantage of the oppressed and the marginal communities.[20] It has become a regular feature with the countrywide associations of the DNTs to organise rallies and marches in Delhi and the state capitals to project their grievances and demands. At the election rallies of the political parties, memoranda of demands are presented and 'profound' assurances are given by the contesting leaders, but nothing materialises when the party, irrespective of its ideology or programme, assumes authority. It goes to the credit of the sabhas or sanghas or associations of these communities that despite their struggles not accruing positive results, they are neither losing hope nor hesitating from expressing their demands without losing an opportunity.[21]

The government, on the other hand, is not ready to apply balm to their wounds even if that does not cost much. It only amounts to diverting their share as SCs to them as STs. This is what the SC lobby does not let happen. But the members of the tribal communities must also realise that even if they are granted ST status, it will not make a qualitative difference to the majority of their members except the few at top in the given socio-political milieu in the country. Mallick's study of the Jamalpur block of district Burdwan (West Bengal), where numerous schemes for tribals are in place, proves the point:

> Reservations in the fields of politics, education and employment aimed at protecting tribal culture and tradition have achieved *strikingly little*. Protection and land and life support system has been poorly implemented. There have been no marked improvements in their social conditions. Planned intervention has not improved the occupational and educational levels of tribals. Non-tribals do not treat them equally.
> (2016, 163)

The creamy layer will emerge eventually to garner all benefits as it happened with the SCs. No doubt, some proportion, howsoever small, may benefit definitely. Xaxa concludes that the Scheduled Castes have benefited from the government schemes more than the Scheduled Tribes. He explains the phenomenon sociologically:

> My contention is that exposure per se is not as important as the social structure they represent and of which they are a part. Besides being considered outside of "civilisation", tribes in India represented a different type of society. Tribal societies on the whole are small in size and are marked by a great deal of homogeneity despite being differentiated along the lines mentioned above. They are characterized more by similarity and resemblance than by differentiation and heterogeneity, especially in terms of their structural features. Thus tribal societies are marked by an absence of interdependence, division of labour and occupation, and correspondingly by a heterogeneity of values, skills, knowledge, income, wealth, status, and privilege.
> (2008, 94–95)

Notes

1. For an extensive discussion on the subject and a critique of the definition of tribe, see 'Introduction', in Birinder Pal Singh (ed.), 2010c.
2. For ethnographic details on each tribe see Singh (ed.), 2010c.
3. Natni is simply a female Nat. When a Mohammedan is referred to as Natni it is used in the sense of 'Nat like' hence as an adjective not as a proper noun. It becomes clear from their referring to them as kabutris, the damsels. In fact, *kabutri* is female pigeon but in local parlance it also means a girl who may be paid for fun by men.
4. Raghavaiah writes that 'The Cheran Banjaras, according to Mr. Cumberlege also first came into Deccan with Asaf Khan in a campaign by Emperor Shahjahan's forces about 1630. Their leaders Bhangi and Jhangi were having 1,80,000 pack bullocks' (V. Raghavaiah, *Tribes of India Volume II, Bharatiya Adimjati Sevak Sangh*. New Delhi, 1972, p. 386). It is also mentioned by him that 'In 1911 the Banjaras' number was 56,000 in Madhya Pradesh, 80,000 in Berar and 1,74,000 in Hyderabad where their number is still the largest in India' (ibid, 385).
5. It is deemed proper to refer to the 'economic activities' of the tribal communities in this chapter than their 'occupations', which were hitherto their way of earning livelihood, generation after generation. Occupation conceptually, in modern parlance means not only a specialisation of work but almost a lasting one, such as, a doctor remains a doctor all her life and an engineer remains an engineer all through. The two occupations cannot be switched on or off at will. Economic activity involves specialisation but is broad in scope and loose in nature. Thus, one may come across tribes specialising strictly in a single occupation such as Nats, Sikligars, Gujjars etc., while others undertake works of different nature at different times. Even then, they would engage in different major and minor occupations or types of work for making their living over different seasons and sometimes even simultaneously. For instance, Gaadi Lohars repair the iron utensils primarily but also sell bullocks and new implements or utensils. Bangalas do snake charming and medicine selling, while Bazigar men entertain people through *bazis* and also engage in making brooms, mats and screens (*chik*) from reed etc.
6. Unlike Nats, who do acrobatics either on the rope or ground, the Bazigars specialise in making jumps (*chhal*) of various types like – *ekehri* (single), *duhri* (double), *teehri* (triple), *uchi chhal* (high jump), *uchi-lammi chhal* (high and long jump), *sidhi-puthhi chhal* (straight and reverse jump), *katria chhal, phattiwali chhal, suli di chhal, chaunki chhal, char kone di chhal* etc. All these refer to jumps of different types with no English equivalents though some have been tried by the author. For details on some of these and more, see Mohan Tyagi (*Bazigar Kabile da Sabhiyachar*, 2013).
7. Such as dental caries, *resha* (phlegm), snake, dog and mongoose (*neola*) bites, arthritis, fever, T.B. (tuberculosis), piles, sugar (diabetes), indigestion, various skin and eye problems. Harinder Kaur (2010b) has given details of almost all the medicines prepared by them even now.
8. There is no such considered decision to discontinue rope dancing; rather there is demand for their shows these days in the fairs and festivals sponsored by the state and cultural institutions.
9. The six tribes are Sansis, Pakhiwaras, Gurmangs, Harnis, Baurias and Biloches (Kaul and Tomkins 1914, 7).
10. According to another source, Bachittar Singh was a Parmar Rajput who joined the Khalsa brotherhood on the historic Baisakhi day of 30 March 1699. He was selected by Guru Gobind Singh to face a drunken elephant brought there to batter down the gates of Lohgarh Fort (*Encyclopaedia of Sikhism*, Punjabi University, Patiala, 1995).

11 It is strange that Gaadi Lohars have no entry in K. Suresh Singh's *People of India* volume on Punjab; instead one finds an entry on Gaddis (pp. 183–87), a nomadic tribe of Bharmaur tehsil of Chamba district and Banghal area of the Kangra district in Himachal Pradesh. These people are in no way related to the state of Punjab. It is an anomaly.
12 For Gaadi Lohars see K. Suresh Singh (ed.), *People of India* volume on *Rajasthan*.
13 After the defeat of Maharana Pratap by Akbar at the battle of Haldighati, the Gaadi Lohars took five vows: (i) They will not return to Chittorgarh; (ii) they will not make houses for living; (iii) they will not sleep on cots; (iv) they will not light the lamp (*deepak*); and (v) they will not use rope to pull water (from the well).
14 Nagaur is a district in Rajasthan. The oxen of this place, called *Nagauri balad*, are famous and much in demand in the agricultural households in Punjab and Haryana. The tractors have now made these animals redundant, hence their trade.
15 Kazak (2005) names a number of such implements such as: *datri, daat, gandasi, phal, kahi, kuhadi, phalah, sangal, dubki kunda, ramba, rambi, tangli, toke, salangan, kalap, jung, loh-tindan* etc.
16 Kazak (2005) names numerous items such as: *chhanane, chimta, chimti, sippi, daat, karad, bhukna, tawa, pipa, pipi, bharholi, pali, pala, dorah, dorhi, kadahi, tasla, mooli-kanda, kuppi, sua, khurchna* etc.
17 See Chapter 8 'In Lieu of Conclusion' under sub-heading '1982'.
18 In March 1979, the chief minister P.S. Badal wrote to the Union Home Minister that all the vimukt jatis in the state viz. Rai Sikhs, Bazigars, Bangalas, Barads, Baurias, Nats, Gandhilas and Sansis including their 33 sub-castes (sic) should be declared as Scheduled Tribes. *The Tribune*, 29 March 1979.
19 Marla is a unit of land measurement. One marla is equivalent to 5.5 yards square or 30.25 square yards.
20 C. R. Bijoy sums up the plight of adivasis in Kerala with respect to their land rights: The lessons from Kerala are: (1) The present arrangement for protection of the interests of adivasis in the state has clearly failed in carrying out its responsibility meaningfully; (2) nor does the present arrangement in the state have the inherent capacity to carry out its constitutional obligations; (3) the judicial response is inadequate; and (4) paternalism and sympathy for the plight of the adivasis, including their land problems, pretended or genuine, are insufficient by themselves to provide necessary impetus or the will to implement the acts that protect adivasis. C.R. Bijoy, 'Adivasis Betrayed: Adivasi Land Rights in Kerala', *Economic and Political Weekly*, May 29, 1999, p. 1335.
21 I have seen a fat file of newspaper clips with an activist from Faridkot covering news items of their protests, rallies, statements, meetings and conferences raising issues concerning their plight and rights.

5 Socio-economic profile of the tribal communities in Punjab

The tribal people constitute the poorest of the poor in Punjab. These communities are designated as the Scheduled Castes and not as the Scheduled Tribes in the state, the status they have been contesting for over the last many decades. The socio-economic status of the regular Scheduled Castes entrenched in the mainstream society is superior to these people. They make a segment of the village or city society and have some regular occupation, howsoever menial but a regular one. They have a permanent settlement, of course, exclusive in a separate colony on the periphery of a village or in a city slum. They have own or rented accommodation, may be *pucca* (bricks/concrete), *kacha* (mud) or the mixed type. The government's policy of reservation and social welfare for them has benefited them, though not to the desired levels. The project of modernisation and industrialisation has helped them positively to an extent. Xaxa writes: 'Despite the attempts at absorption through administrative practices at both the central and state levels over the last fifty years, the attainment of constitutional objectives is still an elusive goal, and is going to become more elusive in the future' (2008, 82). He notes that the Scheduled Castes have benefited from the government schemes more than the Scheduled Tribes.

The tribal communities have been adversely affected by the processes of modernisation and industrialisation since they not only lost their traditional occupations but could not equip themselves with new skills. Thus, they are incompetent to get new occupations due to lack of technical skills. Their nomadic habit also gets in the way of their adjustment in a modern society.[1] Earlier they were nomadic by choice; now they have no choice. The owner of the plot or land forces them to displace. Earlier, nature's plenty attracted them towards nomadism; now it is driven by scarcity. Anyhow, they remain on the move for one reason or another. Those people who have some permanent settlement do not remain there for lack of work opportunities. They keep their families there and themselves move out for livelihood. The senior generation is given to nomadism out of habit, but the younger ones do not wish for it. Everyone now looks forward to a permanent abode, but most of them are yet not able to afford one given the poverty. Such households are found camping temporarily at the government land or vacant plots. Thus, their sole property is the makeshift hutment (*kulli*) or a *kacha-pucca* house.

But whatever accommodation they have made for them is not registered in their name since the land is not in their name. With the loss of traditional occupations, they have no alternative but to go for wage labour, peddling or begging. The children of majority tribes are given to scrap (*kabad*) collection since that does not require any skill. This, in fact, is the fate of tribal communities in the prosperous state of Punjab.

The present study is based on a sample of 763 respondents spread all over the state. All communities in the sample are not found everywhere in Punjab. The largest number of respondents (218) are reported from the Sansi tribe that constitute 28.57 per cent population of the sample, followed by the Baurias with 119 respondents making 15.59 per cent. Gandhilas come next with 100 respondents making 13.11 per cent population, followed by the Bazigar Banjaras with 83 respondents (10.88 per cent). The remaining tribes have a smaller share in the sample, which is commensurate with their overall population in the state. Another reason for their smaller representation is their nomadic nature. No doubt, all these tribal communities had been nomadic earlier, but some amongst them are nomadic still. For instance, Nat, Sikligar, Gaadi Lohar, Bangala and Gujjar fall in this category. Nat are the smallest group in the sample, with 11 respondents only, since they are more often on the move and go even outside Punjab for giving their shows. The Sikligars, Bangalas and Barads hover around 6 per cent population in the sample, followed by the Gujjars with less than that. The respondents of

Figure 5.1 A tribal settlement
Source: Author

108 *Socio-economic profile*

Gaadi Lohar are still less comparatively, as is their total population. They are originally inhabitants of Rajasthan with substantially large population, with whom they retain their contacts still. The large sample size of the Sansis is due to the clubbing of its various sub-groups, such as Dehe, Kuch Bann, Chhaj Bann, Sirki Bann, Bhedkutt, Baan Batt and Gadaria to name a few. Each one is a claimant for individual identity and wants to be known by its name rather than the umbrella name Sansi.[2]

The relation of respondents with income variables has interesting observations both within each tribe at the three levels of income and also across tribes within each level. A look at each tribe reveals that certain tribes have higher concentration of its respondents at the low-income level when others are dominant at the high income level, while for others there is hardly any difference at various levels of income. For instance, a greater number of Sansis (34.78 per cent) are in the low-income group than those (23.52 per cent) in the high-income group. Similar is the case with other tribes as well even if the gap is not that wide, as in the case of Sansis. The share of Sikligar respondents in the low- and high-income groups is 5.31 per cent and 3.59 per cent, respectively. The same is true of Gandhilas with 14.49 per cent and 12.82 per cent, Bangalas with 7.73 per cent and 3.08 per cent and Gaadi Lohars with 6.76 per cent and 0.51 per cent, respectively. On the other hand, Gujjar is one tribe that has a significantly larger share of its population in the high-income group. The gap between the two levels, high and low, is 18.97 per cent and 0.48 per cent, respectively. In the Bazigar tribe, the gap is not that high but double, as there are 8.70 per cent respondents in the low-income and 16.92 per cent in the high-income group. The Barad respondents also lie in the same range of 3.38 per cent and 6.67 per cent, respectively. The case of Bauria and Gandhila tribes is not of large difference between various levels of income but of balance between them, as there is not much gap between the low, medium and high levels of income. For the Bauria, it is 13.53, 16.30 and 16.40 per cent, respectively, and for Gandhilas 14.49, 12.47 and 12.82 per cent, respectively. Of all the tribal communities, Bauria, Bazigar and Gujjar are the three communities that have relatively more households in the high-income group compared to others. The Baurias are a hardworking people, especially as agricultural labour.[3] Some of them have land too as is also true of the Bazigar Banjaras.[4] Gujjars too are relatively better off economically due to land ownership and trade in buffaloes, milk and its products.

The sample of 763 respondents across these communities all over the state is fairly large, given the homogeneity of these people on the scale of socio-economic status (SES) indices. My previous experience of working with these people did not permit me to record their monthly income, which is too meagre; therefore, annual income of the households is noted. The data reveal (Table 5.2) that majority (361) of them making 47.31 per cent of the sample fall in the middle-income group, ranging from Rs. 17,000 to Rs. 39,000 only for the whole year. The proportion

Table 5.1 Tribes

Group/Sub-group	Bauria N	Bauria %	Nat N	Nat %	Sikligar N	Sikligar %	Sansi N	Sansi %	Gandhila N	Gandhila %	Bazigar N	Bazigar %	Bangala N	Bangala %	Gujjar N	Gujjar %	Barad N	Barad %	Gaadi Lohar N	Gaadi Lohar %
Family Income																				
1. Low	28	13.53	8	3.86	11	5.31	72	34.78	30	14.49	19	9.18	16	7.73	1	0.48	7	3.38	14	6.76
2. Medium	62	17.17	3	0.83	34	9.42	106	29.36	45	12.47	36	9.97	28	7.76	4	1.11	28	7.76	15	4.16
3. High	33	16.92	0	0.51	7	3.59	40	23.52	25	12.82	34	17.43	6	3.08	37	18.97	13	6.67	1	0.51
Total All Data	123	16.12	11	1.44	52	6.82	218	28.57	100	13.11	89	19.66	50	6.55	42	5.50	48	6.29	30	3.93

Chi^2 = 143.57** (df:22) C = 0.40;

Source: Author

110 Socio-economic profile

Table 5.2 Family income

Group/ Sub-group	Low		Medium		High	
	−Rs. 17,000		Rs. 17–39,000		Rs. 39,000+	
	N	%	N	%	N	%
Family Income						
1. Low	207	100.0				
2. Medium			361	100.0		
3. High					195	100.0
Total						
All Data	207	27.13	361	47.31	195	25.56

Chi^2 = 1526.00** (df:4) C = 0.82;

Source: Author

of respondents on either side of this group is similar. There are 207 respondents or 27.13 per cent in the lowest group and 195 respondents or 25.56 per cent in the highest income group. In the otherwise prosperous state of Punjab that until lately boasted of high per-capita income and scored relatively high on other indicators of development and consumption amongst other Indian states, the tribal population fares miserably with the above income levels.[5]

After looking into the income of the household, it would be useful to see the income status of the respondents who are the heads of their households. The situation here too is no different and equally dismaying. There are 51 respondents who happen to be women, and they have no source of their own income, as they are looking after the household chores. From the remaining 712 respondents who are male, each one is not economically active and earning. Their old age is a major factor in this respect, yet they are the head of the household, and the total income of the household is the result of the earnings of their sons, daughters-in-law and grand children as well. There are three respondents only who have listed theirs as well as the annual income of the households as nil. These are old-couple households who are infirm and not economically productive but are looked after and fed by their sons living next door. The remaining respondents are significantly dominant in the low-income group as their number hits at 584. The other extreme is the high-income group of seven respondents only. The remaining 121 respondents fall in the medium-income group.

As often projected in the sociological explanations, size of the family is linked to the SES of the family such that the low-income families tend to have larger size than those in high-income bracket. This formulation seems correct in the case of the tribal communities in which the size of the family is invariably large. Table 5.3 below shows that the majority respondents fall

Table 5.3 Family members

Group/Sub-group	Up to 5		6–7		8–9		Above 9		
	N	%	N	%	N	%	N	%	
Family Income									
1. Low	100	48.31	73	35.27	26	12.56	8	3.86	
2. Medium	65	18.01	123	34.07	110	30.47	63	17.45	
3. High	16	8.21	66	33.85	48	24.62	65	33.33	Chi^2 = 144.09** (df:6)
Total									
All Data	181	23.72	262	34.34	184	24.12	136	17.82	C = 0.40;

Source: Author

in the slot that consist of six to seven members in a family. It has 34.34 per cent of households or 262 out of 763. Those households with less than five members constitute 23.72 per cent, while others with eight or nine members make 24.12 per cent. The difference between these two groups is negligible. In the top slot even with nine or more members in a family, that percentage of households is not small that stands at 17.82. It would not be out of place to mention that 76.28 per cent tribal households have six and more members in a family, which is significantly more than the officially advocated prescription of *'Hum do hamare do'* for an ideal Indian family, of course, with a son and a daughter. A look at this data with respect to three levels of income reveals interesting results.

The above-mentioned sociological formulation is in for a shock when the size of the family is related to income levels within the tribal households. There is no clear manifest pattern. For instance, when the smallest family size is related to three income levels, it is found that 48.31 per cent fall in the low-income group, while in the highest group there are a mere 9.21 per cent households. When the number of family members rises to six or seven, there is hardly any difference from the low- to the high-income category, from 35.27 per cent to 33.85 per cent through 34.07 per cent, respectively. And yet, moving to the next slot of eight to nine members, the above pattern undergoes a change. Here the greatest concentration is in the middle-income group that has 30.47 per cent households. In the low-income group there are 12.56 per cent households that doubles to 24.12 per cent in the high-income group. Interestingly, when the number of family members is highest, that is, nine or more members, we notice a systematic rise in the number of households from 3.86 per cent to 17.45 per cent to 33.33 per cent, respectively. This pattern is starkly opposed to the households with the smallest families where their number declines systematically from 48.42 per cent in the low-income group to 8.21 per cent only in the high-income group.

112 *Socio-economic profile*

The total sample of households in Table 5.4 shows a stark preponderance of the male heads of households, that is, 93.32 per cent who provide the necessary information. The number of the female respondents is 6.68 per cent only. The relation of the male heads of households to income levels remains insignificant, as the percentage varies from 89.86 in the low-income to 95.90 in the high-income group through 93.91 in the middle category. On the other hand, the case of households headed by females is different. Their number declines gradually from 10.14 per cent in the low-income group to 6.09 per cent in the medium- to 4.10 per cent in the high-income group. It tends to show that if the male preponderance increases from the low- to high-income group the case of female heads is reverse. Their number declines with increase in income of the household.

The spectrum of age is quite widespread when we look at Table 5.5 below. The number of respondents in the 70 years and more category is not small, that is, 16.91 per cent, thus defying the general proposition that poverty shortens the life span of individuals. It is pertinent to suggest that these

Table 5.4 Sex of the respondents

Group/ Sub-group	Male N	Male %	Female N	Female %	
Family Income					
1. Low	186	89.86	21	10.14	
2. Medium	339	93.91	22	6.09	
3. High	187	95.90	8	4.10	$Chi^2 = 6.26*(df:2)$ C 0.09;
Total					
All Data	712	93.32	51	6.68	

Source: Author

Table 5.5 Age of the respondents

Group/ Sub-group	Up to 50 N	Up to 50 %	50–60 N	50–60 %	60–70 N	60–70 %	70-Plus N	70-Plus %	
Family Income									
1. Low	84	40.58	36	17.39	41	19.81	46	22.22	
2. Medium	104	28.81	98	27.15	105	29.09	54	14.96	
3. High	48	24.62	57	29.23	61	31.28	29	14.87	$Chi^2 = 26.70**$ (df:6)
Total									
All Data	236	30.93	191	25.03	207	27.13	129	16.91	C = 0.18;

Source: Author

senior persons are active respondents and effective heads of their households. The remaining sample of respondents up to 70 years is fairly equally divided in three groups of up to 50 years to two more groups with a difference of ten years span. If these two groups with respondents' age varying from 50 to 70 years are combined, the number rises to 52.16 per cent. This gives them a majority in the sample. The total number of respondents with less than 50 years is 30.93 per cent.

The relation of age with income shows that in the first age group of up to 50 years and in the last one of the senior-most respondents, there is a common pattern of gradual decrease in their numbers from a high of 40.58 per cent and 22.22 per cent, respectively, to a low of 24.62 and 14.87 per cent, respectively, through the medium-income group of 28.81 and 14.96 per cent, respectively. In the middle age group of the respondents, on the other hand, there is a rise in percentage from 17.39 to 29.23 in the 50–60 age group and from 19.81 per cent to 31.28 per cent in the 60–70 years group as we move from the low- to the high-income group.

It has been mentioned above that the tribal communities in Punjab are at the bottom of the socio-economic hierarchy. It is validated further by the education level of the respondents across the state. As expected, it is supposed to be high given the proclamations of the governments from time to time announcing schemes and funds for the purpose, but it is ironical that 70 years after independence the state has failed to provide minimum literacy to this section of a so-called prosperous state in the country. The proportion of illiterate respondents stands at 90.04 per cent. According to the census of India, a person who can read or write four letters put together is literate. Is it not shocking that such a large proportion of these people cannot even read and write their names when we are talking of 'making in India'? The worries do not stop there. There is a single respondent in the whole sample of 763 in 21st century India, who has passed class VIII when the present government run by the NDA (National Democratic Alliance), comprising of numerous political parties but led chiefly by the BJP (Bharatiya Janata Party) aims at 'digital India'. This single respondent is the most qualified person in the whole sample across the prosperous Punjab. There is none other than one. The numbers of respondents who have finished their studies with class II are 3.54 per cent, and those who could qualify the next grade, that is, class III, is 4.98 per cent.

The sample has majority male respondents as heads of the household, and if they are illiterate, one cannot expect their wives to be literate in a male-dominated society. This observation is well borne out in the present study. The data show that 95.01 per cent wives are illiterate. There are 4.98 per cent wives only that have some level of education, and the largest percentage of 2.78 have qualified up to class V. There are 0.88 per cent wives only who studied up to class X and the remaining could finish class II only. From this aspect of the ground reality of the women's education who make a source of providing and promoting education of their children, it is clear that their progeny too will meet the same fate.

The education level of their children is equally dismal, and that is a pointer to their equally gloomy future. A total count of sons in the sample of 763 households is 1,112, out of which 62.14 per cent are illiterate like their parents. A breakdown of their education level is revealing of the poor state of affairs of their education. An attempt is made to check those who are studying, that is, continuing their education and others who have finished their studies. There are 20.59 per cent sons who fall in the latter category and 12.94 per cent in the former category. A further break down of the data informs that those who have finished their studies up to class V, their number is 9.71 per cent, and those who could reach class XII are 10.88 per cent. There is a solitary case of a respondent's son who has got the degrees of master of arts (M.A.) and bachelor of education (B.Ed.). There are two sons only who have obtained the bachelor's degree (B.A.).

Those who are continuing their education, that is, 7.10 per cent, are in the junior classes (up to five), and 5.84 per cent are studying between classes VI and XII. There are seven sons of the respondents who are pursuing higher education, studying in the bachelor's course and above, that is, the master of arts (M.A.) and the bachelor of laws (LL.B.). There is a single, one and only one most qualified person in the category of sons who is pursuing the degree of doctor of philosophy (Ph.D.) in laws after completing the master of laws (LL.M.). The remaining sons (3.68 per cent) are yet not eligible to join a school on account of their age.

The case of daughters, surprisingly, appears less gloomy than that of the sons since only half of them are illiterate, that is, 49.62 per cent. This shows that the tribal communities do not discriminate against daughters which is a norm in the mainstream Punjabi society. Their total number in the sample is 393. Those who are continuing their studies is relatively high (31.29 per cent) compared to 12.94 per cent of sons. Their small number in the sample owes to the practice of early marriage of girls that is continuing still. Thus, so long as they are at home, that is, unmarried, they are sent to school. The sons, however, perform better on the finished level of education that stands at 20.59 per cent compared to 14.75 per cent for the daughters. There is not much difference between two levels of education from class I to class V and from class VI to class XII. The latter percentage is 7.88 and the former 6.87. On the other hand, more daughters, that is, 18.57 per cent, are studying at a lower level of classes (I–V) compared to 12.72 per cent at the higher level (VI–XII). The remaining daughters are yet not eligible to join the school. The most qualified amongst daughters are three only, each one pursuing the bachelors course in arts (B.A.), science (B.Sc.) and education (B.Ed.). There is none studying at the masters level. This number is less than half of the sons who are also doing the masters courses.

It has already been mentioned that the tribal people constitute the poorest of the poor in the state, and they make *kulli*, a hutment, their dwelling either at a vacant plot or the government land along the road or the railway tracks. Some 365 respondents out of 763, that is, 47.84 per cent, dwell in these make-shift hutments. The highest numbers of respondents (43.56 per cent) are in the middle-income group, followed by 38.08 per cent in the low-income group. As the income level rises, the number of respondents falls down to 67 that make 18.35 per cent of the total *kulli* residents.

The remaining 398 respondents live in a proper structure that may rightly be called a house. Table 5.6 shows that 96.23 per cent respondents own

Figure 5.2 A *kulli* in making
Source: Author

Figure 5.3 A *kulli*
Source: Author

116 *Socio-economic profile*

Figure 5.4 A well-built *kulli*
Source: Author

Table 5.6 House ownership

Group/ Sub-group	Own		Rented		
	N	%	N	%	
Family Income					
1. Low	67	100.0			
2. Medium	193	95.54	9	4.46	
3. High	123	95.35	6	4.65	Chi^2 = 3.16(df:2) C 0.09;
Total					
All Data	383	96.23	15	3.77	N.A.:365 (47.84%)

Source: Author

the house, while 3.77 per cent live on rented accommodation. These house dwellers make 52.16 per cent of the sample. This proportion too is a consequence of the government schemes launched for their settlement such as Indira Awas Yojna.[6] Such other development schemes have provided an opportunity to these respondents to invest in their accommodation. The income variable is important here as well. The majority house owners (193) fall in the medium-income group, followed by the high-income group (123).

The low-income group has the fewest (67) house owners. The respondents in this group cannot afford the rented accommodation.

It is not simply the ownership of a house but also its condition that makes an essential component of a household's status, as it is basic for civilised living. The history of civilisation tells us that human living has travelled from living under natural conditions with natural products to cultural products and artefacts. In the age of steel and cement, when some sections of modern society are living under premodern conditions, it becomes an issue of concern. The tribal communities under discussion are seemingly in the transition zone even in 21st century Punjab. As explained above, half the population is living in make shift hutments (*kullis*). Others who own a house are not living in structures that may genuinely be called houses, since almost one fourth of the respondents, 29.29 per cent to be precise, can afford a cemented house (see Table 5.7). The remaining population is inhabiting structures that are yet not fully complete since these are made of bricks only, that means these are yet to be plastered with cement, and the remaining are living in mixed type that means these are partly cemented and partly made of bricks. The latter make 25.86 per cent houses and the former 44.85 per cent. The latter figure is almost touching the limit of half the population.

When the above-mentioned data is seen with respect to the levels of income of the households, there is nothing unusual. In all the three types of houses made of cement, bricks and the mixed type, it is found that the proportion of houses made of cement rises with rise in income. In terms of figures, there is rise from 21.13 per cent in the low-income group to 44.92 per cent in the high-income group. In the case of remaining types of houses, there is decline in proportion as one moves from the low- to the high-income group. If the number of houses with bricks declines from 49.30 per cent in the low-income group to 38.93 per cent in the high-income group, the case is not different with houses of the mixed type, where there is decline from 29.58 per cent to 16.10 per cent, as the respondents' income rises from the low to the high levels, respectively.

Table 5.7 House type

Group/Sub-group	Bricked N	Bricked %	Cemented N	Cemented %	Mixed N	Mixed %	
Family Income							
1. Low	33	49.30	15	21.13	19	29.58	
2. Medium	94	46.84	46	22.63	62	30.53	
3. High	51	38.98	56	44.92	22	16.10	$Chi^2 = 22.04**(df:4)$
							C = 0.23;
Total							
All Data	178	44.72	117	29.39	103	25.87	N.A.:365 (47.84%)

Source: Author

118 *Socio-economic profile*

Whatever may be the condition of a house, it must be sufficiently commodious to give comfort to its inhabitants that depends on the number of rooms it has. Of course, this number must be proportionate to the size of the family and the number of residents. Table 5.8 informs that one-fourth of the total respondents, that is, 28.05 per cent, have houses with a single room. This percentage is very close to those who have a three-room house that makes it 25.82. The largest numbers of respondents (34.86 per cent) have two rooms in their houses, while the number of those that have more than three rooms is significantly low, that is, 11.27 per cent. A comparison with Table 5.3 showing the number of family members is interesting. There are parallels between the two tables such that the households with six to seven members have the largest proportion in the sample as those with two rooms in their houses. The two percentages are completely matching, that is, 34 per cent each. The number of families with five members matches the proportion of one-room houses and those with eight to nine members correspond to three-room-house numbers. These figures decline proportionately as the number of rooms rises to more than three rooms and the number of members grows to more than nine.

A relation between two variables, the number of rooms and the levels of income, shows that if there is a systematic decline in the proportion of households living in a single room from 55.55 per cent in the low-income group to 10.26 per cent in the high-income group, there is consistent rise in their proportion in the case of houses with three and more rooms. On the other hand, the case of majority respondents with two-room houses registers significant majority in the medium-income group. There are 28.99 per cent two-room houses in the low-income group and 29.74 per cent in the high-income group, but the medium-income group shows maximum concentration of 40.99 per cent. This shows that if there are majority families with six to seven members, likewise there is a preponderance of two-room houses and that too in the medium-income group, neither low nor high.

The four walls of a house, whether made of bricks alone or plastered with cement, do not make a house proper if there is no roof. It is the roof that

Table 5.8 Number of rooms

Group/ Sub-group	One N	%	Two N	%	Three N	%	Three+ N	%
Family Income								
1. Low	115	55.55	60	28.99	26	12.56	6	2.90
2. Medium	79	21.88	148	40.99	97	26.87	37	10.25
3. High	20	10.26	58	29.74	74	37.95	43	22.05
Total								
All Data	214	28.05	266	34.86	197	25.82	86	11.27

Source: Author

makes a structure livable and worthy of being called a shelter, safe from sun and rain that touch extreme limits in Punjab. Therefore, it is necessary to look into the nature and type of roof in the living spaces of the tribal people. The discussion above shows that 365 households are residing in hutments (*kullis*) and 398 in houses. One can imagine the quality of life and the quality of houses without a permanent roof. Out of the said total, 208 houses (27.26 per cent) have a permanent roof that may be made of concrete called lentil or bricks and wooden bars (Table 5.9). A small number of seven houses (0.92 per cent) only with corrugated sheets made of cement may also be added to the category of houses with a permanent roof. The mixed houses totalling 42 make a small percentage of 5.50 which may have a room with permanent roof and other with temporary material that may be tarpaulin or polythene. All the three types make 33.68 per cent of the total sample. The remaining population of the tribal households, that is, 66.32 per cent, live in houses or shelters made of tarpaulin, polythene sheets or thatch and a combination of these. This makes two-thirds of the sample population, which is quite a significant proportion of the tribal communities. The polythene sheets are preferred to tarpaulin more for their cheapness and easy availability. The latter is also many times heavier than the former and more cumbersome to handle, which is why it is used in 8.13 per cent of houses. Polythene, on the other hand, is preferred by 32.37 per cent respondents as a material for their roof. These two together make 40.50 per cent of the sample that is no small proportion. Thatch is traditionally used as a roofing material for its easy availability from the forest, but now with the declaration of the Indian Forests Act, its access is denied, but those living in villages still use it to seek shelter for themselves. It is used in 115 or 15.07 per cent of houses. It is interesting to see the relation of type of roof with levels of income. If we leave aside houses with permanent roof, in case of all others – tarpaulin, polythene and corrugated sheets – except thatch, there is a steady decline in the number of houses as the family income goes up from low to high.

Once the safety of shelter is ensured, there arises the need of a floor, a neat and clean one for the health and hygiene of inhabitants. Four types of floor are noted in the study that may be *pucca* made of cement, simple laying of bricks and *kacha* that refers to the natural levelled ground. The fourth type is a mix of these such that the floor of one room is cemented and other one with bricks or *kacha*. It may be recalled that 365 respondents live in hutments and 398 in houses. The possibility of a cemented floor is in the latter type only. The hutments or *kullis* more often have *kacha* floor. Table 5.10 shows that starkly majority residences including *kullis* and houses, that is, 81 per cent have *kacha* floor, which means that it is plain earth without any covering material. But such a floor is usually coated with mud and cow dung, especially in the villages where this is easily available as compared to the urban areas. The number of houses with cemented floor is a mere 10.60 per cent and those with simple bricks 5.90 per cent. The proportion of mixed floors is quite negligible at 2.49 per cent.

Table 5.9 Roof type

Group/ Sub-group	Permanent		Tarpaulin		Polythene		Thatch		Corru. Sheet	
	N	%	N	%	N	%	N	%	N	%
Family Income										
1. Low	33	15.94	21	10.14	90	43.48	29	14.01	34	16.42
2. Medium	92	25.48	26	7.20	119	32.96	46	12.74	78	21.61
3. High	83	42.56	15	7.69	38	19.49	40	20.51	19	9.74
Total										
All Data	208	27.26	62	8.13	247	32.37	115	15.07	131	17.17

Source: Author

Chi^2 = 100.39** (df:16)
C = 0.34;

Table 5.10 Floor type

Group/ Sub-group	Bricked		Cemented		Kacha (mud)		Mixed	
	N	%	N	%	N	%	N	%
Family Income								
1. Low	4	1.93	7	3.38	194	93.72	2	0.97
2. Medium	13	3.60	27	7.48	309	85.59	12	3.32
3. High	28	14.36	47	24.10	115	58.97	5	2.56
Total								
All Data	45	5.90	81	10.60	618	81.00	19	2.49

Source: Author

The relation of this variable with three levels of income is direct and clear. As a family rises on the scale of income from low to high, there is a marked rise in the number of houses with bricks and cement. The percentage of bricked floor type rises from 1.93 to 14.36 from the low to high income level. In case of houses with cemented floor, the numbers rise from 3.38 per cent for the low-income families to 24.10 per cent in the high-income group. Conversely, the percentage of houses with *kacha* (mud) floor falls from 93.72 per cent in the low-income group to 58.97 per cent as income level of the family rises.

The structure of a house is not complete without a kitchen, which is essential for the upkeep of its inhabitants. It makes an important constituent of a house from the time when human beings started leading a settled life. Table 5.11 gives a shock to the modern sensibility when one notices that 698 households out of 763 do not have a kitchen. It makes a whopping 91.48 per cent of the sample. It leaves 8.52 per cent households only that have this essential component of their house. The relation of this variable with income is obvious. As income rises, the number of households with kitchen rises from 2.42 per cent in the low-income to 22.56 per cent in the high-income group. The three levels of income do reflect differences in the number of households without a kitchen in each category, but it is not significant in case of rise in income from low to the medium category, from 97.58 per cent to 95.57 per cent. The fall, however, is significant as one moves from medium- to high-income group. The number of households falls to 77.44 per cent.

There is much hype now on the issue of toilets[7] following the Swachh Bharat Abhiyan started by the Prime Minister, Narendra Modi, on 2 October 2014, the birth anniversary of Mahatma Gandhi. Everyone is advised not to defecate in the open, since that is the only way to keep Bharat (India) clean. The Bollywood celebrities from Amitabh Bachchan to Vidya Balan have been roped into the advertising of this mission.[8] Paradoxically, the state that has failed in its project of providing these basic amenities to its population for the last 70 years is now reprimanding them for going into

Table 5.11 Kitchen

Group/Sub-Group	Yes N	Yes %	No N	No %	
Family Income					
1. Low	5	2.42	202	97.58	
2. Medium	16	4.43	345	95.57	
3. High	44	22.56	151	77.44	Chi^2 = 66.99**(df:2) C = 0.28;
Total					
All Data	65	8.52	698	91.48	

Source: Author

Table 5.12 Toilet

Group/Sub-group	Yes N	Yes %	No N	No %	
Family Income					
1. Low	13	6.28	194	93.72	
2. Medium	34	9.42	327	90.58	
3. High	59	30.26	136	69.74	Chi^2 = 59.72**(df:2) C = 0.27;
Total					
All Data	106	13.89	657	86.11	

Source: Author

the open. The government does not realise that when people do not have houses to live in, how can they have toilets for defecation? The data from a 'developed' state of Punjab depicts the fate of its people in the Table 5.12. It is shocking to notice that 86.11 per cent households do not have the facility of a toilet at their houses; in fact, 47.84 per cent of respondents do not have a house (see Table 5.6 above).

The variable of income, of course, is crucial in this respect too, with which it is directly related. The households that have toilet in the low-income group are a mere 6.28 per cent and those in the high group, 30.26 per cent. In case of those households without a toilet, there is decline from 93.72 per cent in the low-income group through to 90.58 per cent in the medium level to 69.74 per cent in the high-income group.

In a sample of population that does not have the facility of a toilet, there is high likelihood that a bathroom will not be there. A toilet is inevitably more relevant with regard to public sensibility as compared to the bathroom. Table 5.13 validates this point when one notices that 87.55 per cent households do not have a bathroom. It is worth reminding that 86.11 per

Table 5.13 Bathroom

Group/Sub-group	Yes N	%	No N	%	
Family Income					
1. Low	14	6.76	193	93.24	
2. Medium	33	9.14	328	90.86	
3. High	48	24.62	147	75.38	Chi^2 = 36.24**(df:2) C = 0.21;
Total					
All Data	95	12.45	668	87.55	

Source: Author

cent houses are without a toilet. When the privacy of a toilet is necessary to all, males and females both, the bathroom is needed more by women than men, who do not mind taking a bath in the open on a hand pump, a tap, a tube-well or any open water body accessible to them. In the houses that lack a bathroom, the poor women make a makeshift enclosure with the support of a raised cot covered with bed sheets etc. Like in the case of toilets, the facility of a bathroom is similarly related to the three income levels with a high degree of correspondence. The number of households in the low-income group is 6.76 per cent that rises to 24.62 per cent as the income rises. On the other hand, the number of those without this facility declines from 93.24 per cent in the low-income level to 75.38 per cent in the high-income group through 90.86 per cent in the middle category.

The necessity of water for running a household is absolutely essential since it is not only required for civilised living but all living. It is the source of all life, as is made clear by Guru Granth, the Sikh scripture: *Pehla pani jeo hai, jit hariya sab koi*. It is referred to as 'father' in the Sikh scripture.[9] Therefore, it is not out of place to look into the availability of this source of life to the tribal communities living on the margins of the mainstream society.

The field study shows that there are four different sources of water (Table 5.14), and the most commonly used is the tap, as 59.40 per cent respondents make use of this facility. The local bodies' institutions like the municipal committee in the towns and panchayat in the villages have installed water supply systems with grants from the World Bank under the scheme of improving hygiene and sanitation providing clean drinking water and proper sewerage to the poor people in 2008. The availability of municipal and panchayat water supply is regulated according to a schedule depending upon the season. It is not always available for 24 hours. The second most used source of water is the hand pump that may be installed individually by a household or by the municipal committee. About 30.86 per cent of households make use of these pumps for their daily needs. The remaining

Table 5.14 Water source

Group/Sub-group	Hand N	Hand %	Tap N	Tap %	Govt. N	Govt. %	Others N	Others %
Family Income								
1. Low	39	19.40	138	68.66	19	9.18	5	2.49
2. Medium	100	28.90	219	63.29	25	6.92	2	0.58
3. High	86	47.25	76	41.76	10	5.49	10	5.49
Total								
All Data	225	30.86	433	59.40	54	7.07	17	2.33

Chi^2 = 60.22**(df:8) C = 0.28;

Source: Author

source is the common tap installed by the government at a public place or by the roadside for use by all and sundry; 11.53 per cent respondents make use of this facility since they lack their own pump or tap. The 'other' source may be a tube-well or a water channel in the field of a peasant, which is quite small, as 2.33 per cent respondents only use it. The former is used by 7.41 per cent respondents in the sample.

A relation of the source of water (Table 5.14) with levels of income shows no difference at all for the respondents using the government (common) and other source, at all the three income tiers, which is conspicuous for the remaining two sources. There seems an anomaly in the use of these two sources in relation to income levels. The use of a hand pump increases from 19.40 per cent with low income to 47.25 per cent in the high-income group, which is reversed in the case of tap. 68.66 per cent respondents using this source have low income, while 41.76 per cent have high income. It is useful to recall that 52.16 per cent respondents live in houses, and 96.23 per cent from amongst them own houses. This means that even those who live in *kullis* too use a hand pump and tap as source of water, which is why the total number of respondents using these two sources is 90.26 per cent.

Another important component of a 'modern' household is the source of light so that the setting of the sun does not stop the 'life' of individuals. Table 5.15 shows that 58.86 per cent households use an electric bulb to light their houses while the remaining 41.14 per cent use the traditional earthen lamp. The data show that 54.76 per cent households have installed the electricity meters in their own name, while the remaining 4.10 per cent have *kundi* 'connections' that means getting connected directly to the electric supply pole through a hook called *kundi*. Almost one per cent respondents do not have any source of light, not even an earthen lamp. The relation of source of light with income is quite obvious. Despite low income, 7.32 per cent respondents only in the sample are using *kundi* connections, whereas

Table 5.15 Light source

Group/ Sub-group	Lamp N	Lamp %	Electric bulb With meter N	With meter %	Without N	Without %	
Family Income							
1. Low	118	57.56	72	35.13	15	7.32	
2. Medium	152	42.22	196	54.44	12	3.33	
3. High	41	21.47	146	76.44	4	2.09	Chi^2 = 82.29**(df:6) C = 0.31;
Total							
All Data	311	41.14	414	54.76	31	4.10	N.A.:7 (0.92%)

Source: Author

126 *Socio-economic profile*

35.13 per cent have installed regular meters in their name. This proportion increases with rise in income, as in the high-income group their number jumps to 76.44 per cent, that is, more than double. Similar is the case with the use of a lamp. If 57.56 per cent use it in the low-income group, their number is reduced to less than half (21.47 per cent) as income goes up.

Table 5.16 shows quite surprising results in the developed state in which these marginalised communities are still using the age-old traditional sources of fuel for cooking as used in premodern times. The surprising element is that LPG (liquefied petroleum gas) is used in seven households only. At the other end, there is a single household only that depends solely on the cow dung cakes. This is suggestive of the poverty level of these communities who are not able to use the basic amenities of life. There are 5.42 per cent households that too use LPG but along with other sources of fuel. 70.15 per cent households use wood as fuel for cooking which is considered an environmental hazard by the environmentalists who hold the poor doubly responsible first for spoiling the forest and then for adding to the air pollution. But what source may these poor communities use if not the dead wood from the forest? Table 5.16 shows clearly that the use of firewood decreases with increase in income. If 82.27 per cent in the low-income group use it, the percentage goes down to 48.97 in the high-income group. The information above deals with those households that depend solely on firewood, but there are others too who use it but along with some other source such as the cow dung cakes. It is pertinent to mention that out of one-third of the sample that has cattle (see Table 7.2 below), almost half of them own a cow or a buffalo or oxen. Therefore, the share of those who use wood with dung cakes in the sample population is 14.40 per cent. There is another category of tribal households that make use of all types of sources of fuel for cooking except the LPG. Their number is 69, that is, 9.12 per cent.

Table 5.11 above provides information on the absence of a kitchen in 698 households out of 763, a whopping 91.48 per cent of the tribal population. No doubt, traditionally kitchen in the rural areas especially never had a separate accommodation, though a separate space was marked out in the courtyard for the earthen furnace called *chulah*. It burns firewood. This is true only of the houses not the *kullis*. Things have changed now, but these marginalised communities do not have space sufficient enough in their houses even as 398 respondents live in these structures and the remaining 365 live in *kullis*, where the question of a separate kitchen does not arise. In the former category too, 65 households or 8.52 per cent could afford the kitchen. Thus, we find that in the whole sample, 8.52 per cent households have a kitchen, and this fact is worth reiterating. The relation of its construction is directly related to income when we notice in Table 5.11 that from among those who have a kitchen, there are 2.42 per cent households only in the low-income group and as we move to the high-income category the number of households shoots up to 22.56 per cent. But it is intriguing to note that out of 195 households in the high-income group there are 44

Table 5.16 Cooking source

Group/Sub-group	LPG N	LPG %	Firewood N	Firewood %	Wood + Cakes N	Wood + Cakes %	All but LPG N	All but LPG %	LPG+ Others N	LPG+ Others %
Family Income										
1. Low	–	–	167	82.27	21	10.34	13	6.40	2	0.99
2. Medium	–	–	269	74.72	44	12.22	33	9.16	14	3.89
3. High	7	3.61	95	48.97	44	22.68	23	11.86	25	12.89
Total										
All Data	7	0.92	531	70.15	109	14.40	69	9.12	41	5.42

Chi^2 = 87.70** (df:12)
C = 0.32;
N.A.:6 (0.79%)

Source: Author

128 *Socio-economic profile*

households only with a kitchen, while the remaining 151 are without it. This seems plausible because a substantial population is putting up in the hutments.

One may get an impression from the above explanation that it may be due to cultural reasons that a kitchen is not constructed, but the following table (5.17) makes amply clear that it is not culture but poverty is the major cause, since 96.20 per cent of households do not have a stove that runs on kerosene. Table 5.16 above shows that 84.55 per cent households depend solely on firewood and cow dung cakes, though many others use these cooking sources in combination with other sources as well. It is interesting to notice that the variable of income becomes virtually redundant in this case, and 3.80 per cent households only have a stove in their kitchen.

The case of a pressure cooker is no different, as 95.81 per cent households do not possess this gadget so very essential for a modern kitchen to save fuel and time. Table 5.18 makes evident that 95.81 per cent households do not have a pressure cooker. In this sample's high-income group too, 86.67 per cent households do without it, while 26 out of 32 who have pressure cookers

Table 5.17 Stove

Group/Sub-group	Yes N	Yes %	No N	No %	
Family Income					
1. Low	4	1.93	203	98.07	
2. Medium	11	3.05	350	96.95	
3. High	14	7.18	181	92.82	$Chi^2 = 8.63^*(df:2)$ $C = 0.11$;
Total					
All Data	29	3.80	734	96.20	

Source: Author

Table 5.18 Pressure cooker

Group/Sub-group	Yes N	Yes %	No N	No %	
Family Income					
1. Low	1	0.48	206	99.52	
2. Medium	5	1.39	356	98.61	
3. High	26	13.33	169	86.67	$Chi^2 = 54.72^{**}(df:2)$ $C = 0.26$;
Total					
All Data	32	4.19	731	95.81	

Source: Author

Socio-economic profile

belong to this income group. On the other hand, 99.52 per cent households without this gadget fall in the low-income group.

In light of the discussion above, it seems that when the basic amenities are lacking in a household, what would be the incidence of electrical and electronic items in these family units? It is not surprising to note that 40.89 per cent households in the sample have neither a fan nor a cooler. In the light of severe summers in Punjab when the maximum temperature during the day touches 47 degrees Celsius, a simple electric fan is not a luxury item with a family. Table 5.19 specifies that 56.88 per cent households do have an electric fan only with them, while those who enjoy the facility of a desert cooler too along with a fan are a meagre 2.23 per cent. In the scorching heat of the state, a desert cooler too is not a luxury item when the low middle class is using air conditioners. Over the last decade, petty shop keepers too have installed these cooling machines in their small shops even, leave alone their bedrooms. The sense of relative deprivation aggravates the situation. It is dismaying to note that 56.52 per cent households in the low-income category have neither a fan nor a cooler. Not only this, 22.05 per cent households in the high-income category even are sailing in the same boat.

The information on the availability of inverters simply draws a blank, since 99.48 per cent of households do not have this electricity backup device. A mere four households constituting 0.52 per cent of the sample have inverters. This is obvious given the lack of electric facilities detailed above. This share goes to the high-income group only, though the remaining 97.95 per cent in this group draw a blank on this count.

After a day's hard labour one returns home to take food and rest so that the next day may start with recharged energy. The respondents are informed that a cot is the traditional netted *charpai* or *khat* or what is more likely to be understood now as a folding *charpai*, in the present times when the wooden bars are replaced by metallic pipes or rods. The bed refers to the wooden cot with a plywood plank replacing the net and a mattress made

Table 5.19 Fan and cooler

Group/Sub-group	Fan only N	Fan only %	Fan + Cooler N	Fan + Cooler %	None N	None %	
Family Income							
1. Low	88	42.51	2	0.97	117	56.52	
2. Medium	208	57.62	1	0.28	152	42.11	
3. High	138	70.77	14	7.18	43	22.05	Chi^2 = 72.69**(df:4) C = 0.29;
Total							
All Data	434	56.88	17	2.23	312	40.89	

Source: Author

130 *Socio-economic profile*

of cotton, choir or foam over it. In popular parlance, beds refer to a pair of wooden cots that are fixed, hence called the 'double-bed'. These may be simple ones or box beds. Table 5.20 shows that 52.56 per cent households have cots, while the number of the two other categories of having both beds and cots is 23.98 per cent. Those who have none are 23.46 per cent. It makes one-fourth of the sample, no small number by any means. The income variable does not weigh much in the case of householders with cots since the gap between the low- and high-income groups is about five per cent. If there are 54.59 per cent households in the former category there are 49.23 per cent in the latter category. But in the remaining two columns – both and none – the number of households increases with rise in income in the former category but declines in the latter category, and the gap between two extremes is significant.

It is often argued that the slums may not have food to eat, but a television is installed in each and every household. This common sense proposition stands belied in the present study, where Table 5.21 reveals that 40.10 per cent of households have television sets, which means 59.90 per cent are without it. There is a positive correlation between this variable and income.

Table 5.20 Cot/bed

Group/Sub-group	Cot Only N	Cot Only %	Both N	Both %	None N	None %	
Family Income							
1. Low	113	54.59	21	10.14	73	35.27	
2. Medium	192	53.19	85	23.55	84	23.27	
3. High	96	49.23	77	39.49	22	11.28	Chi^2 = 61.33**(df:4 C = 0.27;
Total							
All Data	401	52.56	183	23.98	179	23.46	

Source: Author

Table 5.21 Television

Group/Sub-group	Yes N	Yes %	No N	No %	
Family Income					
1. Low	48	23.19	159	76.81	
2. Medium	149	41.27	212	58.73	
3. High	109	55.90	86	44.10	Chi^2 = 45.11**(df:2 C = 0.24;
Total					
All Data	306	40.10	457	59.90	

Source: Author

As income rises, so does the number of households possessing television sets. If 23.19 per cent households in the low-income group have television, their number goes up to 55.90 per cent in the high-income group. The gap is significant. Similar is the case of households without a television. Their number falls down from 76.81 per cent in the low-income group to 44.10 per cent in the high-income group. But there is an interesting observation in the latter group when seen in relation to having and not having a television. In the same (high) income group, 55.90 per cent respondents have television sets with them, while 44.10 per cent are without it. The gap is comparatively not that significant.

The television seems to have stolen the show from radio, since 99.87 per cent households do not own a radio set, which was an essential component of a household before the arrival of the small screen in the market. It is interesting to note that there is a single household with a radio set.

Table 5.22 also dispels a popular belief that every person is connected with a phone. The Bollywood actress Pretty Zinta in her advertisement for the BSNL (Bharat Sanchar Nigam limited), a government of India enterprise, suggests that having a landline connection is a mark of one's identity. It is ironic that these faceless communities, who have truly lost their identity and are trying to retrieve it, do not possess a landline connection. Not a single one in the whole sample. On the other hand, 28.70 per cent respondents have mobile phones, while the remaining 71.30 per cent have none with them. From among the former percentage, 47.18 per cent in the high-income group have mobile phones, while the number of those who do not have phones with them in the same income group is 52.82 per cent. Such paradoxes as also in the case of television sets (Table 5.21) may be sorted out with more research.

The extent of poverty may be seen, if not measured, from the possession of vehicles in a household. The nature, type, cost and brand of a vehicle is an important indicator of a family's socio-economic status besides other indices. What inference do we draw from Table 5.23, showing the number

Table 5.22 Landline/mobile phones

Group/ Sub-group	Yes N	%	No N	%	
Family Income					
1. Low	24	11.59	183	88.41	
2. Medium	103	28.53	258	71.47	
3. High	92	47.18	103	52.82	$Chi^2 = 62.14^{**}(df:2)$
					$C = 0.27$;
Total					
All Data	219	28.70	544	71.30	

Source: Author

Table 5.23 Vehicles

Group/Sub-group	Bicycle N	%	Two Wheeler N	%	Rebri/Rehra N	%	Rickshaw N	%	Cycl Two-Wh N	%	Many N	%	Cycl Rebri N	%	Cycl/Rick. N	%
Family Income																
1. Low	63	53.85	2	1.71	13	11.11	8	6.84	7	5.98	12	10.26	2	1.71	10	8.55
2. Medium	133	53.41	4	1.61	16	6.43	28	11.24	12	4.82	19	7.63	18	7.23	19	7.63
3. High	70	46.67	9	6.00	1	0.67	19	12.67	9	6.00	15	10.00	7	4.67	20	13.33
Total																
All Data	266	51.55	15	2.91	30	5.81	55	10.66	28	5.43	46	8.91	27	5.23	49	9.50

Chi^2 = 32.17**(df:14) C = 0.24; N.A.:247 (32.37%)

Source: Author

of households possessing the type of vehicle(s)? It is not a surprise, given the economic condition of the tribal communities in Punjab, that 247 households in a sample of 763, that is, 32.37 per cent, do not have a vehicle including the most simple pedalling machine, the bicycle. The remaining 516 households, that is, 67.63 per cent, do have a vehicle, out of which 51.55 per cent own a bicycle only. There are some other households too that own it in combination with a two-wheeler (5.43 per cent), a rickshaw (9.50 per cent) or a *rehri* (cart; 5.23 per cent). Thus, a bicycle is the most possessed common mode of transport that the tribal people use for personal or commercial purposes. The members of Sikligar community have fixed grinders on their bicycles, doing business going door to door from village to village.

After the bicycle, a vehicle most possessed by the tribal households is a cycle rickshaw used to transport people from one destination to another. It is a commercial vehicle whose plying does not require much skill. Those households that have two-wheelers, namely scooters and/or motorcycles, are owned by a small proportion of the sample (2.91 per cent) only, but these are also possessed by others (5.43 and 8.91 per cent) in combination with other vehicles. The majority two-wheelers are owned either by the members of Gujjar community who need to ferry milk to shops and dairies or by those respondents or their family members who are employed gainfully.

Rehri is a cart driven manually for selling items like vegetables, fruits or anything. In the cities there are *rehri* markets selling a wide range of commodities for the consumption of lower classes. An improved version of *rehri* is driven by a cycle that is called rickshaw *rehri*. *Rehra*, on the other hand, is large in size and driven by an animal, more often a pony or a bullock. It transports either heavy materials or in bulk. The data reveal that *rehri* is owned by 22 respondents and *rehras* by 54. The rickshaw *rehri* is more common than other types as it is owned by 109 households. It is used for transporting light materials, carrying a maximum load of two to three quintals.

In the present-day urban society, pets are usually owned by the rich people for status and pastime, but the poor people including the tribals too have them more due to their pro-nature orientation since they consider themselves to be its part. In the market society afflicted with high price rise and inflation, it is becoming difficult to own pets out of economic compulsions. It is more an amusement of the affluent, as is shown in Table 5.24. A significantly large number (74.71 per cent households) do not have pets at all, while there are 5.70 per cent households that have many pets that may include any of cat, dog or hen and in combination thereof. It is interesting to notice that a dog is the most popular pet with these people, as 47.15 per cent households own it, followed by hen owned by 24.87 per cent. The liking for a dog seems more in tune with their traditional practice of hunting.[10] The number of such households owning more than one pet is 25.39 per

Table 5.24 Pets

Group/Sub-group	Cat N	Cat %	Dog N	Dog %	Hen N	Hen %	Many N	Many %	
Family Income									
1. Low	–	–	29	56.86	13	25.49	9	17.65	
2. Medium	3	3.45	39	44.83	21	24.14	24	27.59	
3. High	2	3.64	23	41.82	14	25.45	16	29.09	Chi^2 = 5.06(df:8) C = 0.16;
Total									
All Data	5	2.59	91	47.15	48	24.87	49	25.39	N.A.:570(74.71%)

Source: Author

cent. A relation of this variable with income shows an interesting result, contrary to the above statement, that more households (56.86 per cent) in the low-income group have dogs compared to 41.82 per cent in the high-income group. The percentage of households owning dogs rises with a fall in income, whereas it has no effect absolutely on the ownership of hens. The hen-keeping serves two purposes, one of laying eggs and later for meat. The latter trend is reversed in case of ownership of many pets, since 17.65 per cent households are in the low-income group and 29.09 per cent in the high-income group.

The case of cattle ownership by 33.42 per cent tribal households in Table 5.25 specifies that cow and buffalo are most common with them. About 34.90 per cent households own milch cattle, obviously to meet the domestic need and to sell the surplus milk. The cattle are let loose for grazing, and some fodder is obtained from the nearby fields for free. The ownership of mixed cattle specifically of goat, sheep and buffalo stands at 24.70 per cent households. If the sheep are not considered significant in this column, as may be inferred from the second column, since 1.57 per cent households own sheep only, the figures in this column go up significantly, as 8.24 per cent households own goat and buffalo. The addition of these figures in the previous column makes it 32.94 per cent households with goat and buffalo. Usually, income is an important factor in determining the possession of property, and cattle make an important element in an agricultural society. But in the present case there seems no difference between the low- and high-income-group households with respect to their ownership of cattle. The information in the table is contrary to the above statement. Paradoxically, the households in the low-income group have more cattle, 41.82 per cent cow or buffalo, and 27.27 per cent have goats and sheep along with these, while those in the high-income group are 38.57 per cent and 24.29 per cent, respectively. No doubt, this difference is not much significant, yet it is. The case of bullock ownership is interesting, as more households in the low-income group have more than those in the middle-income group. It is due to

Table 5.25 Cattle

Group/Sub-group	Goat N	Goat %	Sheep N	Sheep %	Buff/Cow N	Buff/Cow %	Bullocks N	Bullocks %	Goat/Sheep N	Goat/Sheep %	Gt/Shp/Buff N	Gt/Shp/Buff %	Goat/Buff N	Goat/Buff %
Family Income														
1. Low	1	1.82	1	1.82	23	41.82	11	20.00	4	7.27	15	27.27		
2. Medium	20	15.38	3	2.31	39	30.00	18	13.85	9	6.92	31	23.85	10	7.69
3. High	15	21.43			27	38.57					17	24.29	11	15.71
Total														
All Data	36	14.12	4	1.57	89	34.90	29	11.37	13	5.10	63	24.70	21	8.24

Chi^2 = 39.34** (df:14)
C = 0.37;
1
N.A.:508 (66.58%)

Source: Author

the fact that Gaadi Lohars fall in this category whose majority households are in the low-income group and none in the high-income group.

The socio-economic profile of the tribal communities with a view to understanding the dismal conditions of their existence has been carried out for the first time in their history for two reasons. One, they do not officially exist in the state, and two, they are a part of the Scheduled Castes. There too they get eclipsed by the dominant Mazhabis or Balmiks and Chamars or Ramdasias or Adharmis. The present study focuses on them exclusively and as tribal communities. This profiling confirms the obvious that was felt strongly in the previous ethnographic study by Singh (2010c). The data has shown beyond doubt that these communities at the periphery of Punjabi society are living in uninhabitable colonies and are bereft of minimum levels of living and hygiene.[11] It is a gross violation of human rights 70 years after independence in a hitherto 'developed' state of Punjab. The shanties of a large number of respondents are devoid of kitchen, bathroom and toilets etc., leave aside other amenities. They are not a part of the *swachh* Bharat[12] and can never be for a long time from now, even if the government takes an active and serious interest to ameliorate their sub-human socio-economic conditions.

Notes

1 To avail benefits of the welfare schemes of the government one needs to have a permanent residence that may be rented. The ration card, the aadhar card, the voter's card, the pan card and the bank account are not issued to the nomadic people.
2 It has been mentioned in the previous chapter that the nomenclatural confusion is common with these people since 1871. Numerous Reports of the administration stand testimony to this fact besides the popular perception of the local people about who is who.
3 The landowners prefer to engage Bauria labour on their farms. Both men and women work as labour seven days a week. They are a hardworking people. The employers inform that other labour often go for a break but never the Baurias.
4 These people are more educated and hence employed in the government and private sectors. One of their members is also a minister in the present Punjab cabinet of Captain Amarinder Singh that assumed power in 2017. He was minister earlier too.
5 The per-capita income of Punjab at current prices for the year 2016–17 is Rs. 1,31,112 compared to the all India average of Rs. 1.03 lakhs. But the state once far ahead of other states is now far behind Gujrat, Haryana and Uttrakhand etc. (www.punjabdata.com/GDP accessed on 7 January 2019).
6 Indira Awas Yojna started in 1985–86 to facilitate the housing of the landless and the poor living below the poverty line. Under this scheme 25.2 million houses have been constructed since 1985.
7 Film *Toilet: Ek Prem Katha* with Akshay Kumar in the lead role was released in August 2017 to promote the government's message against open defecation.
8 A married girl refuses to go to the house of her in-laws because it does not have a toilet.
9 In the *Anand Sahib* part of the Sikh scripture there is this prescription: *Pawan guru paani pita, mata dharat mahatt*. It is recited at the end of each Sikh ceremony before the final prayer, *ardas*.

10 A dog is a synonym of security of property or anything cherished, hence the 'watch dog', but these people have no property to be protected. Yet they have loved to have dogs since olden times.
11 They may be better off compared to their counterpart in other states. For instance, a Sikh Sikligar family with 33 members lives in a single room at Nizamabad (Telengana). See Birinder Pal Singh 2018. Gayatri Jayaraman also reports: 'Perumal's one-room tenement houses 36 members of his family and under Govindan's roof are the off springs of his two wives: 16 children and 50 grand children'. 'The Invisible Nomads of Madurai', *Hindustan Times*, 8 October 2018.
12 *Swachh* Bharat Abhiyan launched by the National Democratic Alliance government on 2 October 1914 for a clean and healthy India.

6 Occupations of the tribal communities

> [M]en only zoologically, they are to be dominated. They may be tamed and trained; when this proves impossible, they may be allowed to live on at the fringes of civilization, without being the object of any of those cruelties that must be avoided against any form of life, but being allowed as a race to die out like those [native] American races who shrank and died . . . when a civilization they could not withstand moved upon them.
>
> Benedetto Croce (1886–1952)

The present chapter describes the occupational profile of the tribal communities in the 21st century Indian Punjab. The difficulty of discussing occupations in the case of these communities is that some of them are still pursuing their traditional occupations, which have become obsolete for others. The previous chapters have given an extensive account of the traditional occupations of the communities and their profile, therefore, the present description is confined to their present occupations only. The problem of definition of traditional occupation(s) arises only in the context of modernisation. No doubt, it is related to social change too that had been occurring in all societies all the times following own pace, either slow or fast. Thus, occupations keep changing with the times. But it is only in the modern era, with the introduction of science and technology, that human society has witnessed a change in this domain experienced never before in its history. New occupations cropped up, and the old ones became obsolete.

The tribes are not to be seen as a static, homogenous, primitive people pursuing certain occupations only who want neither change nor mobility. We may see a continuum of their types specialising in certain occupations depending upon their location in space. Those on the fringes of urban centres did trading, some specialised in making weapons and smelting iron, while others farther away pursued their traditional lifestyle, whatever that was and whatever meagre they could produce for their subsistence. They were seemingly happy and contented with themselves. Baidyanath Saraswati's characterisation of tribe as 'masters of their microworld' with an 'aesthetically perfect rhythm of life' and 'that their lifestyle changes within an unalterable form beyond which they perish' is instructive (1993, 23).

An occupation is usually a specialised activity performed by an individual to earn a living. In the modern society no occupation is specific to any caste, class or community, hence not ascriptive in character. It is a position occupied by an individual on the basis of one's educational qualifications and acquisition of skills and experience, which is why it is achievement oriented and universalistic in character. Ascription versus achievement makes one of the five pattern variables suggested by Parsons (1951) for the distinction of a traditional society from a modern one. Prior to modernisation and industrialisation, occupations were specific to a caste or a tribe. Each one specialised in a specific occupation that may further have its major and minor types. There is no standard division of types based on the raw materials or duration of their engagement, since the cycles of nature influenced not only the availability of raw materials but also the consumption patterns of the population. The Indian caste system has rigidly defined and demarcated the castes and their sub-groups with respect to their occupations, though the reality on the ground had always been somewhat loose (Srinivas 1962).

Max Weber, the father of modern sociology, has given the notion of vocation and the concept of calling in the *Protestant Ethic* (1930), but in the Indian tribes and communities dealing with specialised activities of production have myths and legends associated with them that relate them directly to one god or another. An occupation has three aspects, namely economic, technological and social. The nature of the economic dimension has been changing from barter to cash over the millennia. The technological aspect is also very crucial. There is a great shift from the manual, handicraft and simple technology to a machine driven by some energy other than human or animal. It has also necessitated a sharp and acute division of labour, resulting in high fragmentation of roles and statuses due to specialisation in the factory organisation. To each occupation is attached a social status. It is as true today as it used to be in a traditional society, of course, with considerable degrees of freedom.

With the introduction of science and technology and the capitalist system of production all aspects of the occupations have experienced changes. The economic aspect is confined to cash payment only, to the complete disappearance of the barter system, the mainstay of traditional society. The technological aspect proved more radical. It made the handicraft technology redundant. Machines manufactured in factories by trained specialists proved far more powerful in terms of productivity and efficiency compared to the individual traditional workers. These economic and technological changes together made numerous traditional occupations redundant and changed the nature of others radically. For instance, the water carrier (*mashki*), the oil man (*teli*), the cotton carder (*penja/tadi*), the pot maker (*ghumiar*) etc. have virtually disappeared from Punjab. Many other occupations though remained caste or community specific have also undergone transformation with the times. For instance, the shoe maker, the blacksmith, the goldsmith, the carpenters, the masons etc. are continuing their traditional occupations in the modern market without a significant change but for the adoption of some scientific gadgets etc. All these are caste-specific occupations from which the tribes keep away but for blacksmithery (Sikligars/Gaadi Lohars).

It has been seen in a previous chapter that each tribal community specialises in a particular type of traditional occupation in consonance with its habitat, the type of natural resources and its nomadic nature. The most notable effect on the majority nomadic and other tribal communities has been made with the declaration of the Indian Forests Act 1865 that made nature's greatest resource a property of the colonial government. The forests were no simple groves of shrubs and trees but were home to the tribal communities, from where these people could draw each and every thing for their life and shelter. The Act restricted the tribal peoples' use of the forest resources, and their activities for survival were deemed as plundering.[1]

Another blow to the traditional occupations was hammered, with the CTA 1871 labelling the nomadic and semi-nomadic communities as criminal. The colonisers thought that someone without a permanent abode and a specific occupation was a vagabond indulging in crime for survival. Thus, their movements were not only kept under surveillance but restricted to specific areas. Singh argues:

> Thus such classes of people and communities who lived with and in nature and practised nomadism were not understood by the Imperial rulers and administrators. They considered them not only uncivilized and uncultured but savages and barbarians who posed a potential threat to the law and order of the society. Since they were poor and lacked definite means of production to earn their living, they were assumed to be thieves and dacoits. Thus they were dubbed as criminals.
>
> (2010c, xiv)

According to Arnold, the CTA was used against 'wandering groups, nomadic petty traders and pastoralists, gypsy types, hill- and forest-dwelling tribals, in short, against a wide variety of marginals who did not conform to the colonial pattern of settled agricultural and wage labour' (1985, 85).

In the background of these historical developments when the forces of modernisation and governance are against the very existence of the tribal communities, an attempt is made to look into the nature and types of occupations these people are pursuing to make their living. Despite the above-mentioned factors threatening their survival, we find that some tribes and some percentage within each one of them are pursuing still their traditional occupations. This, of course, is true of the senior generation as the younger one is given to status and income returns. That is why an attempt has been made here to look into the occupational changes of these people over three generations.

An important issue to bear in mind is that each tribal community has a specific traditional occupation, and there are a few respondents in each tribe pursuing these to an extent. The list is long. Thus, small percentages of such occupations have been clubbed together under one column: 'others'. Their share is 14.55 per cent. The majority respondents, however, are given to the 'modern' occupations for earning a living. A simple glance at Table 6.1 regarding the nature and type of occupation of the respondent shows clearly that four types are listed under the category of traditional occupations that have some significant share of the tribal population in the state of Punjab. These four activities in order of decreasing proportion are animal rearing (11.14 per cent), *balti-tasla* (bucket and large shallow pan of iron) repair and *jharni* (iron sieve) making and repairs (10.74 per cent), begging (6.03 per cent) and *chhaj banauna* (making of large sieve of reeds; 4.46 per cent). All these add up to 32.37 per cent or one-third of respondents engaged in the traditional occupations.

One is likely to surmise at 'begging' as an occupation, but the discourse of the dominant communities has made certain tribal communities internalise their labelling as *mang khani jaat*, literally a caste (sic) given to begging. As a matter of fact, the members of such communities like the Bazigar women, the Bangla men or Nat men and women ask for money from the spectators on a voluntary basis after their performance. The Bangala men play *been* on the road side to gather audience for showing snake charming. After the show, the performer moves with a bowl or *patari* cover to collect money. It is in fact a payment for their labour for entertainment or art. No one is coerced to pay, and one may give as much as one desires. This act of moving with a bowl probably got them this label of begging that it is not. Similarly, the Nats too make loud beats on a drum (*dhol*) before showing their acrobatic feats at an open space and ask for money subsequently. The same is true of the bear and monkey show by Madaris. Almost similar is the case with Bazigar women who go to a house in a group where there is some celebration, a marriage or the birth of a son. They perform *giddha*, Punjabi women's folk dance with a wide range of verses (*bolian*) suitable to the occasion, and ask for some reward in the form of cash (money) or kind that may be clothes or grain etc. Now with increasing affluence and expenditure on marriages, they ask for jewellery even. Thus, we may infer from the above discussion that begging is neither their forte nor trait but a misnomer given to them by upper castes and classes to their way of collecting money or material on a purely voluntary basis for making a living. It may also be labelled 'begging' since they do not ask for a specific amount for their performance before the show as is true of a modern enterprise to take advance payments.

The data reveal (Table 6.1) that animal rearing is the most common (11.14 per cent) traditional occupation followed by the respondents. A couple of tribal communities like Gujjars, Gaadi Lohars and Bazigar Banjaras specialise in keeping cattle. The Gujjars among them are dependent solely on buffaloes for the trading of milk and its products (see Table 5.25 above). The Gaadi Lohar and Bazigar Banjara own oxen for their bullock carts and hence indulge in their trade as well. The former tribe is well known for the quality of its bulls. This tribe is making use of the bullock cart since they

Table 6.1 Types of occupations of the respondents

Group/Sub-group	Own shop N	Own shop %	job N	job %	animal rear N	animal rear %	kabad N	kabad %	begging N	begging %	labour N	labour %	chhaj N	chhaj %	hawker N	hawker %	balti-tasla N	balti-tasla %	shoe polish N	shoe polish %	Jharui N	Jharui %	others N	others %
Family Income
1. Low	7	3.38	1	0.48	9	4.35	30	14.49	25	12.08	28	13.53	8	3.86	22	10.63	10	4.83	25	12.08	17	8.21	25	12.08
2. Medium	20	5.54	6	1.66	28	7.76	26	7.20	18	4.99	79	21.88	20	5.54	38	10.52	18	4.99	19	5.26	29	8.03	60	16.62
3. High	12	6.15	14	7.18	48	24.62	16	8.21	3	1.54	38	19.49	6	3.08	18	9.23	2	1.02	6	3.08	6	3.08	26	13.33
Total All Data	39	5.11	21	2.75	85	11.14	72	9.44	46	6.03	145	19.00	34	4.46	78	10.22	30	3.93	50	6.55	52	6.81	111	14.55

$Chi^2 = 136.63^{**}$ (df:22) C = 0.39;

Source: Author

are nomadic still and carry the whole household stuff on their *gaadi* (cart), while the Bazigar Banjaras no longer use the carts. Therefore, they keep not the bulls but cows and goats etc. for milk. The latter cattle are often domesticated by many other communities, especially those residing in the rural areas where availability of grass and fodder is not much of a problem. It is for this reason that animal rearing is still popular with most of these communities even with those living on the urban periphery. The women especially are engaged in this occupation.

The making and repairs of *jharnis* (iron sieves) and *balti-tasle* (buckets and large shallow pans of iron) is another traditional occupation with a high proportion of respondents engaged in them (10.74 per cent), and this is due solely to the nomadic tribes – Sikligar and Gaadi Lohars. These items are used by the agricultural households and by the construction workers, the masons. The bottom of an iron bucket develops holes due to rust, which is either replaced or repaired by these people. No doubt, this particular occupational activity is dwindling due to the availability of cheap plastic buckets and tubs, but still masons and agriculturists use the iron utensils for their strength and durability. The primary identification of Gaadi Lohars, though, is with these utensils (*balti-tasle*), but they also repair and supply numerous other agricultural and domestic iron implements (cf. Kazak 2005). Similarly, the Sikligars are associated with *jharni* making and locks, knives (*chaku-chhurian*) and cutters.

Chhaj banauna, the making of large winnowing pan from reeds for separating grain from chaff, is another traditional activity pursued by some tribes such as Sansis, Barads and Bazigars. No doubt much of such work is now being performed by certain machines, but *chhaj* are still in demand in the grain markets as also in the agricultural households. There is another use of this item (*chhaj*) during the marriage ceremony. *Chhaj todna*, the breaking of a winnowing pan with a stick, is a ritual performed by the maternal side of the groom/bride at her residence before the marriage ceremony in Punjab. These two activities, one agricultural and the other ritualistic, have sustained this traditional occupation. A sub-group of Sansis is called Chhaj Bann. Dhehe are also associated largely with this activity as also many other sub-groups.

To the one-third (32.37 per cent) share of traditional occupations may be added the share of 'others' (Table 6.1) totalling 14.55 per cent of the sample. This takes the total number to 46.92 per cent, which is as good as half the population of tribes. The remaining 53.07 per cent respondents are following the non-traditional or 'modern' occupations, and the foremost amongst these is wage labour, representing 19.00 per cent respondents. This is one category with highest proportion of all respondents. It refers to a variety of activities in the agricultural fields, construction work, grain markets or almost anywhere of any kind of unskilled work. On the other extreme is the service sector called 'doing a job' in popular parlance with monthly salary. A mere 2.76 per cent respondents are engaged in jobs that are more often in the private sector including petty business locally than the government.

144 Occupations of the tribal communities

The latter service is definitely considered more prestigious due to security of service than the former sector.

The hawkers and scrap pickers (*kabadiye*) are the remaining most represented 'modern' occupations with 10.22 and 9.44 per cent, respectively. These activities hardly need any training and specialisation or experience. The hawkers sell petty goods of a large variety for the lower and low middle classes in the villages, urban colonies and slums, bus stands and railways stations. The scrap picking is primarily an urban phenomenon due to the waste that consumer culture produces. The small children including girls are seen collecting urban waste from the roads and the sewerage drains, something that a civilised person cannot even watch. The children are often seen searching for iron filings or nails etc. in the dirty sewer drains with a magnet tied to a wooden stick. Such 'modern' occupations are utterly dehumanising and decivilising that come handy to the tribal people that have lost their traditional occupations.[2]

Another occupation that is quite common with respondents is shoe polishing in the towns and cities of Punjab. The younger generation seems quite comfortable with this work. The crowded places like the bus stands, railway stations and market squares are most suited for such an activity. The polish box is portable, and the shoe polisher may often move about from place to place in search of work. Table 6.1 shows that not the boys only but 6.55 per cent respondents too are engaged in this occupation.

A look at the relation of occupations with income variable is interesting for its different patterns. In certain sectors of activities, there is no significant visible difference at three levels of income, namely low, middle and high, while in others it is manifestly striking. For instance, the shop owners, labour, hawkers and *chhaj* makers fall in the former category while all others represent the latter category. In the latter case, there are some occupations that show a very low percentage of respondents at low income levels and a high percentage at the other end of income level, while in other cases this trend is reversed. The case of jobs and animal rearing are in the former category, whereas other occupations like *kabad* (scrap) picking, begging, *balti-tasle* (bucket and iron shallow pan) and shoe polishing fall in the latter category.

Let us get back to the present generation of respondents to find out the seasonal cycle of their respective occupations. The data in Table 6.2 reveals that there are mainly three responses to the question of seasonal cycle of the respondents' occupations. It is important to note that the first and the last column are synonyms. When a respondent replies the 'whole year' and another one 'no season', the two are saying the same thing. The latter category is a literal translation of *'koi season nahin'* that means they are working for the whole year. The natural and cultural factors have no bearing on their work cycle. One may wonder how this is true in the case of animal rearing and agricultural labour, where nature's cycles are likely to be most dominant. In the case of the former, tribes like the Bauria, Bazigar or others

Table 6.2 Seasonal cycle of work

Group/ Sub-group	Whole year N	Whole year %	Seasonal N	Seasonal %	No season N	No season %	
Family Income							
1. Low	95	45.89	51	24.64	61	29.47	
2. Medium	148	41.00	122	33.80	91	25.21	
3. High	95	48.72	33	16.92	67	34.36	Chi^2 = 19.55**(df:4) C = 0.16;
Total							
All Data	338	44.30	206	27.00	219	28.70	

Source: Author

engaged in agricultural fieldwork are definitely governed by nature, but in the agriculturally lean period they shift to *mandis*, the grain markets for the loading, unloading, gleaning and packing of the grain. Similarly, Gujjars and Gadarias rearing animals keep shifting from region to region depending upon the availability of fodder and grass. This makes clear that the two responses – whole year and no season – are no different but rather are synonyms. Those collecting *kabad* (scrap) or 'begging' or doing a job or selling commodities from a shop or through hawking also know no season. These are whole-year occupations.

On the other hand, the case of those engaged in selling bangles (Barad women) or *vadhai dena* (Bazigar women) or repairing *tasle-balti* (Gaadi Lohar) or of Sikligars' is season specific to quite an extent. For instance, marriages are usually not held during extreme summers or the rainy season besides the fact that astrologers mark out certain auspicious days most suitable for weddings. *Teej* (third day of month) and *karva chauth* (married woman's fast) festivals are especially linked to bangle wearing besides the weddings. In the case of Sikligars and Gaadi Lohars, the harvesting season enhances their production and sales as the farmers invest in their implements. The former are especially busy on certain festivals such as *dhantera*, just before Diwali, when buying new utensils is a norm. Singh notes in the case of Sikligars of the Deccan:

> The Sikligars were quick to mention that in certain months when religious and other festivals fall, for instance Diwali, Dussehra, Dhantera or Navratras, their engagement is doubled which is lean in other periods. Most of them have agreed: "*Hamara season to char mahiney ka hota hai. Aatth mahiney to khatey hi hain.*" That we have a working season for four months only, we eat for the remaining eight months.
>
> (2018, 124)

146 *Occupations of the tribal communities*

Table 6.2 makes clear that starkly majority respondents making three-fourths of the sample, that is, 73.00 (44.30 + 28.70) per cent are engaged throughout the year, and the remaining 27.00 per cent are affected by the seasonal cycle. The variable of income has little effect on the former category at its three levels – low, medium and high – while it becomes manifestly visible in the seasonal category. The number of respondents is highest (33.80 per cent) in the medium-income group of Rs. 17,000 to Rs. 39,000 per month. Their number declines on either side, though significantly more (16.92 per cent) in the high-income group. There are 24.64 per cent respondents in the low-income group.

After finding out the cycle of the tribal communities' occupations, it is pertinent to look into the number of days different respondents are engaged in their work. It is an attempt to be more specific about their occupational engagement, but that purpose has not been achieved, since the responses are more casual than specific. Table 6.3 informs that almost half the sample population, that is, 51.11 per cent respondents, are engaged in their occupations for 300 and more days in a year. The remaining half has 25.43 per cent respondents that remain engaged in work for 100 to 200 days per year. The leftover respondents, 13.24 per cent, are working for more than 200 days and 10.22 per cent for less than 100 days in a year. A relation of this variable with income reveals mixed results. If the numbers of respondents show increase in their proportion even if not very significant, from low to high income levels in 100–200, 200–300 and 350-plus days categories, the reverse is true of the remaining categories of up to 100 and 300–350 days. The difference between different levels of income here too is not very significant.[3]

After describing the occupational schedule and their seasonal cycle of work, it is important to know how the respondents feel about their work. Hence, it is specifically enquired from them if they are satisfied with their occupation. Not surprisingly, Table 6.4 shows that a significantly large

Table 6.3 Number of days of work

Group/ Sub-group	Up to 100		100–200		200–300		300–350		350+		
	N	%	N	%	N	%	N	%	N	%	
Family Income											
1. Low	24	11.59	42	20.29	18	8.70	71	34.30	52	25.12	
2. Medium	40	11.08	95	26.32	56	15.51	95	26.32	75	20.78	
3. High	14	7.18	57	29.23	27	13.85	42	21.54	55	28.21	Chi^2 = 19.81* (df:8)
Total All Data	78	10.22	194	25.43	101	13.24	208	27.26	182	23.85	C = 0.16;

Source: Author

proportion (92.92 per cent) is not satisfied with its occupation. Those who stand on the opposite side are a mere 7.08 per cent. There is hardly any need to explain this dissatisfaction in the present-day market society, as these people are performing either those jobs that are their traditional occupations and perforce they have to undertake such productive activities for their survival since they know no other work or skill, or they take up menial jobs. Even when they are following their traditional occupation, that may be a reason for their satisfaction, but for two reasons they fail here too. One, their younger generation is not following the traditional occupation, since they find it unremunerative and outdated besides the low status. Two, there is hardly anything to celebrate, since there is not much demand for their products in this modernising society. They are performing the menial jobs of collecting rags and scrap (*kabad*), of begging literally in form and content. Those who are still engaged in their traditional occupation, their wives and children do such menial work. A small fraction of the satisfied respondents is that who believe in the ideology of contentment and remain ever satisfied with whatever is given to them. They take it as their 'destiny' and as 'will of the god'.

The level of dissatisfaction is not surprising, but an attempt is made to understand the nature of relations these people have with fellow workers and amongst themselves. Unfortunately, this question 'what are your relations with the employer and fellow workers/dealers in trade of other communities etc.?' has fallen flat. A common answer, almost universal, from the respondents of this sample is: '*changey ne*'; '*vadhia ne*', that is, 'we have cordial relations with every one.' The research fellows were not able to appreciate the nature and gravity of this question despite caution in terms of inter-community interaction and relations. One intention among others is to seek information on the undercurrents of relations between the tribal and other communities who have not only been demonised but declared

Table 6.4 Are you satisfied with your present occupation?

Group/ Sub-group	Yes N	%	No N	%	
Family Income					
1. Low	8	3.86	199	96.14	
2. Medium	19	5.26	342	94.74	
3. High	27	13.85	168	86.15	$Chi^2 = 18.64**(df:2)$ $C = 0.15;$
Total					
All Data	54	7.08	709	92.92	

Source: Author

148 *Occupations of the tribal communities*

'criminal' by the colonial government. Much misinformation is in circulation even now about these people (see Chapter 7). However, their response of 'good and cordial relations' gets substantiated in the field since no inter-community conflict is ever reported by the respondents. This is despite the fact that other communities do feel that Sansi women in particular indulge in thievery and pick-pocketing, yet the relations between communities have never turned hostile.

The discussion above makes clear that 70 years after independence and having removed the tag of criminality in 1952, nearly half the population is still engaged in their traditional occupations for making a living. This means that the government has not done anything worthwhile for securing their future through alternative occupations that it had been claiming since the colonial times and earmarked huge funds for the purpose. On the contrary, the present government does not register their presence in the state, implying thereby that there are no tribes in Punjab, and that they are no different from the Scheduled Castes. The above profiling reveals that the tribal people have tasted nothing of the new developments in economy and society and are at the bottom of all indices of the SES. Their houses lack the basic amenities, their living conditions are worse to none in the so-called developed state of Punjab, and they are engaged in dehumanising activities just for two *chapattis* a day.[4]

Notes

1 'A raid was conducted by Forest Range Officer, Nurpur Bedi, Surjit Singh along with his staff on Bangala Basti, Nurpur Bedi, and Bangala Basti, Kiratpur Sahib, on January 6. During the search of the houses of the accused, two pythons, two cobras, a sand boa and a huge number of animal body parts were recovered.' *Tribune* News Service, 'Snakes, Animal Body Parts Seized in Ropar', *The Tribune*, 12 January 2018.
2 The situation with regard to the working of these communities has not changed over the last more than six decades. In a write-up titled 'Punjab's Young Wage-Earners', the plight of the tribal children is described: 'Children both boys and girls belonging to former criminal tribes are usually found picking dirty rags, scraps of iron and broken pieces of glass from heaps of rubbish in urban areas . . . In rural areas, small boys mostly engage themselves as cowherds.' *The Tribune*, 15 July 1963.
3 It is also enquired from the respondents: 'What do they do when not engaged in regular work?' The idea to obtain this information is to know what sort of activities keep them engaged then. How do they pass their day? etc. But responses to this question defeated the purpose. A significantly large number reply that 'they stay at home', and the research fellow did not probe further. The proportion of such respondents in the sample is 81.52 per cent. From the remaining lot, 5.11 per cent report 'visiting their relatives' during the off days, and the larger proportion of 13.37 per cent mentioned a variety of activities like talking to friends at a common place, gossiping over various issues and playing cards etc. It is interesting to note that for all the three activities, the levels of income – low, medium, high – are neutralised having no bearing on them.
4 It is a popular saying in Punjabi – *sirf do rottian layi*.

7 Intergenerational occupational change

The previous chapter deliberated on the present occupations of the respondents of the tribal communities. Two distinct types of occupations are identified, one traditional and other non-traditional or 'modern', and the proportion of population in these two types is not significantly different, as two percentages are 46.93 and 53.07 per cent, respectively (see Table 6.1). The former is no small proportion seven decades after independence (1947), and additional about 80 years when the CTA was implemented in 1871. This means that nearly half the tribal communities have withstood the pressure of the government, both colonial and the post-colonial/nationalist, for a century and a half to change their traditional occupations and lifestyle, leave aside their cultural norms and values that are still harder nuts to crack than the material elements.

The material forces of course are more potent and rapid than the social factors. The installation of a factory such as a gun coach factory as early as 1864 in the Begur forest of Karnataka (Misra 1982), Chitaranjan Locomotive works in Burdwan, iron ore complex in Singhbhum and the Chaibasa cement works (Das Gupta 1982) and the Bailadila iron ore complex in Bastar (Joshi 1982) did not take long to convert the forest-dwelling hunter-gatherers and small cultivators into unskilled labour begging for employment in the concerned factories. Singh in his volume on the *Economies of the Tribes and Their Transformation* suggests four reasons responsible for the transformation of the tribal economy from food gathering to the food production stage or from the tribe to the peasant:(i) increasing pressure of population on the land; (ii) deepening of cultural contact situation of the tribal with non-tribal population; (iii) reservation of the forest for commercial exploitation by the government and restriction on the customary rights even of the tribal people; and (iv) restriction on shifting cultivation and application of new agricultural policy supported by flow of capital and outsiders into the tribal territories. The colonial policy of reclaiming tribes through plough cultivation and market transformed them thoroughly (1982, xiii).

The forces of industrialisation, modernisation and market have influenced each and every section of the population everywhere, but the communities on the margin such as the Scheduled Castes and the Scheduled Tribes have been hit the hardest, especially the latter. The former have a different and rather a liberating experience with regard to occupational change. They got avenues to escape the menial work over the generations. Judge and Bal (2009) in their study of Punjab dalits show that due to the arrival of capitalism, education and new occupations, they are presently engaged in as many as 46 different occupations. Six per cent amongst them are occupying high-status positions. The tribal people's experience with regard to occupational change is otherwise, though they have been affected directly and indirectly in a huge way. They have been rendered de-skilled and got subordinated to the market. They were, hitherto, relatively free people doing work and enjoying leisure at will. Sinha (1982) informs that the hill Kharia of Purulia who were hunter-gatherers were restricted to small agriculture and from there slowly shifted to making brooms and fishtraps for their survival. Their small children from 8 to 9 years were employed as cow herders and those from 8 to 12 years as field-cum-domestic servants. The case of the Phanse-Pardhis, the hunter-gatherers is no different. Sanave (2005) shows that these people are now selling tamarind, berries and other wild fruits, grass and fish etc. for their survival. Their women weave beads in thread called *manipot* for sale in the local market.

The intergenerational occupational change in the tribes of Punjab, and elsewhere too with some exceptions, is not a case of occupational mobility that is often referred to in the sociological literature. For a starkly large majority, it is a case of downward mobility and loss of their traditional skills and occupations. Lipset and Bendix (1959) followed by Goldthrope (1987) had set the trend for different types of mobility in the populations of the urban and rural areas, within and between occupations, across gender and regions. Very recently Motiram and Singh have shown the intergenerational mobility in India is higher in the urban areas as compared to the rural areas. According to them: 'We find considerable intergenerational occupational persistence – across all occupational categories, the father's category is the most likely one that a son could find himself in (e.g. a likelihood of almost half for agricultural labourers)' (2012, 58). They conclude: 'However, we document considerable (and higher) downward mobility among the SCs/STs. The substantial level of immobility particularly among the low-skilled and low-paying' (ibid, 63). Stretching the comparison further they argue: 'considerable downward mobility for the SCs/STs . . . is higher than the same for non-SCs/STs. For SCs/STs, we also observe higher persistence (as compared to the same for non-SCs/STs) in low-skilled/low-paying occupations' (ibid, 58). Jatinder Singh (1982) has also shown in his study of the tribal people in the rural Jhabua district (M.P.) that with the first generation agriculture was the primary occupation and labour a secondary one. In the second generation, the majority people were migrating to nearby areas for work, but the distance increased further in the third generation (cited in Manpreet Kaur 2018).

Intergenerational occupational change 151

On the basis of his earlier study (2008a) on the Punjab tribes, Singh concludes:

> This diversity of occupations and economic functions gradually became victim of modernizing economy, and education based skills and occupations. The traditional community specific knowledge was outdated and declared unfit for a modernizing society, the project of independent India . . . The account below highlights this change and shows that occupational diversification gave way to occupational homogenization as majority of these people are doing wage labour in the rural or urban areas, *mandis* (grain markets) or farms, picking junk and scrap or as hawkers.
>
> (2010d, 418–19)

An attempt is made in the present chapter to examine the type and nature of occupational shift over three generations of these people in Punjab. The data pertain to respondents that are the heads of households and selected through stratified random sampling in which the focus is on the communities for a wide spectrum of their types. The variable of age for inclusion in the sample is also important so that we may have a sufficient number of senior respondents who could give rich information on their past experiences and their traditional occupations. The age of majority respondents (69.07 per cent) is 50 years and more. Those respondents who belong to the age group of 60 years and plus are 44.04 per cent (see Table 5.5). It is a fairly large sample to obtain quality data on the subject of their respective occupations. The responses of the senior generation about their parents' and ancestors' occupation leave no doubt about the tribal character of these communities that the government refuses to acknowledge.

The issue of their tribal character is first ascertained from the occupations of the respondents' parents. A comparison between the two tables, Table 6.1 (occupations of the respondents) and Table 7.1 (occupation of

Table 7.1 Occupation of the respondents' fathers

Occupation	*Ani*	*Rassi*	*AgriLab*	*Beg*	*Broom*	*Chhaj*
Number	164	26	87	170	27	38
Percent	21.49	3.40	11.40	22.28	3.53	4.98

Occupation	*Circus*	*Kanghi*	*Balti*	*Jharni*	*Others*
Number	24	33	30	52	112
Percent	3.14	4.32	3.93	6.18	14.68

(Occupations at income levels could not be computed due to later tabulation.)

Source: Author

the respondents' fathers) shows distinctly that there are 11.40 per cent respondents that are engaged in agricultural labour, if this is considered a non-traditional occupation in a sense. A look at Table 5.5 shows that 16.91 per cent respondents were born in the last decade or so of the colonial period. The remaining ones are a generation of independent India. But we notice that the fathers of the large majority, that is, 83.09 per cent respondents, were engaged in their tribe-specific traditional occupations. This fact compels us to infer that despite the colonial and the post-colonial/nationalist governments' efforts to wean these people away from their traditional occupations and lifestyle, announcing scheme after scheme for their development and integration in the modern economy and society, could bear no fruit. There are 30.93 per cent respondents that are of 50 years. Their fathers must have been working well up to the 1960s if not beyond. That means the traditional occupations of the tribal communities were quite popular with them until then.

It is worth noticing that most respondents in the higher age group of 60 years and more (see Table 5.5) that make 44.04 per cent of the sample have referred to their father's occupation not as labour (colloquially *mazdoor*, a daily wager or *naukar*) but as *siri*, which means a share-cropper. The *naukar* gets annual salary and some grain, but the *siri* obtains a share in the crop. In Punjab, before the advent of green revolution and even after that for some time, the latter practice was normal that remained in vogue well throughout the 1960s. This practice was withdrawn in favour of the annual payment for *naukar* when agriculture became capital intensive with high investment on technology and high-yield hybrid seeds. The agricultural labour employed annually often takes payment in advance, a practice that is continuing in 21st century rural Punjab. Now for the sowing of paddy, which is not a traditional crop of this region, the migrant labour from Uttar Pradesh, Bihar and Madhya Pradesh primarily is engaged on contract payment. Earlier they were also engaged for harvesting, an activity presently executed by the harvester-combines primarily. The big farmers have bought these machines that are deployed out to harvest the crops of others on payment. The point that is made here suggests that even agricultural labour, a seemingly modern occupation, is largely following the traditional practice but for a change in the mode of payment from kind to cash and in its nomenclature from *siri* to *naukar*, respectively.

Therefore, it is clear enough to suggest that 88.60 per cent fathers of the respondents were pursuing the traditional occupations definitely. One may decisively draw a conclusion that the fathers' fathers must be in the thick of their traditional occupations despite the colonial government's efforts to wean them away from their tradition and lifestyle. This is important to remind that the listing of the respondents' occupations is for the primary occupations only. The tribal peoples' dependence on nature and natural raw material compels them to take up secondary occupations as well. The largest share in the traditional occupations is bagged by animal rearing and 'begging', as often replied by the respondents themselves. The latter one has 22.28 per cent fathers of the respondents indulging in it and the former 21.49 per cent (see Table 7.1). The remaining occupations hover between three to six per cent only. The residual category of 'others' has 14.68 per cent respondents' fathers in a variety of occupations, a number small enough to be listed in a tabular form. It has a long list of 19 occupations including snake charming, making *tokaris* (baskets), *murtis* (sculptures), toys, *desi* (traditional) medicines, ear cleaning etc. It is pertinent to notice that these occupations too are traditional. Therefore, if agricultural labour is also included in the list of traditional occupations, which it is in a way as mentioned above, it would not be an exaggeration to state that the occupation of all the fathers was traditional that amounts to 100 per cent.

A comparison between the two generations, of the respondents and their fathers, reveals that the senior generation was largely nomadic, and there were forests and wildlife enough for subsistence in the nomadic state and for their traditional occupations that relied heavily on nature and natural resources. Thus, all the respondents invariably listed 'nomadism as an occupation of their parents', since that was a way of their living, their livelihood and their heritage. The same is not the case with respondents who have started living in permanent settlements. There has been a consistent effort on the part of the colonial and the post-colonial/nationalist governments to facilitate settlement of these nomadic communities, and they had been allocating funds for this purpose, though without much success. The present respondents, therefore, do not list 'nomadism as an activity or an occupation'. There is loss of traditional occupations and depletion of forests as well besides the laws against the use of forest and its resources. Moreover, nomadism is not a cherished value in modern society.

The prevalence of traditional occupations is also due to the resilience of certain communities who are not willing to leave their old lifestyle. The Sikligars are engaged in making *jharnis* and *chimte* still, as Gaadi Lohars are dealing with *bathal-balti* repairs and the Chhaj Bann are making *chhaj* etc. Table 7.1 shows that there is hardly any difference in the engagement of their numbers across the two generations. If the respondents' proportion (see Table 6.1) in these occupations is 6.81, 3.93 and 4.46 per cent, respectively, their fathers' share is no different. Their respective figures are 6.18, 3.93 and 4.98 per cent. It is worthwhile to note that out of a sample of 763, the fathers of five respondents only were collecting scrap, and eight were hawkers that are professedly the 'modern' occupations.

In certain occupations such as animal rearing and 'begging', there is a definite decline in the proportion of respondents compared to their fathers. If 21.49 per cent fathers were engaged in animal rearing, the respondents' (sons) share is 11.14 per cent. Similarly, 'begging' has seen a fall from 22.28 per cent for fathers to 6.03 per cent for the respondents or sons. On the other hand, agricultural labour is another occupation common between the two generations that has reversed the above trend. There are 11.40 per cent fathers engaged in labour, but the number shoots up to 19.00 per cent for the sons (respondents). The number of respondents' fathers engaged in shoe polishing and *kabad* (scrap) collection is virtually non-existent. One may thus draw a clear inference that there is a definite loss of certain traditional occupations, and the workforce released from there has joined 'modern' occupations like wage labour, scrap collection and shoe polishing etc.

The same is also true of running a shop and doing a job. These two engagements are absent too in the fathers' generation, while its combined percentage for the respondents is 7.86 (Table 6.1). A count of the numerous occupations stands at 35 for the respondents' generation[1] and 31 for the past generation, that is, their fathers'.[2] There is hardly any difference between the two counts of occupations, but there is a difference of quality between them. The traditional occupations were tribe specific, and each one specialised in its own way, unlike the 'modern' occupations that need no skill such as owning a corner shop, taking a petty salaried job, doing wage labour, becoming a hawker, pulling a rickshaw or *rehri*, collecting scrap or polishing shoes etc. It is made possible because the processes of urbanisation and industrialisation have broken the spine of the traditional occupations, and the tribal people are forced to undertake work that comes their way or they can lay their hands on. Sachidananda in *The Changing Munda* (1979) explains that the tribes people earlier dependent on forests and agriculture are now reduced to labourers or small farmers due to industrialisation.[3]

After looking into the occupation of the respondents' fathers, it would be useful to examine the same for their mothers. It would further validate the prevalence of the traditional occupations in the senior generation. An important point that one needs to keep in mind while discussing women's or the respondents' mothers' occupation is that their engagement in traditional occupation(s) is in addition to the household chores that inevitably fall in their lap. The older women do take the assistance of young daughters, grand daughters and daughters-in-law in executing the domestic chores, from which the males often keep distance. These women were not only marginally engaged in the traditional occupations in the sense of helping their husbands but had active involvement, depending on the nature of work. No doubt the majority women as mothers more often carried out their occupation at home but for 'begging', as is true of the Nat and Bazigar women, which activities are executed inevitably in the public domain. The latter go out to houses for giving *vadhai* (felicitations) and the former for showing acrobatics. The Bangala women do assist their husbands in making medicines from herbs that they have collected from the forest. The Gandhila and Barad women particularly, among others, make brooms from the leaves and reeds collected by their men folk. There is a clear division of labour in the Barad households, where men make *kanghis* and women make *jude* and *binne* or *innu*. The Barad women themselves go out to sell their products besides selling the bangles. The Bauria women go to the fields with their husbands, and Sansi women too help their men in their economic pursuits.

Intergenerational occupational change 155

The Gujjar women look after the buffaloes and the milk. If Sikligar women help their husbands at home, the Gaadi Lohar women go out to collect items for repair to be done by their husbands. The point worth noticing is that there is neither a fixed pattern nor certain rigid norms to regulate the women's engagement in productive labour. But it is certain that women in each tribe contribute significantly to the economy of the household. It is worth recalling the comment of a senior respondent on the Bazigar women: '*Is kabile da loon-tel toran vich bazigar aurtan da bahut vadda yogdaan si.*' That is, the women of this tribe had great role in running their households. The gender division of labour is tribe and production specific.

The size of the family too affects the role of women's engagement at home doing household chores, including the care of the old and the young. The joint family is prevalent still, which is why the size of the family is large. Table 5.3 shows that 23.72 per cent families have five members while 58.46 per cent families have six to nine members and 17.82 per cent have more than that. Manpreet Kaur (2018) has also noted that 80 per cent of the Barad households have an average family size of 6.84 who live in just two rooms. These figures suggest that the domestic confinement of women owes to the large size of their families, but it is commendable that yet they find time to go out for productive labour, giving domestic charge to the young girls in the family, who not only look after the household chores but also play mother to infants. These women combined domestic chores with productive labour in traditional occupations, whatever that may be, since that was the domestic system of production.

Table 7.2 reveals the range of occupations that mothers of the respondents were engaged in. It is pertinent to recall that once again this listing is about primary occupations apart from the domestic chores that women were performing inevitably. The largest share goes to broom making as a singular occupation in which 13.10 per cent mothers of the respondents were engaged. But this figure is not farther from their share in agricultural

Table 7.2 Occupation of the respondents' mothers

Occupation	Ani	Rassi	AgriLab	Beg	Broom	Chhaj	Circus	Jude-	Balti-
Number	53	37	96	50	100	66	11	39	30
	6.94	4.84	12.58	6.55	13.10	8.65	1.44	5.11	3.93

Occupation	Jharni-	*N/Vadhai	Bangles	Kuch-	Shepherd	Hawkers	Others	Total
Number	52	95	15	19	71	18	26	763
	6.81	12.45	1.96	2.49	9.3	2.35	3.41	

(Occupations at income levels could not be computed due to later tabulation.) (*N = needle selling)
Source: Author

156 *Intergenerational occupational change*

labour (12.58 per cent), followed yet again closely by needle selling and *vadhai dena*, a speciality of the Bazigar women with 12.45 per cent. Two occupations, namely, shepherding and animal rearing, though, appear to be one are different but their combined proportion is highest amongst the mothers of the respondents with 16.24 per cent women engaged in this activity. The difference between the two is that the latter is executed largely at home or around while the former involves taking the animal stock – sheep, goat or buffaloes – en bloc away from home and the village for the whole day and may be to distant places. It may be recalled that 33.42 per cent households in the sample have cattle with them. The larger share of cattle stock holders goes to Gujjars, Gaadi Lohars, Bazigar Banjaras and Gadaria Sansis. And this activity is invariably carried out by women.

What is most significant in this discussion is that five mothers only are engaged in the collection of *kabad* or scrap and six only in exchanging old clothes for new utensils made of steel. Both of these, of course, are non-traditional occupations practised in the urban areas. And 98.56 per cent mothers of the respondents were engaged in the traditional occupations characteristic of each tribe. It is interesting and significant to notice that women as mothers were engaged in all those traditional occupations that their husbands were doing but for *kanghi* making done by the Barad men. On the other hand, the Bazigar men would not perform activities like *vadhai dena* (felicitations) performed by their women only. This argument goes to prove the point that the tribal women are twice as skilled as men, in the domestic chores and in the traditional occupations.[4]

The middle generation of wives of the respondents make a total of 694 persons, and the majority of them, that is, 37.75 per cent, are engaged in domestic chores followed by animal rearing, 10.24 per cent. The *kabad* collection, 9.38 per cent, and 'begging' 7.78 per cent, dominate the remaining occupational distributions of these women. The wage labour is performed by 5.76 per cent women. The hawkers are 4.18 per cent selling petty commodities for use by women and children largely, while 3.02 per cent specialise in selling toys only. The category of others includes 12.82 per cent wives performing a variety of sundry jobs whose share each is small enough to be accounted for in the discussion. One worrying issue in the case of wives is that a large number of them, that is, 6.19 per cent, have been reported to be ill, which means they are unproductive and dependent on other members of the family.

The nature of occupations has undergone a sea change in the third generation of daughters and daughters-in-law, whose total numbers are 349 and 574, respectively. The unmarried daughters are staying with their parents. In both cases, the largest proportion is invariably engaged in the household chores, and their respective percentages are 30.65 and 60.27. It seems to be the duty of the daughter-in-law to do the household chores. Interestingly, if 26.64 per cent daughters are taking education, there is none in the category of daughters-in-law. For the latter category, animal rearing involves

9.58 per cent – that is three times less at 3.43 per cent for the daughters. On the other hand, if 8.18 per cent daughters-in-law are doing labour to earn a living, the percentage of daughters is mere 2.57. *Kabad* collection engages 5.22 per cent daughters-in-law and 4.58 per cent daughters, and as one goes to begging, the gap between the two disappears, since their respective percentages are 3.31 and 3.72.

A perusal of the intergenerational change in the occupations of the tribal communities described above shows that there is a definite trend in the decrease of traditional occupations over three generations from the respondents' fathers and mothers to their children. It may still be seen in its best and clear form if we look into the proportion of the respondents and their parents engaged in three occupations that are more likely to be characterised as 'modern' than others, such as wage labour, hawker/peddler and scrap (*kabad*) collection. These unskilled occupations are a consequence of recent developments in agriculture and industrial production systems, urbanisation and generation of waste material following the consumer culture of 'use and throw'. Let me clarify that hawkers are not simply those who are selling products roaming around, but their products are generally cheap industrial goods for the consumption of relatively economically poor classes in the rural or marginalised urban areas. A large number of them are also selling cold drinks (*thhande bechna*, as they call) at the bus stands. This is different from the bangle or needle selling by the Barad and Bazigar women, especially the latter, who draw peoples' attention through their loud and well-tuned melodious calls (*hokre*). The proportion of hawkers in the sample of the respondents is 10.22 per cent (Table 6.1), while that of their fathers is 1.04 per cent and mothers, a mere 0.65 per cent.

The case of *kabad* or scrap collection also shows a similar trend from the senior generation of the mothers to the present one of wives of the respondents. When a mere 0.65 per cent mothers were engaged in this occupation, its percentage goes up to 9.38 per cent for the wives of the respondents, while their own proportion stands at 9.44 per cent (Table 6.1). There is no difference between the gender roles in this activity. The daughters and daughters-in-law of the respondents are also engaged in it, and their proportion in the sample is 4.58 per cent and 5.22 per cent, respectively. This decline in the third generation is due to the education of their daughters, who are sent to school, after which they are hurriedly married off. The daughters-in-law have greater share in this occupation and also in the household chores.

The loss of traditional occupation invariably pushes the tribal people into the unskilled job market, which is why the peasants and tribes, uprooted from their work and places, enter the market as wage labour. This work does not require any special skill, and sundry jobs may be given to them by the one who hires them. There are 19.0 per cent respondents doing wage labour in agriculture to make a living, while the percentage of their fathers doing the same is 11.40. Incidentally, 12.58 per cent respondents' mothers were engaged in this occupation, while this figure for their wives stands at

5.76 per cent. It is important to note that the Bauria men and women, especially, feel comfortable doing agriculture labour, while others too engage in this activity in the rural areas. It is for this reason that with the shrinking of natural resources and restrictions on the forest wealth, more women are drawn to wage labour in agriculture and elsewhere for making a living. There seems an anomaly, because mothers are less likely to be engaged in labour than the wives of the respondents who make the present generation. A plausible explanation is the crisis of viability in the Punjab agriculture that has become a significant trend over the last few decades. The stagnation in agricultural growth has reduced the small and marginal farmers to agricultural labour (Gill 2010). Besides, more wives are confined to domestic work that does not make a separate category for mothers' occupation (see Table 7.2). The proportion of wage/agricultural labour declines further in the case of the daughters (2.57 per cent) of the respondents and goes up to 8.18 per cent for their daughters-in-law. The difference and discrimination between the two roles is obvious, as explained above. The daughters are married off, and the unmarried ones go to school or do household chores. This is a conservative value to keep daughters safe at home.

Sharmila Rani (2019) in her study of the Bangala tribe in the Malwa region of Punjab has also seen a shift in their occupations over three generations from the traditional to the 'modern' type. The sample of 250 respondents informs that 88.4 per cent of their grandfathers' generation was engaged in traditional occupation, while their fathers' percentage came down to 61.6 per cent, which is lowered further to 34.8 per cent in their own generation. There is a fall from 88.4 to 34.8 per cent. On the other hand, if 65.2 per cent respondents are engaged in 'modern' occupations, their fathers' proportion was 38.4 per cent, which fell down to 11.6 per cent in the case of their grandfathers. There are 8.8 per cent respondents only engaged in snake charming, and all of them are above 41 years. The making of desi medicines is another traditional occupation of the Bangala tribe, in which 15.6 per cent respondents are engaged, and a large majority of them are 51 years and above. Interestingly there is none in the age group of 21 to 30 years in both the occupations.[5]

Another study of a different tribe in the Doaba region of Punjab by Manpreet Kaur (2018) corroborates the above trends in the occupations of these communities. She finds that 64 per cent respondents are engaged in labour which is also followed by their sons (51.51 per cent) and sons-in-law (51.95 per cent), while their fathers' occupation was *kanghi* making, a traditional occupation of the Barad tribe and a mark of their identity. Their share is as high as 80 per cent. She quotes a senior respondent: '*Sadda jaddi kumm ehi si-kanghian banaun da, ehde naal hi saddi pachhan si*' (Kaur 2018). That *kanghi* making was our ancestral work and that was our identity.

She also looks into the occupations of their women. 81.50 per cent mothers of the respondents were engaged in the making of *jude* and *binne* (*innu*), a traditional occupation of the Barad women and 15.50 per cent in the allied occupation of bangle (*vangan-churian*) selling. On the other hand, none of the respondents' wives is making *jude-binne*, though 56.82 per cent are still engaged in bangle selling. And 62.02 per cent daughters-in-law are simply housewives, while 50 per cent daughters are engaged in domestic work. If unskilled wage labour is considered a 'modern' occupation that majority respondents (64 per cent) undertake, their fathers' share is 19 per cent and their mothers' a mere 2 per cent. The respondents' wives in this occupation are 9.85 per cent. The remaining ones are either housewives (19.70 per cent) or work as maids (13.64 per cent). The slide becomes more conspicuous in the case of their children, who are engaged entirely in the non-traditional occupations[6](Kaur 2018).

A look into the activities of the respondents' children, especially sons as the proverbial bread winners, further proves the point that these communities are going away from their traditional occupations. They are taking recourse to petty occupations in the urban areas such as peddling, rag-picking, begging in the actual sense of the term (without any performance as is true of their elders), taking employment at tea stalls, restaurants and *dhabas* (roadside eateries) etc. Usually, the children of these communities drop out early without completing even the junior school. A study by Narinder Singh (2015) of 266 tribal children between 6 and 15 years in the Patiala city reveals that 98.90 per cent studied up to the middle school, that means class VIII. The majority among them, 77.80 per cent, have studied up to class V. Their age structure reveals that 47 per cent children are in the age group of six to nine years, which means they are beginners in the school; 31.9 per cent are in the age group of 10 to 12 years, and the remaining 21.0 per cent are between 13 to 15 years. Paradoxically, it is in this age group (6–9 years) that 77.90 per cent children are engaged in various occupations, and 57.90 per cent of these children are in rag-picking only. These figures are from amongst the 140 children (out of 266) doing various occupations to raise the income level of their family. 93.57 per cent children work round the year to add income to the household, and 95 per cent of them contribute up to Rs. 1500 per month.

A further break down of the 266 respondents shows that 140 of these, that is, 52.63 per cent, are not studying in any school but are engaged in various occupations, out of which rag-picking secures the first position with 58.76 per cent children. The remaining 20 per cent are domestic workers, called *chhotu* in popular parlance, while 11.42 per cent are waiters at eateries or *dhabas* who too are called by the same name. Shockingly, in the era of right to education and ban on child labour, 67.86 per cent amongst them are in the age group of six to nine years.[7] When the tribal children's fathers' occupation is noted, the highest percentage (68.53) is of the hawkers. The remaining 15.54 per cent and 13.15 per cent are shop workers and wage labourers, respectively (Singh 2015).[8]

The discussion above manifestly shows a decline in the traditional occupations of the tribal communities in the state. The labour thus released

160 *Intergenerational occupational change*

is absorbed in the so-called menial unskilled jobs in the modern employment sector. An aggregation of the three main occupations, namely wage labour, *kabad* (scrap) collection and peddling, shows that 38.66 per cent respondents are engaged in them. Interestingly and rightly so, the number of respondents' fathers in agricultural labour is 11.40 per cent, and those engaged in scrap collection (*kabad*) and peddling is a mere 0.65 per cent and 1.04 per cent, respectively. The same is true of their mothers, whose percentage in the three 'modern' occupations is 15.58 per cent. A significantly large majority (12.58 per cent) is engaged in agricultural labour. The hawkers or peddlers are 2.35 per cent and the scrap collectors a mere 0.65 per cent. This figure goes up to 22.34 per cent in the case of wives of the respondents. These collective percentages (without hawkers) in case of the daughters and daughters-in-law are 7.15 and 13.40, respectively. It is suggestive of the pitiable plight of the tribal communities that despite the proliferation of jobs and services in the urban society, their members are adopting such jobs that have low status and require no special skill.

Manpreet Kaur's (2018) study shows that the majority of sons in the Barad community of Punjab (51.51 per cent) are engaged in wage labour. The remaining half is engaged in occupations like barber (22.22 per cent) or in some workshop or service station (16.16 per cent). The remaining 4.55 per cent pull the rickshaw, and 5.56 per cent do some odd jobs. The case of their sons-in-law is no different: 51.95 per cent are doing wage labour, and 22.72 per cent work as barbers. Those working at some workshop or service station are 16.24 per cent, and the remaining 9.09 per cent follow sundry jobs. The occupational profile of the Barad daughters and daughters-in-law is no different. Exactly 50 per cent daughters are busy doing domestic chores. The number goes up to 62.02 per cent in the case of daughters-in-law.

The findings of the present study are in consonance with an earlier study by Singh (2008a). It reports that besides Bangalas, Bazigars and Nats, whose senior generation is earning to some extent from their traditional occupations, 'All others are given to daily wage unskilled labour in villages and towns, rag-picking or selling petty goods as "pheriwalas". In all the communities we studied an insignificantly small section is working in the service sector, more than 98 per cent are given to petty jobs and errands' (Singh 2008a: 63). Let us now try to seek an explanation for the occupational change in the tribal communities to their detriment, in the concluding chapter. What led to this change? What are its consequences? Why does there seem no hope for the amelioration of their lives and living conditions?

Notes

1 The number and types of occupations of the respondents' generation: shop (own), beekeeping, job, acrobatics, animal rearing, agriculture on own land, begging, medicine selling, maid, *bagle pharna* (catching egrets), *dhol bajauna* (beating the

drum), entertainment, ear cleaning, hawker, domestic chores, snake show, *balti-tasle* making, *kabad* collection, *kath putli* dance (puppetry), labour, *murti* making, *giddar singhi pharna*, needle selling, *vadhai dena*, exchange old clothes for utensils, *jharni-chimte* making, rickshaw pulling, *rehra* plying, circus, shoe polishing, *siri*, *tokri* making, *chhaj* making, toys/crockery selling and flower decoration. The total number is 35.

2 The number and types of occupations of the respondents' parents: nomad, animal rearing, *rassi vatana* (rope making), exchange old clothes for utensils, *kabad* collection, labour, *desi* medicines, begging, *murti* making, *siri*, shoe polishing, entertainment, hawker, *tokri* (basket) making, agriculture on own land, domestic chores, agricultural land on *theka* contract, *balti-tasle* making, *chhaj* making, acrobatics, needle selling, job, ear cleaning, maid, toy making, *kath putli* dance (puppetry), circus, snake charming, *bagle pharna*, bangle selling and *vadhai dena*. The total number is 31.

3 Many respondents say: '*kise kumm nu na nahin karidi. Je aap na karna hove tan naalwale nu dus deyid'ai.*' That they never say no to a work that comes their way. If one is unable to do something, it is suggested to a fellow tribesman.

4 For details see 'De-skilling of the skilled women', paper presented at Indian Association for Women's Studies national conference on 22–25 January 2017, University of Madras, Chennai.

5 All the respondents engaged in snake charming earn between Rs. 25,000 and Rs. 50,000 per annum, while others making desi medicines may earn up to Rs. 75,000 annually, but all hawkers and scrap collectors earn between Rs. 50,000 and one lakh (Rs. 1,00,000), and some amongst them, 10.64 per cent and 16.13 per cent respectively, earn more than Rs. 1,00,000 annually (Sharmila Rani 2019).

6 The Barad women, however, are continuing with selling of bangles over generations. If the respondents' share in it is 15 per cent, their mothers' proportion is 15.50 per cent, which goes up to 21.53 per cent in the case of the daughters-in-law. The daughters are a mere 3.12 per cent (Manpreet Kaur 2018).

7 According to the Ministry of Human Resource Development, the Right to Education Act passed in 2009 ensures free and compulsory education as a fundamental right to all children in the age group of 6 to 14 years in the country. Every child has a right to full-time elementary education of satisfactory and equitable quality in a formal school, which satisfies certain essential norms and standards.

8 The hawkers include those collecting junk and selling chairs, utensils, cloth and vegetables etc.

8 In lieu of conclusion

> To accept that hunters are affluent is therefore to recognise that the present human condition of man slaving to bridge the gap between his unlimited wants and his insufficient means is a tragedy of modern times.
> Marshall Sahlins (*The Original Affluent Society*)

> When we came amongst them (the Andamanese) and admitted the air of the outside world, with consequent changes, to suit our necessities, not theirs, they lost their vitality, which was wholly dependent on being untouched . . . the end of the race came.
> Maurice Vidal Portman (*A history of Our Relations with the Andamanese, 1899*)
>
> Where the European has trod, death seems to pursue the aboriginal.
> Charles Darwin cited in Bauman (2004)

The social and economic history of the tribal communities tells us that in their early phases of forest dwelling and nomadic existence each one of them specialised in certain activities that were helpful not only in eking out a living but in sustaining them over centuries. They were also fulfilling the material and cultural needs of the settled communities by supplying them the products of their labour and with their art of entertainment. It has been taken note of in the preceding chapters that their traditional means of livelihood and diversified ways of doing so have not only been marginalised but negated aggressively by the forces of industrialisation and modernisation. Their specialised skills have been rendered obsolete, and they have been coerced to undertake such occupations that do not need any art or skill. The heterogeneity of the tribal work and culture has been homogenised much in tune with Engels's dictum that the road roller of capitalism will homogenise all societies/communities. The preceding chapter on intergenerational occupational change has shown clearly that for the majority of tribal communities in the state there is a distinct slide from the traditional occupations of the respondents' parents to their children adopting 'modern' occupations like wage labour, peddling, petty jobs and scrap collection etc. The modernisation of economy and society paradoxically increased their poverty and pushed their marginalisation to the extreme. It is a shift in their dependence on nature to their subjugation by the market.

Two issues manifestly stand out about the tribal communities in Punjab. One, the tribes are very much present in the state that its government refuses to acknowledge.[1] Two, these communities are losing their traditional occupations and getting disabled by the processes of modernisation and development adopted by the state. They have not been enabled by the state, leave aside adequately, to acquire new skills necessary for modern occupations.

(I) Presence of the absent

Let us take up the first issue of their physical presence in the state, verified in person by talking to them and collecting their responses to a detailed questionnaire. All these tribes are very much present in the state as they were in the last quarter of the 19th century, documented beyond doubt by *A Glossary of the Tribes and Castes of the Punjab and North-West Frontier Province* by H. A. Rose in 1883 based on the census data collected by Denzil Ibbetson in 1881. It is a comprehensive three-volume compendium whose first volume provides rich ethnographic details of all the major tribes that are present even today. Another attempt in this regard, more than a century later, that provides rich ethnographic details of these communities and supplements the earlier work in some ways is *'Criminal' Tribes of Punjab: A Social-Anthropological Inquiry* (2010c) by Birinder Pal Singh.[2] This work updates the details on seven major tribes in the *Glossary* notified as 'criminal' under the CTA 1871.

The present study intends to take the issue of tribal presence in Punjab a little further by asking the respondents what occupation their parents, fathers and mothers both, including their grandparents were pursuing. The proportion of respondents above 60 years of age is 44.04 per cent, and if we take all those above 50 years, the figure goes up to 69.07 per cent. If the parents and grandparents of 70 per cent respondents had been engaged in their traditional occupations characteristic of each tribe, then it would be fair enough to conclude that the tribes then were very much present in the state as is their progeny now, and they had been pursuing their occupations as well. Besides oral testimonies of the senior respondents in detail about their ancestors' occupation, another clear evidence reflected in the data itself is that a large majority of that generation was nomadic. Nomadic lifestyle is characteristically a tribal feature, so much so that majority respondents mention 'nomadism as occupation' of their parents. They were *'ghumantru'*, a nomad, is the reply. The senior respondents too attest this information in their interviews.

It is not a case of a misunderstood question and an incorrect or a vague reply. Their ancestors were nomads and nomadic primarily. They were used to the abundance of natural resources in the forest that was their home. They were hunters and had to be so, which is why we find all such people having a palate for certain type of wildlife that was available in their habitat. Sahlins talks of the 'original affluent society' of the hunters and gatherers that the human society was in its earliest stages and probably for the longest period. He opposes their way of life to the modern Western weltanschauung:

> But there is also a Zen road to affluence, which states that human material wants are finite and few, and technical means unchanging but on the whole adequate. Adopting the Zen strategy, a people can enjoy an unparalleled material plenty – with a low standard of living. That, I think, describes the hunters. And it helps explain some of their more curious economic behaviour: their "prodigality" for example – the inclination to consume at once all stocks on hand, as if they had it made. Free from market obsessions of scarcity, hunters' economic propensities may be more consistently predicated on abundance than our own.
> (*The Original Affluent Society*, p. 1)

It is the market-governed consciousness of scarcity and hoarding that makes the modern person believe the animal-like existence of the primitive nomadic people who wandered for their livelihood. They know what is where in the forest and around, and how much. They have to go there simply and obtain the desired object(s) for consumption, unlike the modern person who knows what is available where but has to pay a price for that in currency. And each one every time does not have the requisite money to buy the essential commodities. In this context Sir George Grey writes that it is a mistake to suppose that the native Australians 'have small means of subsistence, or are at times greatly pressed for want of food'. He continues:

> Generally speaking, the natives live well; in some districts there may be at particular seasons of the year a deficiency of food, but if such is the case, these tracts are, at those times, deserted. It is, however, *utterly impossible* for a traveler or even for a strange native to judge, whether a district affords an abundance of food, or the contrary ... But in his own district a native is very differently situated; he knows exactly what it produces, the proper time at which the several articles are in season, and the readiest means of procuring them. According to these circumstances he regulates his visits to different portions of his hunting ground; and I can only say that I have always found the *greatest abundance* in their huts.
> (quoted in Sahlins, p. 3; emphases added)

Sahlins's argument is developed further by Bird-David, who argues that the natives develop a relation with natural agencies what Abramson calls 'the cosmic economy of sharing'. She suggests:

> Moreover, irrespective of what they obtain in any particular hunting and gathering event – in any momentary episode of the life-long engagement of sharing – the very fact that they have obtained something in their eyes reaffirms their relationship with the natural agencies and

therefore secures the recurrence of sharing. In a sense, then, they do have "confidence in the yield of the morrow" – a confidence born of the view that the environment is morally bound to share food and other material resources with them and that under normal conditions it will.

(Bird-David 1992, 31)

Tim Ingold appreciates that 'Bird-David correctly recognises that for hunter-gatherers themselves environment is not "nature" in this Western sense but rather the world as it is gathered within the ambit of an all-embracing nexus of personalised relationships whose quality is aptly conveyed by the notion of trust' (in Bird-David 1992, 42).[3]

Karl Polanyi in his famous work *The Great Transformation* also authenticates the 'richness' of the tribal people. He argues:

No Kwakiutl "ever ran the risk of going hungry." "There is no starvation in societies living on the subsistence margin." The principle of freedom from want was equally acknowledged in the Indian village community and, we might add, under almost every and any type of social organization up to about the beginning of sixteenth-century Europe . . . It is the absence of the threat of individual starvation which makes primitive society, in a sense, more humane than market economy, and at the same time less economic.

(1957, 171–72)

The tribes in Punjab as also elsewhere subscribe to Sahlins's catch phrase 'want not, lack not', may be via Zen way directly since Buddhism flourished here but also as an amalgam of Lord Mahavira's teachings like *aparigraha* and nonviolence, and other nature-loving and nature-caring ways of life advocated by saints and sages conceptualised lately by Gandhi (1908) in his theory of *swaraj*. Gandhi says that nature has everything for human needs but not for her greed. Thus, the principle of sarvodaya must be invoked, because that is the only way to allow sustenance of all natural species including *homo sapiens*. That is why he likens it to *yajna* (sacrificial ritual). And sarvodaya cannot be realised without practising poverty voluntarily (*aparigraha*). Gandhi strongly recommends the 'principle of non-possession' for attaining sarvodaya. He writes to Narandas:

Non-possession is allied to non-stealing. A thing not originally stolen must nevertheless be classified as stolen property if we possess it without needing it. Possession implies provision for the future. A seeker after truth, a follower of the law of love, cannot hold anything against tomorrow. God never stores for the morrow . . . If each retained possession only of what he needed, no one would be in want and all would live in contentment.

(Iyer 1993, 377)[4]

166 *In lieu of conclusion*

It is very likely that the philosophy of *aparigraha* or voluntary poverty resurrected from the ancient times in the age of capital and weaved by Gandhi into his theory of non-violence and swaraj has tribal origin. It could be a theorisation of their practical existence as observed by the ancient sages and philosophers like Lord Mahavira, who had a holistic vision of reality. This Eastern wisdom is directly opposed to the Western perspective rooted somewhere in the early Greek thought of philosophers like Euripides, who says that 'poverty possesses this disease, that through want it teaches man to do evil'.

Gandhi reasserts: 'Civilization in the real sense of the term consists not in the multiplication but in the deliberate and voluntary reduction of wants . . . If anyone appropriates more than he really needs, he reduces his neighbour to destitution' (ibid, 378). Grann also notes about the natives of the USA: 'When an Osage chief was asked why he didn't adopt the white man's ways, he replied, "I am perfectly content with my condition. The forests and rivers supply all the calls of nature in plenty"' (2017, 39).

In the Indian context Furer-Haimendorf explains the richness and lavishness of the tribal life compared to the present generation. He writes:

> We have seen that Gonds have become used to purchasing a number of consumer goods in shops or markets, and this may give the impression that their standard of living has raised in the past thirty years. This impression is partly deceptive, however, for the parents of the present generation had similar resources but spent them in different ways. While they bought few items of outside manufacture and no Gond would have aspired to own such a thing as a bicycle, they were more lavish in entertaining and in the celebration of festivals and rites. The expenditure of food stuff on weddings and funerals was far greater than it is today . . . the rewards these artists received for their performances were more generous than they are nowadays.
>
> (1989, 108)

The nomadic tribal people moving from place to place with all their baggage necessary for living never bother about their food or shelter because they are sure to get it the way they are used to, à la Max Weber: 'A man does not "by nature" wish to earn more and more money, but simply to live as he lives and as he is accustomed to live, and to earn as much as he is required to do so' (1930/1992, 24). If this is true in the age of capital, what would the people be thinking and feeling in the 'sleeping societies' inhabiting the forests anywhere? If they do not find things to their liking they will simply move ahead. They know no boundaries of states and nations, so very central to the modern mentality, though they know well their ecological territories.[5] They have no sense of acquisition and hoarding considered so very essential by the urban middle class whether in the West or in the East. The *bhramankari* (roaming) Jain *munis* (monks) do not stay at a place for more than a month lest they feel attached there because love for worldly things generates greed for possession, a hindrance in attaining *moksha*, the spiritual liberation. The affluence of the nomadic people lies in not wanting things, what Sahlins calls 'want not, lack not'. Wanting is largely a creation of the industrial capitalist market's consumer culture. The pre-capitalist people subscribe to the theory and philosophy of contentment, hence *Rabb di raza'ch razi rehna*. The tribal people too subscribe to the god's will. The oriental wisdom also focuses on the uselessness of *maya*, the wealth which is an illusion and never goes with the dead to the other world. Such philosophy of life is weaved into the Indian folk wisdom, and the tribal people are no exception to this.

Punjab, the land of five rivers, had plenty of forests given the fertility of land and heavy monsoons in the pre-green revolution times without the presence of tractors for cultivation. It must have been an ideal place for the nomadic tribes, which is why, it seems, they travelled from the deserts of Rajasthan some three or four centuries ago. All tribes trace their origin from there. Unlike Rajasthan, this region has a variety of seasons, from extreme summers to harsh winters through autumn, spring and heavy rains. It provided adequate fodder for the animals and rich diet to their masters. These conditions, to my mind, are congenial for the growth and spread of the nomadic tribes.

The modern colonial masters from the land of the industrial revolution were far from the nomadic ways of life and thought. There are a host of prescriptions from the police officers and the administrators in the colonial Punjab against such a lifestyle. They considered the nomadic tribes a dangerous people. It justifies the declaration of the CTA and an excuse to apprehend them. The Punjab Administration Report of 1905–06 also focuses on the relation between wandering and criminality and expresses problems with regard to the implementation of the CTA. It records:

> The crime committed by wandering tribes continues to increase; no real surveillance can be maintained over these gangs, and the law as it stands is a direct encouragement to them to continue wandering, as so long as they have no fixed place of residence they cannot, however, criminal, be registered under the Criminal Tribes Act.
>
> (*Report* 1907, 18)

The colonial administration's perception about wandering and criminality has not changed over the decades. The *Annual Report* for the year 1936 notes: 'Increase in the number of convictions under the Criminal Procedure Code (from 46 to 92) indicates a revival of lust for wandering' (1938, 5).

There is no change in the perception of the colonial administration since then about the relation between criminality and nomadism: 'They do, however, include a considerable proportion of men who are either homeless or have no fixed and paying occupation and if such men remain unrestricted there is of course a danger that they may take to crime sooner or later' (*Report* 1927, 2). Nomadism is linked not only to criminality but also to the loss of revenue to the colonial exchequer. There are numerous complaints with the administration about the incorrigibility of certain tribes not only with respect to their thefts but also spoiling the forests through grazing by large herds of cattle and the banks of the canals too by their movements. However, a deputy commissioner sympathetic towards the tribes remarks, 'These complaints are true enough. The land allotted to them was insufficient and this gave grounds for the excuse that they could not live honestly and therefore must steal' (*Report* 1912, 5). According to Arnold, the CTA was used against 'wandering groups, nomadic petty traders and pastoralists, gypsy types, hill- and forest-dwelling tribals, in short, against a wide variety of marginals who did not conform to the colonial pattern of settled agricultural and wage labour' (1985, 85). Singh concludes elsewhere: 'These citations and examples from numerous researchers make it amply clear that labelling the tribal communities as criminal was not based on serious consideration but mere articulation and imposition of the British administrators' preconceived notions about them, their work and lifestyles etc.' (2008b, 64)

It is important to note that attempts of the colonial and the post-colonial/nationalist governments over a century and a half to make these communities become sedentary and leave their traditional occupations and nomadic lifestyle have not been successful. A large number of tribes are nomadic still despite allotment of plots for the construction of a house. Even if the family is settled, the male bread winner, say a Bangala or a Sikligar, remains a nomad. Some other tribes like the Gaadi Lohar, Gujjar and Nat, engaged in traditional occupations, remain on the move despite odds. They move with the family in a band unlike the Bangala men who tread the lonely path. The discussion above, thus, attests to their presence in the state.

(II) Occupational change

The shift in occupations over three generations is obvious. It shows that the forces of modernisation have impacted these people more than anyone else, and to their utter disadvantage. Each tribe, depending upon its location in space, has pursued major and minor occupations specific to the material conditions. They specialised in various productive activities, making items of domestic use and crafted them aesthetically. They exchanged their products with non-tribals, earlier in kind and later in cash. Each tribe in Punjab has been affected adversely in terms of loss of traditional occupations made redundant by industry and the market. Despite this, nearly half the respondents are engaged in the traditional occupations while their parents were entirely into these. This also validates the tribal presence in the state. Now more and more tribal people are joining the streams of the unskilled labour force, of scrap collectors and peddlers primarily, and this trend cuts across gender and age. These streams of occupations have been labelled 'modern' vis-à-vis their traditional occupations. With lack of education and skills for modern occupations, the tribal people have been coerced to undertake menial jobs.

The tribal people have a specific lifestyle, characteristic of each community. Their senior generation does claim that despite limited resources and facilities earlier, they were leading a life of satisfaction and contentment. The degree of relative deprivation was low, and the inertia of tradition was high. Their belief in destiny and god kept them contented and going. The present generation is dissatisfied with their work/occupation more than their elders due to numerous factors, the most important being the loss in status and economic returns from the traditional occupations, their lack of skills for modern occupations, the rise of competitive society and the consumer culture. A common worry of the elders is *'bachian vaste rozgar hi nahin'*, that there are no jobs for their children. They have not been enabled by the state in the modern skills through proper training in ordinary and technical schools.[6]

I am sure the tribal people would be happy and contented with their occupations and lifestyle had they not been forced by the CTA and the Indian Forest Act to abdicate their habitat. Both these exogenous factors drove them to confinement, poverty and humiliation at the hands of the police and administration. The occupation change has coerced them to leave the clean forest environment for the dirt and squalor of the city slums. To understand these predicaments in the lives of the tribal people, it is useful to look into certain crucial events in their history and identify factors that are responsible for the loss of traditional occupations. Even if these factors were instrumental negatively, the overall inclusive development of Punjab's economy and education could restore balance in their lives, but that was not to be. When the state of the political, economic and educational institutions is deteriorating since long consistently there can be no respite to the re-skilling of the de-skilled tribal people. Thus, they will meet the same fate as elsewhere, that is, detribalisation.

Four eventful years

A peep into the social history of the tribal communities in Punjab declared criminal under the CTA 1871 marks out the following four eventful years. Each one of these has left an indelible mark on the lives and thoughts of these people.

(i) **1852**: In this year, H. Brereton, the Superintendent Thuggee Investigations, Punjab, reaffirmed the linkage – that Sleeman reached in 1835 that the Thugs and the criminal tribes were one and the same people – observing that Thugs in the Punjab, although mostly Mazhabis (the Chuhra Sikhs), were recruited from the general criminal class: 'Chuhra thieves, Sainsee burglars, and Child Stealers, and Jat dacoits' (Major 1999, 662). He also cites the proceedings of the Legislative Department then:

> The Judicial Commissioner of the Punjab then wrote to the seven Division Commissioners to obtain their views. Not surprisingly, the seven were unanimous in agreeing that a system of surveillance, which had since annexation been in operation against the Mazhabi "Thugs", should be applied to tribes like the Baurias and Sansis: in the words of one Commissioner, "the existence of a criminal class, living notoriously on robbery, is an outrage on civilized society, and their suppression is urgently called for". . . . Under the authority of this Circular all Sansis, Harnis and Baurias were to be registered at the local *thanas* (police stations), the *lambardars* of the villages in which these tribes nominally resided were to be answerable for their conduct and movements, registered tribesmen were not to be allowed to sleep away from their villages without a ticket of leave from the *thanedar*, and any tribesman found absent without leave was to furnish security for good behaviour or, failing that, be sent to jail.
>
> (ibid, 665)

(ii) **1871**: This is the most crucial year in the life history of the tribes not only in Punjab but all over the country. The CTA was passed then. This is the single most crucial year that changed the destiny of the tribal communities categorised as criminal by the colonial authority. The Bauria and Sansi were the first to be notified in Punjab followed by others. They were registered with the local police stations or posts, where they were roll called sometimes thrice a day. Their movement from the settlement was restricted. It is pertinent to remind that the fear of the police is so deeply entrenched that even the present generation is not willing to reveal their tribal identity. At the end of the colonial rule, certain officers did realise the real effects of the CTA on these people. An Indian Civil Service (ICS) officer, C.M. Lloyed Jones, stated before the CTA Enquiry Committee of 1947: 'Declaring them a criminal tribe by birth affects morally their future generations as they know that as soon as they attain the age of 15, they would be registered even if their character is not bad and they are not inclined to commit thefts, etc. It is *the Act itself that makes* them to think that *they are thieves*' (cited in Sher 1965, 246–47; emphases added).

(iii) **1952**: On 31st August the tag of criminality on these communities was removed by the government of independent India. A wrong done by the colonial government now stands corrected. The CTA is repealed, and these tribes are called the denotified tribes or vimukt jatis. They celebrate this day as the 'day of their independence'. In their self-perception, their ancestors were rebels against the Mughal invaders and later fought against the British rule.[7] Therefore, their criminal labelling was out rightly misplaced and uncalled for.[8] On 4 September 1952, 'half a century old infamous Reformatory Settlement at Amritsar housing 232 members of the criminal tribes has been finally wound up and all the inmates have been freed from all restrictions' (*The Tribune*). A Bawaria of the Ferozepore district, Wazira challenged the CTA in the Punjab High Court in 1952 for declaring the whole community of the district as criminal. The petition was admitted (*The Tribune*, 18 May 1952). Before that, a Sikh Bawaria filed a suit in the same court challenging the Constitution (SCs) Order 1951 promulgated by the President (*The Tribune*, 18 January 1952).

(iv) **1982:** The denotified tribes got relief from the Punjab and Haryana High Court on a civil writ petition filed by Buta Ram Azad and 17 others against the Union of India and the State of Punjab in 1975, challenging the Constitution (Scheduled Castes) Order 1950 for their caste status. Justice Ajit Singh Bains, having examined the criteria of the Government of India for defining the Scheduled Castes (extreme social, educational and economic backwardness arising out of traditional practice of untouchability) and the Scheduled Tribes (indications of primitive traits, distinctive culture, geographical isolation, shyness of contact with the community at large and backwardness), concluded:

> The argument of the learned counsel for the respondents (Government) that the petitioners' tribes do not fulfil the criteria for inclusion in the list of Scheduled Tribes is misconceived. The petitioners' Vimukt Jatis are not untouchables . . . I am of the view that the Vimukt Jatis to which the petitioners belong have been *wrongly included in the list of the Scheduled Castes*. In fact they should have been *included in the list of Scheduled Tribes* and the Government of India may consider their deletion from the list of the Scheduled Castes and they may be included in the list of the Scheduled Tribes.
>
> (Bains 1982; emphases added)

The verdict not only clearly recommended their inclusion in the list of STs but also declared their inclusion in the list of SCs as wrong. This boosted the morale of the tribal communities, who accelerated their efforts at various planks to obtain the Scheduled Tribes (ST) status.

Three factors

Three main factors are coming in the way of the majority of tribal communities' dependence on nature, the forest. First one is the promulgation and implementation of the Indian Forest Act that made the forest a state property. The second one is the project of green revolution that Punjab implemented so aggressively that the Punjabi peasant made a model for others

172 *In lieu of conclusion*

for its progressive orientation and hard work. The third factor is rapid and unplanned urbanisation.

1. Forest (as state property)

The declaration of the Indian Forest Act 1865 made all forests the government's property. The traditional rights of the tribal communities dependent on them stood withdrawn. Furer-Haimendorf writes:

> While they were forbidden to take even enough wood to build their huts or fashion their ploughs, they saw contractors from the lowlands felling hundreds of trees and carting them off . . . Where tribals were allowed access to some of the forest produce, such as grass or dead wood for fuel, this was considered as a "concession" liable to be withdrawn at any time. The traditional de facto ownership of tribal communities was now replaced by the de jure ownership of the state, which ultimately led to the exploitation of the forest resources with total disregard for the needs of the tribal economy.
>
> (1989, 80)

Commenting on the British exploitation of the Indian forests, Guha writes:

> Whereas the first century of British rule was characterized by a total indifference to forest conservancy, by 1860 Britain had emerged as the world leader in deforestation, devastating its own forests and the forests of Ireland, South Africa, northern United States, and parts of coastal India to draw timber for ship building, iron smelting and farming. In India, a generally hostile attitude to forest preservation was reinforced by the belief, widespread among colonial administrators, that forests were an impediment to the expansion of agriculture and consequently to the generation of land revenue.
>
> (1994, 22)

Singh also notes in the Pangi valley of Himachal Pradesh: 'The opening up of hitherto landlocked valley to the outsiders has resulted in huge losses to the forest and its people. Earlier, the Chenab Timber Agency axed 5,04,955 high quality Cedars (Deodar) in this valley for the colonial government between 1852–87 but 4,47,133 were cut only in three years (1860–63)' (1996, 117).

Guha continues:

> The edifice of colonial forestry was inherited by the government of independent India, and immediately put to work in the service of the state's primary goal of rapid industrialization. The national forest policy of 1952 underlies the continuity of colonial and post-colonial policies:

upholding the "fundamental concepts" of its predecessor, the forest policy of 1894, it reinforced the claim of the state to exclusive control over forest protection and production.

(1994, 29)

Guha quotes Thomas Weber that the 'destructive energy of the British race all over the world was rapidly converting forests into desert' (ibid, 23).

The nationalist government's policy is no different from its colonial predecessor. The forest under state control is leased out to the contractors, who let hell loose on its produce without any regard for the people surviving on them. Furer-Haimendorf cites the case of a south Indian tribe:

For the Chenchus, the destruction of bamboo in their habitat will be catastrophic. They depend on bamboo not only for the construction of their huts and for making many of their utensils, but above all for the manufacture of baskets and mats, which they traditionally sell or barter for agricultural produce. It is no exaggeration to say that the depletion of the stocks of bamboo in the forests of the Amrabad plateau would make the area virtually uninhabitable for its original denizens.

(1989, 84)

The natural mixed forests provided food, fodder, fuel-wood and shelter to its inhabitants, virtually everything necessary for their survival. The colonial government replaced them with mono-cultural plantations for commercial purposes. The forests were denuded, and pine was planted to begin with, for resin, paper pulp and timber. The programme of commercial forests was faithfully carried forward by the Indian government. Furer-Haimendorf argues: 'An extreme example of such a commercialisation of forests at the expense of the local tribal population is a project in Madhya Pradesh where Rs. 46,000,000 are to be spent on converting 8,000 hectares of forest in Bastar Hills to pine forests to feed the paper pulp industry' (ibid, 80).

The Superintendent, Deccan and Gujrat Revenue Surveys, writes in 1864, ten years after his first visit to the district (Shahada):

I was hardly prepared for the change that has taken place. Miles of high jungle, I might almost say forest, had been cleared off, and places which gave cover to wild animals, such as nilgai and sambhar, were now clothed with luxuriant crops of wheat and gram. The whole of the area is now, in effect, under good cultivation and the absence of wild animals is conspicuous.

(Kulkarni 1982, 419)

Furer-Haimendorf notes: 'In Northeast India there are to this day tribes among whom specific forest tracts with clearly defined boundaries are claimed as clan or village property, where only members of the clan or village in question are allowed to hunt or cut firewood' (1982, 79). He explains the general situation in India:

> Tribal communities dwelling in enclaves inside the forest were either evicted or denied access to the forest produce on which they had depended for many necessities. Thus arose a conflict between the traditional tribal ownership and the state's claim to the entire forest wealth. Numerous revolts, . . . were the direct result of the denial of the local tribals' right in the forests which they had always considered their communal property.
>
> (ibid, 80)

Singh also notes in the Pangi valley:

> [T]he tribal villages had their specific tracts of forest in which all the households had equal right and share in its wealth be it fuel wood, fodder, timber, fruit, herbs and other edibles . . . the forest there was very rich in a variety of edibles. The village panchayat used to fix a date for the collection of these items some of which are commercially expensive. These could fetch them a good price in the neighbouring plains. The tribal people used to exchange these for items of domestic use.
>
> (1996)[9]

The problem of encroaching the tribal wealth and property cuts across the colonial and the post-colonial/nationalist governments. It has now become more rampant. The large manufacturing and trading corporations are invited to the mineral-rich tribal belt in central India, home to the oldest living tribes, to establish plants for development. The natives resisting the loss of their land and forest are persecuted as Maoists who are posing a threat to the nation's development.[10] Paradoxically, the tribal people are not interested in the 'development' being done in their name. Recently, the president of the Niyamgiri Suraksha Samiti Lada Sikaka vented his anguish: 'The government is offering us a 30 ft (feet) road under the pretext that it will be useful during a health emergency. But we don't want forests razed to the ground for a wide road' (Barik 2019).

The situation in Punjab was no different with regard to tribal oppression, though there was no rebellion of any significance, probably because all the tribes were nomadic without a sense of belonging or attachment to a place. The whole region was theirs, where they could wander at will. There was no single region that may be called a tribe's territory or home. But the neighbouring Hurs did declare autonomy. 'Hurs Set up Parallel Government' was the title of a news item in *The Tribune* of 20 May 1942. It reads: 'Not only have they appointed a leader whom they call their King but have appointed commanders, captains etc . . . They are said to have divided themselves into groups and assigned separate jurisdiction to each group.' If this is true, then the Sind Government is pitched not against a criminal tribe but a huge military organisation.

In the colonial and the post-colonial Punjab there is no mention of any rebellious activity but for their peaceful protests. The Punjab experienced plenty of turmoil and disturbances from partition in 1947 to another division in 1966. In between and afterwards there was Punjabi suba movement, the Naxalite movement, anti-Emergency protests, Kapoori canal morcha against SYL (Satluj-Yamuna Link), the farmers' struggles and the Sikh militancy etc., but the tribal people remained ever aloof. However, it does not mean they remained unconcerned about their eviction from the forest and their shrinkage.[11]

The problem is not with the forest but how one looks at it. Is it nature's bounty to be exploited for accumulation of profit, by an individual, a corporation or the state, or is it an abode for nature's creatures, big and small, with plentiful resources to thrive on? In Indian thought, forest is neither a house of wilderness nor an abode of savages. It is also simply not a storehouse of nature's bountiful resources to be exploited by the humankind but a space where the saints and sages meditated to understand their own selves and the world around them.[12] It was the abode of *gurukul ashrams* where the princes came to seek knowledge and the kings visited their heads (the guru) for advice in matters of society, rule (*rajya*) and *dharma*, the righteous, the ethical and the moral. Mahatma Buddha too got enlightened under the Baniyan tree (*Ficus bengalensis*), now known as Boddhi *variksha* or Buddha's tree. In the Hindu philosophy of life and ethics, to attain the highest *purushartha* called *moksha* (salvation), one is supposed to proceed to the forest called *vanprastha*. That means after completing family obligations (*grehastha ashrama*), a person is prescribed to spend one-fourth of her life span in a forest. This span mediates between *grehastha* (family) and *saniyas* (renunciation) that leads ultimately to *moksha* (salvation). Thus, unlike the Western perspective of forest being an abode of the wild and the beastly, with roving bands of savages, it is nature in its pristine form away from the world of human problems and evils. There exists a possibility of spiritual liberation and getting released from the cycle of rebirth by attaining union with God, the individual soul (*atma*) merging with (*parmatma*). Ayurveda, the Indian system of medicine, also prescribes that the nomadic way of life is most healthy. The humankind will be afflicted with diseases and ailments when it makes permanent settlements.

2. Green revolution

The green revolution is the name of a state-sponsored capital-intensive 'scientific' agriculture that drastically changed the socio-cultural and economic landscape of the Punjab. It was the government's policy to meet the nation's food requirement to ensure food security. 'In 1961, the Ford Foundation thus launched its Intensive Agriculture Development Programme (IADP) in

India, intended to release Indian agriculture from the "shackles of the past" through the introduction of modern intensive chemical farming'[13] (Shiva 1992, 2).

The greed for more production and high profit brought more and more land under cultivation, hence the loss of pastures, ponds and forests in the densely populated state.[14] It has the average density of 482 persons per square kilometer, according to the *Census of Punjab* 2011. 'The area recorded under forest is only 3.1%. Besides, area under agroforestry plantation including orchards is 0.37%. However, as per Forest Department this amounts to 5.9%, probably due to the fact that the forest department includes areas under strip plantation along canals and roads also into forest area' (*State of Environment Punjab-2007*, 81). According to a state forest survey report the dense forest cover in Punjab has decreased by a whopping 80,600 hectares since 2001. It has been reported in *Punjab Newsline* by G.S. Bhalla and Hema Khanna that the forest cover of the state is merely 3.14 per cent which is lower than the 4.62 per cent of the desert state of Rajasthan.[15] The dependency on forests is the need of all tribes not only for procuring raw material but also their food. A wide range of fauna made their food when the forests were aplenty despite the enforcement of the Indian Forests Act. Where does such a possibility exist when the forest cover is merely 3.14 per cent?

The green revolution has disturbed the ecology and ground water in the state by concentrating on two crops, wheat and rice. Rice is a crop of the humid high-rainfall region.[16] Its adoption in a hot and dry weather of Punjab has increased tremendous pressure on the ground water aquifers.[17] According to an estimate, in 1984 out of the total 138 development blocks, 53 were dark zones. The number rose to 84 in 1995 and 108 in 2005. The *State of Environment* report affirms: 'The present ground water development in the state is 145% with 75% of total area of the state being over exploited as per data provided by Central Ground Water Board (CGWB) & Department of Irrigation, Punjab (2004). Out of 137 blocks, 103 blocks are over exploited, 5 blocks are critical, 4 blocks are semi critical and only 25 blocks are in safe category' (2007, xxv).[18] Hira mentions that in 1964, the entire area of central Punjab had water table above the depth of 15 feet. With the inception of the green revolution, the water table started declining, and the area having water table below 30 feet depth increased from 3 per cent in 1973 to 90 percent in 2004 (2008, 200). Thus, paradoxically the very state named after water (*punj* + *ab*), the land of five rivers, is gradually running out of it.[19]

The *Statistical Abstract of Punjab* (2005) notes a 'spectacular' development in agriculture in Punjab during the last few decades. Nearly 80 per cent of the water resources of the state are used by the agriculture sector. Of the total cropped area, which stands at 86 per cent of the total area, 97 per cent of the area is irrigated out of which conventional canals' share stands at mere 27 per cent, whereas tube wells account for 72 per cent. There is phenomenal rise in the number of tube wells, which increased from 1.28 lakhs (1,28,000) in 1970–71 to 11.68 lakhs (11,68,000) in 2004–05.

The shrinkage of natural resources at such a fast pace is affecting the socio-economic fabric of these tribes. The Bangala men move to Himachal Pradesh to collect snakes and herbs necessary for their survival. K.S. Singh also suggests a relation between the tribes and the forest: 'forest has been associated with the early life of mankind where they domesticated plants and invoked early forms of agriculture and gradually moved from gathering and hunting to advanced and primary modes of subsistence' (2004, 46).

The developmental project of the green revolution no doubt raised the income levels of the peasantry initially (Bhalla and Chadha 1982) and filled the country's godowns with grain, but its ill effects on ecology and economy have now started manifesting.[20] These have reached to a worrisome extent that seems irretrievable. The *State of Environment* report notes: 'A study by International Food Policy Research Institute (IFPRI) has put out the red alert on the farm sector in Punjab. The study has warned that Punjab needs to diversify from wheat and rice, urgently, otherwise the food bowl of India could well turn into a begging bowl by 2030' (2007, xxiv).[21] The study, *Withering Punjab Agriculture: Can it regain its leadership?* carried out in August 2006 by IFPRI, India has warned that Punjab is in the middle of a serious agricultural crisis. The study reports that Punjab's agricultural economy has lost its place among the fastest growing in the country, surpassed by a number of other states including Karnataka, Madhya Pradesh, Maharashtra, Rajasthan and West Bengal (*State of Environment Punjab-2007*, 45).[22]

3. Urbanisation and the real estate economy

The third factor is the rampant urbanisation, which is not only reducing the tree cover but also the area under agriculture due to rise in the real estate business. The sprawling high rise residential colonies around the tricity – Chandigarh, Mohali and Panchkula – is a glaring case of speculative investment of the black money in real estate. Most of the residential flats are vacant, and in the majority of enclaves, the occupancy rate is as low as 25 per cent. Such colonies are growing around all big cities in the state, developed by the builders with English names, Western design and exotic outlook of the apartments, houses and malls.[23] It becomes a status symbol to own a residence there and be a part of the modern elite. This is a matter of grave concern not only for the Bangala and other tribes dependent on the forest but the Punjabi peasantry too thriving primarily on agriculture. The *State of Environment Punjab* report also notes: 'Data also indicate that with increase in developmental activities, more and more good agricultural land is being used for industrial zones, housing complexes, transport systems, recreational purposes, etc. thus indicating that now marginal lands are being brought under the plough, thus adversely affecting the ecology' (2007, xxiii).

All these developments are telling on the ecological health of the state in general and the habitat of the tribal communities in particular. They have been worst affected by the development processes. The economic returns from agriculture are also inadequate, and other institutions such as health and education too are in shambles; then how could the transition of tribal communities from traditional occupations to the modern and from tradition to modernity be smooth? Punjab is a victim of misregulated modernisation.[24] To understand the plight of the tribal communities, it is therefore necessary to look into the functioning of the systems of economy and education in Punjab that are so very essential for empowering people for ushering them into a modern society. The tribal youth could be given cheap quality education for suitable employment. The following discussion throws light on these twin aspects that are crucial in the context of occupational change.

Post-colonial Punjab's economy and education

The governments, colonial and post-colonial, tried to wean these communities from their traditional occupations and cultural moorings by teaching them new skills. The funds were allocated for their children's education and welfare, but somehow these measures failed to ameliorate their socio-economic conditions over the decades. The cultural strings are too hard to break. It seems the governmental efforts were either not sincere enough and for name sake only, or there was a problem with the path of development itself. To my mind, the problem lies on both the counts. The former issue concerns the implementation of schemes and the pilferage of funds. The funds are allocated, but corruption does not let them reach the target groups. It has become more deep rooted under the nationalist government than under the colonial rule. A *Report of the Evaluation Committee* for the period 1947–1966 shows: 'There had been, of late, a good deal of criticism both in the Press and in the Legislature regarding the implementation of these schemes and, by and large, it has been felt that corresponding benefit has not accrued to the individuals or the community as a whole, due to *erroneous execution and inefficient implementation* in the field'(n.d., 1; emphasis added).

There was no improvement over the next 30 years. The Institute for Development and Communications (IDC), Chandigarh, tries to see the impact of the government's welfare schemes on the depressed castes in the state in 1996. It finds 10 per cent only of the 13 depressed castes own a house, out of which 2.4 per cent were *pucca* (concrete). And 97 per cent of households were landless and 84 per cent were living below the poverty line. A community wise break up shows that 80 per cent Bangali(a), 96.7 per cent Bauria, 73.8 per cent Bazigar and 92 per cent Sansi live below the poverty line (1996, 12). The overall literacy rate of these castes (sic) is 20.4 per cent, while that of the denotified tribes is abysmally low. Bangali(a) and Bauria have 10 per cent each, Bazigar 12.31 per cent and Sansi 14 per cent (ibid, 14).

It is dismaying to note that despite threefold increase in the annual Special Component Plan for the Scheduled Castes from Rs. 711.5 million in 1990–91 to Rs. 2,050 million in 1996–97, the benefits reaching the target groups are negligible. The survey reveals: 'Lack of awareness about government schemes for the welfare of the Scheduled Castes was one of the important reasons . . . It was found that only 8% of the respondents had availed themselves of the schemes. Out of these 8%, only 5.2% had benefited from the schemes' (ibid, 43). The study points out that more than 60 per cent respondents are not aware of the schemes.

How is it that despite the government's efforts things did not change in their favour? There is something wrong with the model of development adopted by the post-colonial government. Kohli (1997), focusing on the 'crisis of governability', argues that the Indian state's capacity to govern has declined, especially after 1967, which is followed by the erosion of order and authority. Following a comprehensive survey of literature, Pantham hints at the deinstitutionalisation of the Indian political system that includes the following phenomena:

> the erosion of intra-party democracy, the concentration of power in the Prime Minister's Office, the declining role of legislatures, growing centralization in Union-State relations, decreasing neutrality of the civil servants, electoral malpractices, the rise of person to top political positions by non-institutional pathways, the rise of "coteries" of power and the increase of political violence.
>
> (1995, 54)

When the steering institution goes awry, other ones down the line cannot function properly. And this is what has happened in the country over many decades. Saberwal provides a sociological explanation in noticing a conflict between the formal institutions of modernity based on rationalist liberal principles of impersonality and the entrenched logic of segmentation of the traditional order. He suggests that Indian tradition is not compatible with modern Weberian rationality. Madan and Nandy also believe that the crisis is a result of imposition of alien Western institutions controlled by an 'arrogant and unbending elite' (in Kaviraj 1997, 367–78). Kaviraj has given a different explanation elsewhere: 'The Indian bourgeoisie is strong enough to prevent a collapse of the bourgeois industrialization . . . but weak enough to leave the institutional structures largely untransformed despite internal efforts' (Kaviraj 1984, 225). It happened because the institutions of parliamentary democracy could not take roots on the Indian soil. Randhir Singh (1999) argues that all problems – economic, political, social – of this country are a consequence of 'India specific capitalist development'. The state and politics in Punjab is no different from the mainland. The education and health systems were doing well until the early 1970s but collapsed subsequently. It is not the people who failed them but the government, and the political elite in particular.[25]

Economy

The robust Punjabi farmers enhanced the SDP (state domestic product) and per-capita income and consumption following the green revolution. It started stagnating subsequently, so much so that the BIMARU[26] states got ahead of Punjab on many levels of economic development. Its per-capita income at 6.32 is lower than the national per-capita income of 9.62 in 2006–07 at 1999–2000 prices (Punjab Government 2007, 133).

Despite the *Best State Awards* there is no dearth of problems afflicting the state (Singh 2005). Lakhwinder Singh and Sukhpal Singh comment on this slide in the Punjab economy and the lofty claims of political leadership and liberal intellectuals: 'The empirical evidence does not support such a claim. The growth of per capita income was only 2.72 per cent during the period 1991–98, which is clearly and significantly lower than the rate of growth recorded in the 1980s (3.42 per cent)' (2002, 580–81). They conclude: 'Punjab economy is facing an economic crisis of unprecedented scale. The rate of growth of state domestic product has declined in the 1990s and as a consequence of it, the per capita income has gone down' (ibid, 585–86). Ghuman also notes: 'It is clear from the foregoing analysis that State's priorities have undergone a sea-change since 1990s . . . In 1991–92, 60 per cent of state budget was spent on development. The situation totally reversed by the year 2005–06 when around 58 per cent of state budget was spent on general services' (2008).[27] The economists argue that one major problem with the Punjab economy is its overstay in agriculture.

What then is the fate of poor people in the rural areas and more so of the tribal communities, already marginalised as a result of their traditional occupations, becoming obsolete? The problem lies with the political and the administrative system steering the processes of development. The World Bank report notes: 'While official rules provide for the possibility of punitive action in the case of repeated absence disciplinary action for absences are rare. Teachers and health workers are almost never fired'(Chaudhury et al. 2005, 2).[28] It is apt to invoke the concluding remarks of Major in his paper with reference to such elite in the colonial Punjab since there is much in common with their counterpart in the post-colonial state:

> Interestingly, Act VI of 1924 provided for individual provinces to repeal the Criminal Tribes Act within their territories if they wished, but the Punjab Government never took up this option . . . A reading of the Punjab Legislative Assembly Debates for the period 1937–46 is instructive: during these years no elected Punjabi politician officially questioned the need to retain the Act, and while several assemblymen did query the registration of specific criminal tribes in particular districts, an equal

number rose to put questions concerning the communal distribution of posts within the Criminal Tribes Department. For the Punjabi elite, *there were clearly more important issues at hand than the social salvation of the criminal tribes.*

(1999, 687–88; emphasis added)[29]

How can the tribal people ever hope to get into the mainstream economic development under such conditions? B.P. Singh sums up the discussion elsewhere in this context:

Thus, it may be concluded that the existing modern state is theoretically, ideologically and practically pitted against the tribes. Its policies rather promote their physical dislocation and social decimation. I repeat, their physical dislocation and social decimation. Whatever measures might be taken and howsoever honestly, the twin processes of physical dislocation and social decimation remain unavoidable since the state is given to modernization of economy and society.

(2012, 202)

Education

In a 'developed' state like Punjab, if the government is shying away from its responsibility of providing education to its people, how can the hitherto marginalised communities ever hope to compete with others? The agency of education so very necessary for enabling a population for self-dependence has been spoiled by the political and administrative elite.[30] The state is a holy cow for them to milk. The strong and sturdy peasantry is in turmoil. The government schools providing cheap and quality education to the urban and rural people alike are now in shambles. There is neither infrastructure nor the teachers to teach. According to a report on Punjab (2005) 552 government schools do not have a single teacher, 2500 have one teacher each and in 7000 primary schools there are only two or three teachers. Each day 36 per cent of primary teachers abstain from schools. Of the remaining 64 per cent, only half go to classes (Chaudhury et al. 2005, 5–6).[31]

Punjab is no better than many states of India that have been historically backward and poor. The *Annual Status of Education Report* (ASER) of 2005 on Punjab shows 'that over 82 per cent of kids from standard II to V could not read a simple story in Punjabi and 62 per cent were a zero at subtraction' (ASER 2007). The situation has not improved since then. The data compiled from more than 11,000 primary schools of the state show: 'More than 50 per cent students studying in primary schools of Punjab are not able to read a single story in Punjabi; around 25 percent are not able to write Punjabi letters and 40–70 percent students are not able to subtract and divide' (*India Edu News* 2008). If this is the level of the students' comprehension of their mother tongue, whose development is an objective of the state government, one can imagine their performance in English language and mathematics.[32] What then is the fate of poor children in the rural areas and more so of the already marginalised tribal communities?

The system of education has hardly shown an improvement over a decade. The ASER 2015 report informs that the proportion of students in the age group of 6 to 14 years is 50.00 per cent in the private schools. This is despite their charging hefty tuition fees compared to the government schools. This suggests people's lack of trust in the quality education of the government schools. This is no longer a prejudice against them, as the report validates that 40.10 per cent students of standard III could read the standard II level text. This proportion rises with class level, as 64.5 per cent of standard V and 80.9 per cent of standard VII could read the same text (level II). It is dismaying still, as 10 per cent of students of standard VII could not read the level II text. It is not only their poor reading skill, but mathematical skill is equally dismal, as 56.6 per cent of standard III, 68.8 per cent of standard V and 77.9 per cent of standard VII could 'at least do subtraction'. This means that 22 per cent students of standard VII could not do simple subtraction (ASER 2015).

The latest report on the performance of school children in Punjab is equally disturbing. The National Achievement Survey (NAS) was conducted in the state by the Union Ministry of Human Resource Development in November 2017 to assess the competency levels in elementary classes. The assessment test was conducted by the National Council of Educational Research and Training (NCERT). The report says: 'Of 24,046 children of Class 5 who took the test in select schools in all districts of the state, 37% could answer more than half the questions of their class . . . The numbers for Class 8 were worse, as only 12% of the 24,920 students could answer more than half the math questions meant for class-appropriate competencies correctly' (*Hindustan Times*, 5 February 2018). The results of the class VIII maths test for three districts, namely Muktsar, Fatehgarh Sahib and Patiala, is as low as 4.6, 6.0 and 6.2 per cent, respectively. In languages, their results were: 52% of class V and 55% of class VIII could answer half the questions correctly (ibid).[33]

The decline in the standard of teaching and education in the government schools has compelled the middle class to send their children to the private schools. Kingdon shows that the recent growth of private primary schooling in urban India has been nothing short of massive and that the pace of privatisation has accelerated over time in both urban and rural India (2007, 185). The *ASER* survey by Pratham in 2007 shows that among the major Indian states, in Punjab, Haryana, and Kerala, the percentage of children attending private schools has increased by more than 10 percentage points between 2005 and 2006 (ibid, 186).

It is interesting to note that the Punjab government itself realised the dismal state of the existing schools. It started special schools called Adarsh (ideal) for the meritorious students in the science/commerce stream, providing free boarding, lodging and teaching to those who score 80 per cent and more marks in the tenth grade. In 2017, none of the schools had full occupancy. The government decided to close many schools in 2017 for lack of students. This problem plagues other states as well. The Odisha government too decided to close as many as 828 government schools with fewer than ten students. 'Between 2000 and 2015–16, the drop-out rates fell sharply from 41.8% to 2.82% and 57% to 3.87% in primary and upper primary levels respectively. Of the 828 schools closed during the past two years, the tribal dominated Rayagada and Kandhamal districts accounted for 121 and 101 schools. Ganjam, Chief Minister Naveen Patnaik's home district, has 70 such schools' (*The Hindu*, 7 January 2018). The extent of rot may further be gauged from the fact that 'Odisha still has 2,425 schools (2,335 primary and 90 upper primary) with *fewer than 15 students*. It is *not that only interior districts* are experiencing this trend' (ibid; emphases added).

The decline in government school education coupled with high unemployment (PSA) in the state has marred the future prospects of the tribal people altogether. Whatever little employment is available is grabbed by the rich and the powerful. Now with the political clout, heavy cash (bribe) is also required. The tribal people see no future for their wards even if they make them study. Singh notes: 'A 65 year old Bauria respondent expresses sorrow: "Whatever is granted to us by the government, only one per cent reaches us. 99 per cent is taken away by "others". One respondent of Araianwala (Faridkot) retorts: "We do not get employment. Not one person in a thousand gets it" (2010a, 25).

Social ostracism is a major cause of drop-out for the tribal students. They are ridiculed on account of their typical traits not only by their fellow students but by the teachers too. Singh informs:

> The Jatt and other high caste children in the school do tease the Bauria children and address them as "*giddarkhane*" (Jackal eaters), "*raulla*" (who eats too many chapattis or *rottian*), "*bhukhad*" (always hungry), "*petu*" (who eats too much), "*mirchan-khane*" (chili eaters), "*sale choruchake*" (bloody petty thieves) etc. Such disparaging comments given to the Bauria children deter them from going to school and they are forced to take to child labour.
>
> (ibid, 24)

An old man attested: 'Teachers usually of high caste invariably ask the Bauria children for domestic work but those belonging to low castes (Scheduled Castes) beat them so that they may leave the school and do not compete with them' (ibid, 24). The Bazigar respondents register similar treatment of their children at school: '*Gariban de bachian nu kutt-maar ke bhaja dende ne*' that the teachers thrash the children of the poor and make them run away (Singh 2010b, 50). Kaur notes about the Barad students: 'They were made to sit on the back seats and were not given attention. Teachers and other students used to thrash them. They also used abusive language for them like *Oye Barada;* Barad *kamini jaat; sale kanghi bannh; oye binne vechanwale di aulad*. [O' Barad; Barad, the mean caste; bloody comb makers; O' son of a *binnu* seller](2010c, 90).

Kaur informs about the Bangalas too:

> Literacy rate is negligible . . . Through out the field investigation, the researcher could find only one person who has passed 12th class (Grade). A few of them have studied up to fourth or fifth class (Grade) only, otherwise they are not even able to write their names . . . Further: "We do not have money to provide education to our children. Moreover, even if one gets education s/he will not be able to get a job under such conditions."
>
> (2010b, 72)[34]

The above discussion shows that despite freedom from the colonial rule, a grim situation persists in the arena of education, a significant tool for self-empowerment. According to the Nobel Laureate Amartya Sen: 'The remarkable neglect of elementary education in India is all the more striking given the widespread recognition, in the contemporary world, of the importance of basic education for economic development. Somehow the educational aspects of economic development have continued to be out of the main focus, and this relative neglect has persisted despite the recent radical changes in economic policy' (Dreze and Sen 2002, 38). The problem of neglect lies with the political and administrative system. The political elite are not interested in the literate masses, leave aside the enlightened ones, which is why the educational institutions working well after independence are now dying. It includes not only the government schools and colleges but the universities as well.[35]

Detribalisation

The issue here is not the loss of traditional occupations of the tribal communities but the tribes themselves. They are an endangered species on the way to their extinction. Their physical dislocation and social decimation is unavoidably inevitable. This is their fate everywhere, universally, all over the globe, thus validating the Maori proverb: 'A white man's rat has driven away the native rat so the European fly drives away our own, and the clover kills our fern, so will the *Maoris disappear before the white man himself*'(Sharma 1994; emphasis added). The 'white man' is a metaphor for modernisation and its attendant processes. It was not the fear of an indigenous and an illiterate primitive wise man but a visionary pronouncement that has come true. Interestingly, it has been corroborated by the theorist of evolution, Charles Darwin: 'Where the European has trod, death seems to pursue the aboriginal'(Bauman 2004). The fear of the alien in the tribal person's mind is not out of place. It is no phobia emerging out of her much maligned closedmindedness. In fact, it was their farsighted vision about the potential threat to them from the strangers (*diku*).[36]

Levi-Strauss's lamentation is equally relevant, that the Europeans had been so obsessed with power that in their desire to remake the world in their own image, they had willingly destroyed most of the technologically primitive societies on this planet and paved the way for a new age of 'monoculture' (1986, 60). He stressed the urgent need to preserve the native cultures, since these are disintegrating faster than radioactive bodies. Thus, we have an indigenous wise person, a great biologist and an anthropologist par excellence, all expressing fears about the threat to the very existence of the tribal communities anywhere.

Banaji informs about their extinction in concrete terms:

> [T]here are about 40,000 natives left in Australia as opposed to 2,50,000 at the beginning of the 19th century, most, if not all, of them hungry and disease ridden, threatened in their deserts by mining plants, atom bomb testing grounds and missile ranges. Between 1900 and 1950 over 90 tribes have been wiped out in Brazil . . .
>
> (1970, 85)

Oommen also quotes figures: 'In 1787, Australia's population was entirely aboriginal, but after 200 years of colonisation in 1988 it became a mere 1 per cent. The estimates of Native Americans at the time of European contact vary between 2 to 5 million, but after 500 years of European occupation it dwindled to a mere 2,50,000' (2007, 144). According to another count, the Red Indians in the USA numbered 8,46,000 in 1492 but 3,37,366 in 1937. Now only 300 tribes survive out of a total of 2,000 who still have 250 languages and dialects (Raghavaiah 1971, 5). More recently, Vinay Lal writes: 'In Tasmania, the Aboriginals were rendered entirely extinct; on the Australian mainland, when Aboriginals were not hunted and scalped, they were trafficked and exhibited. The children became, even as late as the twentieth century, part of the "lost generation"' (accessed 2018).

The modernisation got a booster dose in globalisation, that like its predecessor intends to overcome the disparities not within a region or a nation but all over the globe, because the world is becoming a global village á la McLuhan (1964). This will be done by supplying commodities of consumption from the developed countries to the industrially poor nations; by training their populations in the institutions of the developed countries; by financing their developmental projects through human resources and material; by the to-and-fro movement of capital, people and culture across borders. Some scholars consider globalisation a new phenomenon that started in the middle of the 20th century but for others (Giddens 1990) it is an extension of the project of modernisation, while for others it is invigorating as 'hybridisation' (Robertson 1992). For certain critics it is an extension of capitalism, primarily American capitalism (Ahmad 2002). Whatever it may be, both modernisation and globalisation claim to raise the levels of living of the poorer nations and its peoples. The reality is otherwise. Both these processes have worsened the fate of the majority people worldwide, and the tribes have been hit the hardest. Inequality has also increased over the last one scentury (Piketty 2014).[37]

The tribes in India and in Punjab[38] are no exception to this global phenomenon of their marginalisation and subsequent decimation ultimately. Such tribes like the Sentinelese living on an isolated Island (North Sentinel) have merely 50 surviving persons. Others that fail to integrate with the mainstream modernisation processes of development and corruption will meet the same fate.[39] And those who join the bandwagon of modernisation will cease to be tribal anymore. Thus, in both cases extinction of the tribes is a certainty.[40]

The tribal communities are believed to be a blot on the face of modern scientific and civilised society. There is no space for such communities on the landscape of modernity because they represent its exact opposite. The hallmark of a tribal society is sustenance and praxis of tradition and gradual change, while modernisation stands for a fast and radical change. The primitive culture and lifestyle is a direct opposite of the modern. There is an antagonistic contradiction between the two life worlds. The evolutionary thinkers would be asking, why should the tribal people be living like this? They represent the early phase of human society when the means of production and communication had not developed due to the lack of modern science and technology then. The human society has now come of age, and the new philosophies and methodologies of dealing with nature and the world around us have developed to such levels that the human mind can control and alter the natural forces the way it suits her.[41]

Thus, the primary objective for each and every human society is to be an industrially developed civilised society based supposedly on reason and rationality. It is in direct contrast to the primitive animistic tribal societies that are sleeping still and will hardly ever come out of slumber on their own. Not because they cannot, but they do not wish to, following Weber.[42] These people have to be shaken up vigorously for their awakening, but if they refuse to get up, these may be exterminated physically for the sake of development. The resilience of these communities in conserving their culture and society and resistance to change has put them on the road to their extinction. The Western society has caged such people in reserves.

The dominant systems of politics and administration around the world are negatively disposed to the tribal societies, since their presence is an index of backwardness. These people are either eclipsed in ghettos, slums and reserves or eliminated physically, since that is the quickest way to achieve a high score on the scale of modernisation and development.[43] The modern Indian state does not care for their civil or human rights. If these people are resisting change, as most people anywhere always do, then they should have been coaxed to come out of their tradition bound mindset by inculcating in them new ways of doing things in the modern times. A cue in this direction is seen in the comments of C. Brown, the Inspector-General of Police (Punjab), about the conduct of the Bilochis: 'The conduct of the tribe has been good. This improvement is no doubt due to the promise of more land which the Colonization Officer has made to them' (*Report* 1903, 5).[44] Some officers in the colonial administration, no doubt, were sympathetic to the problems of the criminal tribes and their sustenance. The annual *Report* of 1923 has this to say in this respect:

> The obvious improvement effected in the behavior of the criminal tribes in the province generally has sufficiently established the predominant importance of the economic factor in dealing with them. The criminal habits have in most cases been found to have originated with poverty and also owing to want of opportunities. Given *opportunities and controlled and directed properly most of them have been found as industrious and well behaved as any other class of men*. The wandering tribes who, prior to 1917, were driven from place to place, rolled hither and thither, always in their primitive state, living constantly from hand to mouth by begging or stealing. Society shunned them and they in return retaliated by divesting them of their belonging as frequently as circumstances permitted.
>
> (1923, 2; emphasis added)

Thus, they should have been trained in new skills in tune with their traditional occupations and cultural moorings.[45] For instance, the members of the hunting and gathering communities, such as Baurias and Gandhilas, could be asked to guard the wildlife reserves and forests, and the Sansis as local brewers (cf. Dida brand of whiskey) could be prompted to specialise in the making of wines and whiskies. Likewise, the Baurias and Bazigars engaged in agricultural works could be given land and modern implements to do agriculture and the Noongars for developing horticulture. Similarly, the herders (Gadaria and Bazigars) could be asked to keep flocks of sheep and goat and made to develop the allied cottage or small-scale industry dealing with wool etc. The Gujjars, specialising traditionally in the dairy business, could be facilitated to develop large-scale modern scientific dairies and dairy farms. They could also extend it to market cheese and other milk products. There is huge demand for milk and its products in the growing urban centres all over the state and the country.

Likewise, the members of Sikligar and Gaadi Lohar tribes could be motivated to become small entrepreneurs in the steel and iron industry for manufacturing agricultural implements, utensils, locks and other products of domestic use. The Gandhilas could be encouraged to develop pisciculture and beekeeping, and the Bangala people could be gainfully engaged in the production of antidote for snakebite and other herbal (*desi*) medicines. They

188 *In lieu of conclusion*

may make good ayurvedic doctors. The Barad who supplied *kanghi* (comb) to the cloth weavers (*julahas*) may be trained to undertake that work and produce coarse and fine cloth for earning a respectable living. Besides these major tribes, there are numerous others in smaller numbers who specialised in one or other art and occupation. They were engaged in them for their subsistence, which may now be fruitfully revived in the name of the ethnic and the folk that make saleable commodities in the era of global market.

It is unfortunate that under the influence of modern theories of evolution, the nomadic people have been termed criminal. There is nothing more criminal than calling the whole community criminal. Such mass labelling of people is outrageously immodest. A great wrong has been done to these people, and when the time came to redress their grievances, they are thrown into the open market, de-skilled and deprived of their traditional occupations. When there is an opportunity to make use of their traditional skills and engage them in gainful occupations, they are handed a bowl for begging in a competitive market society.

These are a few stray thoughts for the development of tribal communities that should have been executed by the directorates and ministries made for them over the last more than a century and a half. But nothing concrete happened on the ground, as we may notice that the socio-economic and cultural problems of these communities have gone from bad to worse. There is nothing impossible in implementing such schemes and achieving the desired targets peacefully and amicably and in the best interests of the tribal communities, who could be saved from the painful pangs of transition from tradition to modernity. Such modes of development have not been practised in India anywhere, to the detriment of these communities. Giving a weekly dole and a few permissions within the confines of a reserve is no favour to them. It is no panacea to the indignity and humiliation they have suffered at the hands of modernisation and capitalist development.

The colonial government, no doubt, tried to wean them from their culture and occupations by interning them in reformatories, but they did so after the declaration and implementation of the CTA 1871. The tribal people were presumed to be thugs and criminals, which is why they were hunted, trapped and interned. More than this is the irresponsible and amass application of the CTA. It was not the criminal only who were registered but all members of a community. The administration itself is on record that all members of a tribe are not criminal. That some members of the same tribe at certain places are considered not only not criminal but good and well behaved. But the *Report* of 1911 informs that after considerable discussions it was decided to include all members of a tribal community under the CTA. It records: 'it was deliberately decided that people of tribes generally proved criminal ought to be registered even in districts where their record did not appear to be a bad one' (1911, 5).

A *Report for the Criminal Tribes Act* for the year 1910, for instance, reveals a variety of traits in the community of Sansis in different parts of the state. 'In the districts of the Eastern Range the behavior of the Sansis has been generally satisfactory. No serious offences are recorded against them' (ibid, 4). But, 'The Sansi-Kanjars of the Karnal district . . . are reported to be a bad lot' (ibid, 4). 'In the Central Range, with the exception of those in the districts of Sialkot, Gurdaspur and Gujranwala, their general conduct has been good.' On the other hand, 'In the Western Range, the Sansis have, on the whole conducted themselves well and have comparatively given little trouble' (ibid, 4). The Commissioner of Rawalpindi says that 'the remarks about the diminishing criminality of the Sansis in the Shahpur district raise an interesting question, which can hardly be discussed within the limits of an annual report' (ibid, 4–5). The situation has not changed over the next three decades. The *Report* of 1940 notes:

> While the Sansis of Amritsar, Ferozepur, Gujrat, Jhang, Lahore, Ludhiana, Lyallpur and Rohtak were well spoken of, there were general complaints of petty pilfering and theft against the members of this tribe from the districts of Gurdaspur, Karnal, Gurgaon, Hissar, Hoshiarpur, Jullundur and Sheikhupura. The ostensible means of livelihood of Sansis of these districts is the rearing of sheep and goats, working as tenants and watchmen, but they generally resort to petty thieving.
> (1940, 11)

The same is true of other tribes, for instance, the Bauria. The *Report* 1902 records: 'in Ferozepore the members of the tribe (Bauriah) were largely taking to an honest life . . . In Hissar the criminality of the Bauriahs was not held to be clearly proved and proposal for their registration were rejected in 1897' (1902, 1). 'The Baurias are the next important tribe. They are said to have behaved well on the whole but there are serious complaints of the Bidawati Baurias of the Eastern Punjab and of the Central Punjab Baurias of Ferozepore, Jhang and Multan' (1918, 18). Williams, a deputy superintendent of Punjab police notes a variety in the character of the same tribe that has nine sub-divisions. Referring to the Baurias in the Hissar district of Punjab, he notes, there 'reside Deswali, Bidawati, Raldhablia and Gandhila. The Deswali are agriculturists and the Raldhablia entirely pastoral; Gandhila are chiefly shikaris; and Bidawati purely thieves' (*Report* 1903, 3; no italics). The *Encyclopaedia* also notes about them: 'Their skill in tracking also is notorious. They are by no means always, or indeed generally criminal, in this province at least; and in Lahore and Sirsa seem to be sufficiently inoffensive. But in many parts of the Panjab, and generally I believe in Rajputana, they are much addicted to crime' (*Encyclopaedia*, 448).

The *Reports* of 1911 and 1912 as also others have authenticated the notoriety of the criminal Pakhiwaras of Kot Mokhal 'throughout the Province, and are more or less in touch with the resident Pakhiwaras of other districts' (1912, 5). But the Commissioner of Lahore Division remarks: 'The Pakhiwaras of Gurdaspur district are not criminal. Sialkot was the only district in which they have all along been registered. Lahore, Gujranwala and Gurdaspur all speak well of them' (ibid, 5).

A great wrong, thus, has been done to them by labelling the whole people as criminal. The CTA made the simple and the innocent too, criminal or at least developed such tendencies in them following the rationale *bad achha badnam bura* that it is better to be bad than to have a bad reputation. But the colonisers thought that was right and probably the only way since they had a well organised paraphernalia to exercise force and coercion to tame them. They represented the world power whose sun never sat then. Moreover, they were equipped with the scientific knowledge of evolution of nature and culture and had developed the theories of human psychology and criminology. Above all, there was religious legitimacy to their crusade against savagery. They were burdened with the white man's mission to civilise the nomadic savages. Paradoxically, the CTA made the peace-loving forest-dwelling people 'criminals'. It is said in the context of Sultana, the dacoit: 'The Act did nothing to remove crime, but on the other hand it turned many innocent people into hardened criminals and Sultana Sansi – the Robin Hood of India, was the unique product of this Act' (Sher 1965, 322).

The colonial power and the Salvation Army were working together to civilise the Indian 'savages'. The colonisers failed to appreciate the theory and philosophy of nomadic existence, of *aparigraha* (voluntary poverty) and of remaining content with oneself following god's will (*rabb di raza*). It is instructive to look into the proposition made by Syed Hussain Nasr in restoring the balance between man and nature that has been ruptured by modern science because Christianity 'came as a spiritual way without a Sacred Law'. He argues: 'A re-discovery of metaphysical knowledge, and a re-vitalization of theology and philosophy of nature could set a limit upon the application of science and technology. In the old days man had to be saved from nature. Today nature has to be saved from man in both peace and war' (Nasr 1976, 135).

Crime is no monopoly of a tribe or a community. An individual is not born a criminal but made one by adverse circumstances. The colonial takeover of the forest and its resources – over the ground and underground – and their exploitation by the merchants and contractors disturbed the living patterns of the tribal communities. Those with large numbers and cohesive formations rose in revolt against the outsiders, *diku*, while those who could not do so collectively chose to become rebels of their own type. The individual rebels were reacting against ignominy at the hands of the local police or district authorities in league with the merchants and the local lords.[46] What would be the reaction of a person or a community thrown out of its home or habitat and threatened with dire consequences in case they offer resistance? Almost all the nomadic tribal communities claim to be Kshatriya Rajputs. They trace their descent from the much-valorised kings of Rajputana. It really does not matter if they are the actual descendants, but the fact is that they believe so. In that case they must also act bravely in case of a confrontation, because their 'ancestral heroes' are known for saving their grace, honour and respect, for which they laid their lives in wars fighting the mighty Mughals. The tribal people believing in the lineage of brave warriors will not take their insult lying down.[47] Some among them rose against the injustice and disgrace done to them and became 'criminal'. What was the crime they were committing and against whom? It was against the colonial encampments, the rich contractors and merchants. They looted the rich not for amassing wealth but for subsistence while others distributed that amongst the poor. They were Robbin-Hooding. Sultana 'daku', one among others, was a famous character in the Chambal Valley.[48] It is instructive to read Jim Corbett writing about Sultana in his *My India*:

> Having known what it was to be poor, really poor during his long years of confinement in the Najibabad Fort, Sultana had a warm corner in his heart for all poor people . . . he never robbed a pice from a poor man, never refused an appeal for charity, and paid twice the price asked for all he purchased from the small shopkeepers.
>
> (cited in Sher 1966, 156)

He continues: 'He was tried under the law of the land, found guilty, and executed. Nevertheless, I cannot withhold a great measure of admiration for the little man who set at naught the might of the Government for three long years, and who by his brave demeanour won the respect of those who guarded him in the condemned cell' (ibid, 166).

The criminal people are considered to be unscrupulous with no principles. They have no ethics and morality.[49] But the case of tribal communities is directly opposite. Shekhar writes about the Santhals: 'We Adivasi are very bad at stealing. Corruption isn't in our blood. And even if we do commit a crime, we are pathetic at covering our tracks' (2017, 32). The tribal people are a humane lot who have compassion for animals and treat them equal to human beings as members of their family, unlike the modern people who consider them as filthy and infectious. Singh writes about the Gujjars: 'Something like a regular *siapa* (breast beating) is observed on the death of a buffalo, the women mourning for it almost as if for a human being . . . with veiled faces weeping over the death' (2003, 217).[50]

It is said about Sultana, who belonged to the Sansi or Bhantu tribe of Uttar Pradesh, that he did not kill the English police officer deputed to kill him: 'They could not see Sultana but Sultana saw all the three of them and unmistakably recognised Mr. Young. Sultana was sitting along with his ten companions, with their loaded guns but did not kill them *for the sake of his principle* of never taking a man's life without being offended' (Sher 1966, 157; emphasis added).[51] The Baurias would burgle that house only whose residents do not wake up despite stones thrown thrice over the roof. They believe that one with hard-earned wealth will wake up with the first throw.

192 In lieu of conclusion

The Barwar of Gonda (UP) is a notorious tribe for thefts, but they follow a strict code of conduct, the violation of which leads to expulsion from the community. Its members are forbidden from stealing in the dark. The light must be switched on before stealing. They must not carry weapons on them, and the choice of the house for theft must be made very carefully not randomly.[52] A Sikligar is not allowed to make a duplicate key or go to a non-Sikligar house to open the lock. Once, because someone gave the duplicate key of a treasury to a thief, the whole community of lock makers was excommunicated by other Sikligars. A former Inspector-General of the Punjab Police writes about the ethics of the Biloch tribe:

> Their code of honour binds a Biloch to give complete accounts of his activities and movements if and when called upon by any other traveller en route to explain. It may look incredible nevertheless it is a fact that once a Biloch came across a Superintendent of Police who asked him for an account (Haj De Cha Saven). The Biloch who was returning after a successful burglary made a clean breast of the whole affair.
> (*The Tribune*, 3 March 1961)

Those who steal justify their action, which is not without reason. The *Report* for the year 1926 records:

> The Bhura Brahmans of the Kangra (old Punjab) District think that in their case stealing is not a crime; they merely exact a form of charity which was given willingly in the good old days but is withheld in these sinful times. The Chhamar thinks that a little stolen from the house of Bania who robs others by falsifying his accounts or the goldsmith who invariably cheats by mixing his alloys, is no crime. The Bhedkuts, Bhangalis and others have their own views, and the space at my disposal does not permit of further explanation.
> (*Report* 1927, 6)

Shekhar explains the rationale of the Santhals in post-colonial India:

> Then, using nails, fingers, hands, and whatever tools we can manage we steal coal. The drivers can't stop us nor can those pot bellied Bihar(i) security guards . . . For they know that if they do not allow us to steal the coal, we will gherao the road and not let their trucks move . . . But a few stolen quintals, when the company is mining tonnes and tonnes, hardly matters . . . After all, they already have our land, they are already stealing our coal, they don't want to snatch away from us *our right to re-steal* it.
> (2017, 174; emphasis added)

Thomas Aquinas, a staunch theorist of the 'just war', has this to say in this context: 'When a poor person, out of his need, steals, he is not committing a sin and should not be punished by the church. The bread he stole was due him from the rich man; and if the poor man stole, it was because of the rich man's hardness of heart' (Ellul 1969, 18).

It is strange that the modern theories of knowledge could not appreciate the life and lifestyle of the tribal communities that lived with and in nature without destroying it. It did not understand their simple living and frugality but rather debunked them on all counts as savages. On the contrary, it generated models of development that are devouring nature and natural resources in the name of progress and displacing the tribal people from their home. The liberal-democratic states spearheading such development find these communities blockades in their way and hence do not fight shy in eliminating them altogether.[53]

Alas, the words of wisdom of a Maori wise person have come true. The chief of Aseenewub tribe in the Red Lake Ojibwe region in Canada, too, cautioned his people at the time of their colonisation. 'This is what was spoken by my great-grand father at the house he made for us . . . And these are the words that were given him by the Master of Life: "At some time there shall come among you a stranger, speaking a language you do not understand. He will try to buy the land from you, but do not sell it; keep it for an inheritance to your children."' Are these words of wisdom from north to south coming out of the fear of the indigenous and the illiterate? I believe not. The old visionary persons could foresee the trends of modernisation. They could sense the colonising element in this process and their incapacity to fight the state steered projects empowered with modern science and technology. Thus, they could foresee their extermination. Charles Darwin and Claude Levi-Strauss too are in league with the indigenous visionaries. All of them have been proved right. The Eurocentric model of modern society is road-rolling all nations worldwide, sometimes endogenously and often exogenously, sometimes overtly and often covertly, sometimes as modernisation and now as globalisation but all to the detriment of the tribal communities.

Notes

1 Interestingly, other states too are joining the bandwagon of eclipsing these communities such as Haryana. Surprisingly, the commissioner of the National Commission of the Nomadic, Semi-nomadic and Denotified Tribes, Bhiku Ramji Idate, informed the conference at Kodaikanal in 2017: 'Tamil Nadu did not have denotified and nomadic tribes any longer, but rather three denotified communities.' On the other hand, a local activist, Rajangam, working with these people in Tamil Nadu, estimates their population to be five lakhs across twenty nomadic communities. He disgruntles that 'the nomadic communities have never been part of any census.' Gayatri Jayaraman, 'Hazards of fictional fear mongering', *Hindustan Times*, 9 October 2018.
2 The government of Punjab had given a project to the department of Sociology and Social Anthropology, Punjabi University, Patiala, to ascertain the tribal character of 14 communities who were demanding the Scheduled Tribes status. The *Report* (2008) identifies eight of these as tribal.

194 *In lieu of conclusion*

3 Tim Gold suggests: 'Sahlins uncritically accepts the "Western" view of the environment as a world of nature outside of, and opposed to, the human world of society and its interests; moreover, he allows this view to inform his own characterization of the hunter-gatherer attitudes towards the environment, epitomized in the notion of confidence' (1992, 42).
4 The modern Western culture is a product of the industrial production system and ups and downs of the market that generate insecurity in the minds of people, hence the risk society of Ulrich. There are depressions of the 1930s and the bank crashes of 2008 in the US and so on. Profit and hoarding are a regular feature of the capitalist market that generate insecurity in the peoples' minds. Inequality is on the rise globally. Thomas Piketty (2014) has shown the U-curve of inequality over a period of the last century.
5 'How is it possible for us to be treated as belonging to Afghanistan? We stay for a few months there and for a few months in Pakistan. The rest of the time we spend moving. We are Pawindahs and *belong to all countries or to none* . . . Our animals have to move if they are to live. To stop would mean death for them. Our way of life harms no body. Why do you wish for us to change?' (emphasis added; Jamil Ahmad, *The Wandering Falcon*. New Delhi: Hamish Hamilton/Penguin, 2001, p. 53).
6 The Bollywood icon Shah Rukh Khan prescribes in an advertisement: 'Don't be *santusht* (satisfied). Wish for Dish.' Dish is one of the innumerable objects in today's consumer market that further deepens the scope for a huge plethora of choices and possibilities for entertainment in popular culture. The young, vulnerable audience is sure to follow his prescription of 'desiring more and more' than Gandhi's advice for non-possession.
7 The case of Thela Kanjar of Amritsar is chilling. The people were protesting against the arrest of Dr. Satyapal and Dr. Saifuddin Kitchlew on 10 April 1919, just before the Jallianwala Bagh massacre. Muhammad Tufail, alias Thela Kanjar of the Kanjar tribe, was one amongst them when the army opened fire. He decided to avenge the killing of fellow protesters. He was unarmed. But he urged few persons around him to hone their anger against the actual aggressors. The firing became rapid but they kept moving. Yadav writes: 'Like a wounded tiger, Thela Kanjar leapt at a British soldier and throttled him to death before dying' (Bhupendra Yadav, 'Many Narratives of the Massacre', *The Tribune*, 25 November 2018). The infuriated army wanted to avenge the death of their fellow soldier. Thela's two sisters were not only beautiful and talented but excellent dancers, on whom the troops wanted to vent their anger. Despite mourning, the girls were brought to the army camp for a performance by the police. They thrilled the audience and 'Amid the applause in the end, they stripped themselves naked. After which they told their shocked hosts. "We are the sisters of Thela Kanjar. You sprayed his body with bullets because you couldn't bear to see a young man like him possessing a nationalist soul. You may come and satisfy your lust now. But, just once before that, we wish to spit on your faces."' (ibid) Saadat Hasan Manto has given a graphic account of the incident in his story, '1919 di ik gall' (*Punjabi Tribune*, Chandigarh, 13 April 2019). The same story is carried in Rakhshanda Jalil (ed.), *Jallianwala Bagh: Literary Response in Prose & Poetry*, Niyogi Books, New Delhi, 2019.
8 For instance, *The Tribune* dated 22 February 1947 reports that 'the Bawari community made a representation that they be called in future by the name of "Bahir Rajput Chhatri Hindus" and they be removed from the list of criminal tribes . . . On the basis of jail census they maintain that they are most law abiding and peaceful citizens of the State.'
9 The collection of these edibles is exploited by labour from outside (Bihar and Nepal) employed for road building. To save these natural resources from the

In lieu of conclusion 195

outsiders, the Pangwals harvest them prematurely although it impacts their yield and quality. The government officers too caused havoc to the fine timber of Cedar and Walnut that make high-quality furniture. For more details see Birinder Pal Singh (1996).

10 (a) Arundhati Roy writes: 'Over the past five years or so, the governments of Chhattisgarh, Jharkhand, Orissa and West Bengal have signed hundreds of MoUs (Memorandum of Understanding) with corporate houses, worth several billion dollars, all of them secret, for steel plants, sponge-iron factories, power plants, aluminium refineries, dams and mines. In order for the MoUs to translate into real money, tribal people must be moved. Therefore, this war' ('Walking with the Comrades', http://coto2.wordpress.com/2010/03/22/arundhati-roy-walks-with-the-comrades-indias-resource-wars/(Accessed 12 May 2011). (b) Bhaduri, calling it internal colonisation, informs about the economic dimension: 'In Chhattisgarh, tribals are being forcibly evacuated in thousands from their villages in the name of fighting extremism under the Salwa Judum and carted off to huddle in Vietnam-style concentration camps while the corporations greedily eye their mineral resource rich land'(Amit Bhaduri, *The Face You Were Afraid to See: Essays on the Indian Economy*. New Delhi: Penguin, 2009, p. 132). (c) According to the Centre for Science and Environment (CSE) Report of 1984–5, 'Bastar generated an annual revenue of Rs. 470 million, yet only Rs. 50 million was spent on the region itself'(Sundar 2007, 252). (d) Odisha has 700 million tonnes of bauxite reserves, of which 88 million tonnes are estimated to be found in Niyamgiri. 'In the rush to acquire mining rights stringent environmental laws were violated, and the Dongria consent was not sought. Court cases and local opposition did not deter the company. Then, on April 18, 2013, the Supreme Court gave a clear direction that mining clearance can only be given if gram sabhas, comprising Dongrias, agreed to the project. In what is perhaps India's first environmental referendum, *all 12 villages selected* by the government *voted against the project*' (S. Barik, 'The Guardians of Niyamgiri', *The Hindu*, 17 March 2019; emphases added).

11 The present rules governing the forest in Punjab are a result of the Punjab Forest Act of 1927, which does not allow anyone to take anything out of the forest for sale in the market. The Act defines the 'forest produce as anything found in or brought from the forest. The forest guards keep watch on any infringement of the forest property that, technically speaking is also applicable to the grass as fodder for cattle, not to talk of the fuel wood or timber. In 2006, the Forest Rights Act (FRA) for the first time defined minor forest produce as including bamboo and tendu and many other things. It also gave tribals and other traditional forest dwellers the 'right of ownership, access to collect, use and dispose of minor forest produce, which has been traditionally collected within or outside village boundaries' (Sunita Narain, 'Is Bamboo a Tree or a Grass?' in *CSE's Fortnightly News Bulletin*, 7 December 2010). But by then the forests have disappeared in Punjab.

12 The *rishis* in olden times dwelling in the forests, running *gurukuls* developed the holistic systems of medicine (*ayurveda*) and health (*yoga*). A whole lot of *yoga asanas* are named after animals. Those sages must have been great ethologists who drew lessons for human life and social relations from the behaviour of the animals and their types or traits that have been integrated in Indian culture and society.

13 The term 'green revolution' was first used in 1968 by the former USAID director, William Gaud, who noted the spread of the new technologies and said: 'These and other developments in the field of agriculture contain the makings of a new revolution. It is not a violent Red Revolution like that of the Soviets, nor is it a White Revolution like that of the Shah of Iran. I call it the Green Revolution.' It is, thus, an ideologically loaded concept.

196 *In lieu of conclusion*

14 More than 83% of the total land in the state is under agriculture (as compared to national average of 0.38%). Though the total land under agriculture increased by about 5% from the sixties to the seventies, it remained more or less constant thereafter. However, barren, unculturable, fallow and other uncultivated lands have recorded a sharp decline between 1960–61 to 2004–05 (*State of Environment Punjab-2007*, xxiii).
15 The worst affected districts of Punjab in terms of forest cover depletion are Ferozpur (111 per cent), Amritsar (106 per cent), Hoshiarpur (84 per cent), Bathinda (76 per cent) and Ludhiana (55 per cent). The data show that since the depletion of forest cover in the Malwa region of Punjab (there are three socio-cultural tracts: Malwa, Majha and Doaba), that is, the districts of Ropar, Sangrur, Patiala, Bathinda and Ludhiana is low, hence the concentration of Bangala community in this area is high.
16 Prior to the green revolution, 41 varieties of wheat, 37 varieties of rice, four varieties of maize, three varieties of bajra, 16 varieties of sugarcane, 19 species/varieties of pulses, nine species/varieties of oil seeds and ten varieties of cotton were reported to be in use in Punjab and propagated through pure line selection by various workers. However, the number of varieties in use by farmers has decreased since then (*State of Environment Punjab-2007*, 85).
17 A high cropping intensity has also led to heavy requirements of water for irrigation purposes. The total demand of water for agriculture presently stands at 4.38 mham against the total availability of 3.13 mham. Hence, the deficit of 1.25 mham is met through over-exploitation of underground water reserves through tube wells, resulting in rapid decline of the water table in the entire state (except south-western parts due to limited extraction because of its brackish and saline quality) (*State of Environment Punjab-2007*).
18 All the blocks of various districts like Amritsar (16), Jalandhar (10), Moga (5), Kapurthala (5), Sangrur (12), Fatehgarh Sahib (5), Patiala (8 out of 9) and Ludhiana (9 out of 10) are reported to be over-exploited. The water table is thus depleting at an annual average rate of 75 cm in these districts and by 55 cm across the whole of the state (*State of Environment Punjab-2007*, xxv).
19 The Sikh scripture, *Guru Granth Sahib*, says: *Pehla pani jiu hai jit hariya sab koi* that water is the source of all life, and it assumes high and respectable status so prescribed by the scripture: '*Pawan guru pani pita mata dharat mahat*' literally, that air is teacher, water is father and the mother earth is great.
20 '[O]ut of about one million operational holdings, about 63% are smaller than 4 ha, indicating fragmentation of land. These farmers have been forced to over use their land by increasing cropping intensity (that increased from 126% in 1960–61 to 189% in 2005) and adopting the wheat-paddy mono-cropping practices' (*State of Environment Punjab-2007*, xxiii).
21 (a) Further, in place of a broad range of traditional varieties which were naturally suited to the climatic and edaphic conditions of the state, farmers have adopted a narrow range of high-yield varieties (HYVs). The area under input intensive HYVs of wheat has increased from 69% in 1970–71 to 100% in 2000–01. Similarly, area under HYVs of rice comprised 33% of total area under rice in 1970–71. It increased to 100% in 2005. This has resulted in the loss of domesticated floral biodiversity of the state (*State of Environment Punjab-2007*, xxiv). (b) The Punjab government appointed a commission for the diversification of crops. See S.S. Johl, *Diversification of Agriculture in Punjab*, Report of the Expert Committee. Chandigarh: Government of Punjab, 1986.
22 For details on various aspects of peasantry and society in the state, see Birinder Pal Singh (ed.), 2010e. Also see Birinder Pal Singh, 'Farmers' Suicides and the Agrarian Crisis in Punjab: Some Sociological Observations', *Sociological Bulletin* (forthcoming).

In lieu of conclusion 197

23 The residential colonies with modern amenities and 'foreign' outlook are also emerging on the periphery of large towns. This trend is dangerous because it not only segregates the already stratified and segregated population but takes the rich residents away from the city at a relatively more secure and insulated place. They may simply avoid the congested and filthy parts of the city. This is also indicative of the distrust that the elite are developing against the state and its apparatus, namely the police. They trust their own surveillance and security.
24 See Birinder Pal Singh, 'Farmers' Suicides and the Agrarian crisis in Punjab,' *Sociological Bulletin* (forthcoming). By misregulated modernisation I mean that the political and the administrative institutions have not regulated the modernisation of the traditional society like an expert driver sitting on the wheels. The elite of these institutions are unto themselves indulging in self-aggrandisement and indifferent to the people. The state to them is a holy cow to be exploited for their enrichment. As a matter of fact, the modern state is responsible for steering modernisation.
25 The elite too preferred the government schools and hospitals. For instance, the Rajindra Hospital and the Government Medical College, Patiala, then used to attract patients from Jammu and Kashmir, Himachal Pradesh and Rajasthan, but now even poor people of the city prefer to go to multi-speciality private clinics mushrooming around it.
26 It is an acronym that means 'sick'. The states of Bihar, Madhya Pradesh, Rajasthan and Uttar Pradesh were then economically poor and least developed in the country.
27 He computes data on the state expenditure from the *Punjab Statistical Abstracts* (1967–68 to 2005–06) to show how social services (education and health) became victims at the hands of general services i.e. administration etc. The figures for the latter rose from 39.84 per cent (3.39 per cent of the NSDP) in 1967–68 to 57.76 per cent (10.80 per cent of the NSDP) in 2003–04. The corresponding figures for the former fell from 30.35 per cent (2.61 per cent of the NSDP) to 19.79 per cent (3.70 per cent of the NSDP). A breakdown for education and health expenditure tells us that in 2005–06 the latter accounted for only 0.71 per cent of the NSDP and the former 2.35 per cent, which is far below the ideal 6 per cent level recommended by the Kothari Commission on Education (Ghuman 2008).
28 It is questioned, why doesn't the political system generate demands for stronger supervision of providers? The Report continues: 'Most of the countries in our sample are either democratic or have substantial elements of democracy. Yet provider absence in health and education is not a major election issue. Apparently, politicians do not consider campaigning on a platform of cracking down on absent providers to be a winning electoral strategy' (Chaudhury et al. 2005, 19).
29 The situation has not changed in the post-colonial Punjab, whose elected representatives 70 years hence are showing no concern for the public institutions. They are more concerned about increasing their perks and salaries many times than ensuring funds to the languishing government schools and health centres. They have funds for buying high-end vehicles for themselves and renovating their offices and residences, but for the public, the 'government treasury is empty'. [For instance, each MLA (117 in all) was given a Tata Sumo in one term and Bolero in another. The ministers were given Toyota Camrys and later Fortuner SUVs. In 2017, all newly appointed ministers spent between Rs. 15–50 lakhs on the renovation of their residences, but the government teachers were not given salaries for months. 26 Teachers' Unions are protesting for the last 22 days (on 28 October 2018) at Patiala (CM's residence) for the regularisation of 8886 contractual teachers. They are working in two central government schemes – Sarva Shiksha Abhiyan and Rashtriya Madhyamika Shiksha Abhiyan getting salaries between Rs. 40,000/- to Rs. 45,000/- per month. The government is asking them to join at Rs. 15,000/- per month (*Hindustan Times*, 29 October 2018).

30 An old Bauria respondent lamented: 'We have no money for the education of our children. Moreover, there is high level of corruption in the state.' Another respondent, a Sansi, remarked: 'Even if some of our children get educated they will not be able to get a job. There is too much corruption.'

31 The scene at the all-India level is equally dismal, thus proving the point that the problem is structural and not incidental. It is a systemic problem. (a) The World Bank report reveals: 'Across Indian government-run schools we find that only 45 per cent of teachers assigned to a school are engaged in teaching activity at any given point in time – even though teaching activity was defined very broadly to even include cases where the teacher was simply keeping class in order and no actual teaching was taking place . . . Less than 30 per cent of schools in the sample had more teachers than classes . . . only 50 per cent of teachers in Indian public schools who should be teaching at a given point are in fact doing so (Nazmul Chaudhury et al., 'Missing in Action: Teacher and Health Worker Absence in Developing Countries', *World Bank Report*, May 19, 2005, pp. 5–6). (b) Geeta Kingdon also notes: In half of the sample schools, there was no teaching activity at the time of the investigators' visit . . . Inactive teachers were found engaged in a variety of pastimes such as sipping tea, reading comics, or eating peanuts, when they were not just sitting idle. Generally speaking, teaching activity has been reduced to a minimum in terms of both time and effort. And this pattern is not confined to a minority of irresponsible teachers – it has become *a way of life* in the profession . . . (2007, 182; emphasis added). (c) Pratham conducted a survey of learning achievement on about 3,30,000 households from 549 Indian districts in 2006, and interacted with all children aged 6–16 years. Kingdon interprets the data: 'The findings make grim reading . . . 47 per cent of children who were in school and studying in grade 5 could not read the story text at grade 2 level of difficulty . . . In arithmetic, nearly 55 per cent of grade 5 and nearly 25 per cent of grade 8 children could not solve a simple division problem (three digits divided by one digit)' (2007, 180). (d) The situation of rural education at the all-India level is more disturbing. The latest ASER survey about education in rural areas of the country reveals: 'One-fourth of the 'country's youngsters in the 14–16 age group cannot read their own language fluently, while 57% of them struggle to solve a simple sum of division . . . Shown a map of India, 14% couldn't identify it, 36% couldn't name the country's capital and 21% could not answer the state they live in' (*Hindustan Times*, 'One-Fourth Students Aged 14–16 Years Not Able to Read', 17 January 2018). The chief economic adviser, A. Subramanian, also commented on the survey: 'This scenario is pretty staggering and makes you think what's going on and what should be done?' (ibid). (e) Rukmini Banerji of the Pratham Foundation suggests: 'While there may be ongoing debates on the different methodologies used in the ASER measurement and in the National Achievement Survey (NAS), there is consensus on the fact that years spent in school do not satisfactorily translate into years of learning' ('The Education System, as It Stands Today, Doesn't Quite Make the Grade', *Hindustan Times*, 4 April 2019).

32 The present Punjab based on the linguistic criterion was formed in 1966 following the Punjabi suba movement in the early 1960s launched by the Shiromani Akali Dal.

33 (a) Paradoxically, of all the cities in the state Patiala is an educational hub, with three national-level universities and numerous reputed schools, and colleges in all streams of education. Fatehgarh Sahib was earlier a part of this district. It has two colleges of general education and technology and Guru Granth Sahib World University. Muktsar is the constituency of the five-times chief minister of Punjab, Parkash Singh Badal. (b) The situation at the hub of industry and affluence Ludhiana, also known as the Manchester of India, is equally dismal. The ASER

2018 reveals that, 'around 44.8 % of students studying in classes 3 to 5 in the district can't do basic subtraction' (*Hindustan Times*, 17 January 2018).
34 Malkit Kaur too writes about the rampant illiteracy among the Gandhilas, focusing more on female literacy: 'Girls are still more disadvantaged. Their level of literacy is very low. Even when they go to school, majority drops out. Only a few study up to primary (Grade V) or at the most middle (Grade VIII) level. Among the whole population only 5–6 persons are in the government service' (2010, 102).
35 Ravish Kumar of NDTV did a serial on 'Higher education in India' during November–December 2017. It has 27 episodes showing the plight of institutions of higher education in terms of faculty recruitment, salaries, teacher–student ratio, library, laboratory and other infrastructure. These episodes are subtitled, 'Class *mein nahin guru, Bharat kaise banega vishwaguru?*' following the Prime Minister Narendra Modi's slogan of 'making India a *vishwaguru*'. Later, Ravish Kumar focused on the issue of employment. It is a routine with the State Public Service Commissions all over the country to announce recruitments, invite applications with heavy fees and take years to hold examinations. The result more often gets challenged in the High Court for some irregularity like leakage of question papers etc. It is cancelled subsequently. In both the serials the manifest message is the indifference of the government and the political elite towards education and employment of the youth in 21st-century India.
36 Diku, Deko, Dikku are variously spelled in different texts but all have the same meaning – the outsider. Singh writes: '*Diku* is a territorial and ethnic concept applicable to the categories of the land-grabbers and money-lenders belonging to both Hindu and Muslim communities, who came from outside the identifiable culture area'(K. Suresh Singh, 'Agrarian Issues in Chotanagpur', in K. Suresh Singh ed., *Tribal Situation in India*. Shimla: Indian Institute of Advanced Study, 1972, p. 377).
37 (a) According to Joseph Stiglitz, the chief economist and senior vice president of the World Bank,'among the 80 percent of the world's population that lives in Asia, Latin America, and Africa, 1.4 billion of whom subsist on less than $1.25 a day' (Stiglitz, 'Wall Street's Toxic Message', *Vanity Fair*, July 2009). He had written earlier: 'what I saw radically changed my views of both globalization and development . . . I saw firsthand the devastating effect that globalization can have on developing countries, and *especially the poor* within those countries' (Joseph Stiglitz, *Globalization and Its Discontents*. New York: W.W. Norton & Company, 2002, p. ix; emphasis added). (b) The British political philosopher John Gray also commented: 'Globalization is only a perverse and atavistic form of modernity – that, roughly of nineteenth century English and twentieth century American economic individualism – projected worldwide' (John Tomlinson, 'Vicious and Benign Universalism', in Frans Schuurman, ed., *Globalization and Development Studies: Challenges for the 21st Century*. New Delhi: Vistaar Publications, 2001, p. 46). (c) And in India, 75 per cent of people live below two dollars a day (Arjun Sengupta et al., 'India's Common People: Who Are They, How Many Are They and How Do They Live?' *Economic and Political Weekly*, 15 March 2008).
38 Given the density of population and advancing early on the path of development in India including expansion of agriculture and disappearance of forests, the tribal people in Punjab are hardly living in a manner expected of them as outlined in the 'definition of tribe' by the ministry of tribal welfare (see p.63, ch. 4).
39 Ajay Saini informs 'all other indigenous communities – the Jarawa (498), the Onge (120), the Great Andamanese (56) and the Jangil (extinct by 1920s) – lost their traditional habitats and were critically depopulated. These communities are now on the verge of extinction and fall in the category of PVTGs (particularly

200 *In lieu of conclusion*

vulnerable tribal groups)' (Ajay Saini, 'The Stolen Generations', *The Hindu Magazine*, 28 October 2018).

40 The twin processes of modernisation and globalisation have only added to the speed with which the tribal communities are going to witness their own extinction. There is absolutely no chance of their survival in the liberal-democratic system of Punjab/India or anywhere.

41 The protagonists of this weltanschauung have named definite stages of society's development from the savage to the civilised society (Morgan), from the military to the industrial society (Spencer), from the theological to the positive society (Comte).

42 'A man does not "by nature" wish to earn more and more money, but simply to live as he lives and as he is accustomed to live, and to earn as much as he is required to do so' (Max Weber, *The Protestant Ethic*, 1992, 24).

43 The tribal communities are settled in all the cities of Punjab, but their localities are hardly visible because a narrow alley leads to a cluster of irregularly packed houses. The neighbouring shop-keepers too are oblivious of their identity. They are often mistaken as migrant labour etc.

44 A Deputy Commissioner opines otherwise. 'The old practice of giving these criminals land grants in the expectation of giving up crime for agriculture should be definitely abandoned. It has not been a success, land grants should in future be reserved for the good characters and not for the thieves' (*Report* 1917, 6).

45 The Commissioner of the Multan Division notes: 'It is a difficult problem. They (Bilochis) are not taking to agriculture but only grow crops to feed the cattle. We must devise some measures of making them reduce their cattle and enabling them to pay off their burden of debt' (*Report* 1917, 7).

46 The Inspector-General of Police (Punjab) H.T. Dennys reports about the Bhats: 'In the Sialkot district the members of this tribe in Kot Chak Lala still continue to give trouble. Over one-third of the crime of one police station is attributed to them. They are violent criminals and instances of their daring assaults even on government servants are not wanting. The Bhats in other Kots of Jhammat, Jharianwala and Ratta Dhara are better behaved and make an attempt to earn a living by agriculture' (*Report* 1917, 6). The *Report* also mentions the case of Pakhiwaras: 'The continued and strenuous endeavours on the part of the district authorities as well as the Salvation Army have entirely failed to make any good impression on these criminals (ibid, 5).

47 One may note that various tribes have taken vows of different sorts justifying their nomadism and lifestyle until they regain their lost kingdom.

48 '[I]n the words of Mrs. Kirkland, because if the rich and the rulers of that time were generous too, the gentlemen like Sultana would not have become dacoits' (Sher 1966, 159).

49 B.D. Sharma, IAS collector and district magistrate of Bastar, in a personal interview in February 2008 narrated an anecdote that when their team, including the concerned minister, went to a tribal village and asked people for some aid etc., none responded. After much insistence, one fellow came to him and returned two hundred-rupee notes saying: 'Last time you gave me this money. It is your's'.

50 B.P. Singh notes about the Pangwals where he interviewed a pony owner who would take uphill three trips of load only per day to a construction site in Mindhal. On asking why he did not take five trips per day that he could, the reply was, *bechara thak jayega phir kal kaam kaise hoga? Iski bhi to jaan hai.* The poor guy (pony) will get too tired to resume work the next day. He too is a living being (Birinder Pal Singh, *Economy and Society in the Himalayas: Social Formation in Pangi Valley*. New Delhi: Ajanta, 1996).

51 Kaul and Tomkins write: 'They knew their own powers, and though they never unnecessarily used violence, they never scrupled to use force if it was necessary for

securing the jewels, or for rescuing one of their party (1914, 66). The Inspector-General of Police (Punjab) mentions the trait of a notorious community called Janglis in the colonial times: 'They are generally averse to homicide and garrotting is not in their game' (*The Tribune*, 3 March 1961).

52 *The Tribune*, 13 April 1983 reports the case of an expert member of this tribe who was never caught: 'Mangroo was caught because he was looking for a lantern to light it up since there was no electricity at that time. He hit a utensil in the kitchen that woke up the members of the house and nabbed him.'

53 There could be some respite to these people, at least in theory, in the socialist system of politics and administration that intends to fight exploitation of nature and in culture. But there too it is impossible because that system too is given to modernisation and development, which inadvertently debunks tradition, the hallmark of tribal communities. The tradition, however, stands qualified. It means to retain those features of the tribal culture and society that promote harmony between nature and culture; that integrates an individual with the cosmic; that which supports all-inclusive organic growth without generating toxic wastes; where every person labours to fulfil basic human needs.

Glossary

adivasis   indigenous people
amrit   nectar; sweetened water for baptising to Sikhism
amritdhari   khalsa; lit. one who has taken *amrit*
anna   old Indian rupee had 16 annas, now it has 100 paisa
aparigraha   voluntary poverty; non-possession
atma   soul
atta   flour
balti   bucket
baltian   buckets
baoli   small water reservoir
basti   colony, settlement
bathhal/tasla   shallow iron pan
baur   an animal trap
bawar/wanwar   noose
bazi   play; acrobatics/jumps
been/bin   a musical instrument made of gourd pipe
begaar   unpaid labour; wages
behrupia   with many faces/forms
bhapas   khatri Sikh traders that migrated from west Punjab in 1947
bhari   a bundle of wheat corn
bhart   bards
bhukki   poppy husk
bigha   land measuring a thousand square yards
billi da panja   cat's paw
billi di jer   cat's placenta
biradari   brotherhood; community
bolian   folk verses
botianwale   owners of female camel
chaku-chhurian   knives
chara   green fodder
charpai/khat   netted cot
chhabrian   baskets
chhaj   winnowing pan made of reeds

chhaj todna   breaking of a winnowing pan (in marriage ceremony)
chhanra   sieves
chhiku   small iron container
chhotu   little lad or boy
chimte   tongs
chittha   an identity card (of Bauria)
chowkidar/chaukidar   watchman
chula utarna   to dislodge the pivot (of the gate)
chulah   earthen furnace
dakaiti   dacoity
daku   dacoit
daru   liquor; medicine
deras   camps
desi juti   traditional shoes of leather
desi   traditional
dhaar or *badh*   sharp edge of the blade
dhaba   Punjabi eatery (roadside)
dhantera   custom of buying new utensils before Diwali
dharna   squatting in protest
dhol   drum
diku   outsider
doab   area between two rivers – Satluj and Beas – in Punjab
gadha   donkey
gadhewalas   who keep donkeys
gadhuian/kadhuian   large needles
garam kam   heated-iron work
gharana   school of Indian classical music; lineage
ghee   butter oil
gherao   to encircle; to block
ghumiar   pot-maker
giddha   Punjabi women's folk dance
goras   white men
gotra/got   clan name; surname
grehastha   family life
gur   jaggery
gurukul ashram   traditional residential school (usually in the forest)
haat   bazaar (temporary); a shop
hafta   a week; 'weekly' bribe
hansli   neck ornament
hath-khaddis   handlooms
hokre   hawker's cry
hukka   smoking pipe
innu   cushioned loop for head to carry load
janj ghar   marriage palace
jatha   a band of persons

jauhar   self-sacrificing ritual by Rajput women
jeb-katri   pickpocket
jharni   iron sieve
jholi   sling bag
jude   small brooms
julahas   weavers
juratwala   one with guts
kabad   scrap
kabadiye   scrap pickers
kabutri   female pigeon; a damsel
kacha   mud house; not made of concrete (*pucca*); unripe
kadahiyan   frying pans
kadi-jindra   a kind of secure lock
kahi   Saccharum spontaneum
kalan   pedigrees
kanal   one eighth of an acre of land
kanghi   comb
kanian   reeds
karva chauth   day of married woman's fast before Diwali
keshadhari   a person with uncut hair
khaddar   coarse cotton
khanda   double-edged sword
khoji   tracer
khura-khoj labbanwale   tracers
kirat karo   doing labour
kot   settlement
kulli(s)   hut(s)
kundi   hook
lambardar   village headman
lassi   butter milk
loh-sandan   iron implements
loh-vastuan   iron items
lun   salt
maanje   large brooms
mahant   priest
mandi   market
mashki   water carrier
matkas   pitchers
mazdoor   a daily wage worker
miri   temporal
misls   confederacies
mittha   sweet
moksha   salvation
murha   sitting stool made of reeds
murki   small earrings

murtis   sculptures
Naam japo   recite the name (of God)
nath   nose ring
Natni   female Nat
natya   drama
naukar   a servant; one paid monthly or annually
pakhis   temporary shelters
panj piaras   five loved ones (Sikhs)
pardhan   local head; president
parmatma   supreme soul, that is, God
patari   cane basket
peehri   genealogy
penja/tadi   cotton carder
phirni   outer road of the village
pir (*pirh*)   threshing ground for the harvested crop
piri   spiritual
poni   small sieve
poorna swaraj   complete self-rule
praja   public
prandas   braids
pucca   concrete; ripe
purushartha   lit. meaning of being human
putt   son
rabb di raza   god's will
rajya   rule; state
rehra   large cart
rehri   small cart
riri or *phakka*   part of harvested grain given free from the last threshing floor
rishi   saint/sage
saan   hone
saf   mattress
sahsi/himmatwala   a courageous person
saiqal   to polish
salwar   loose trousers
Sammi   a form of folk dance
sampark   contact
saniyas   renunciation
shajra-i-nasab   genealogy
siapa   breast-beating
sila   ears of wheat
sindhoor   vermillion
siri/seeri   share cropper
sirkanda   elephant grass
sirkis   huts
sucha/pavittar   sacred

suian   small needles
swachh   clean; fresh
tanda   caravan; a Banjara camp
tangli   pitchfork
tasle   iron pans
teej   third day of the month
teli   oilman
thana   police station
thanda   cold; unheated
tharah   platform of bricks
theka   contract; liquor shop
thhande bechna   selling cold drinks
tokaris   small baskets
tokre   large iron containers
toori   wheat chaff
toshakhana   treasury
ull   nickname
vadhai   felicitations
vadhai dena   to felicitate
vadhayian   felicitations; congratulations
vanaj   business
vangan-churian   bangles
vanprastha   march towards the forest
variksha   tree
vimukt jatis   denotified tribes
wand chhako   to share one's earnings with others
zamindar   landlord

References

Ahmad, Aijaz. 2002. *On Communalism and Globalisation: Offensives of the Far Right*. New Delhi: Three Essays.
Annual Report on the Administration of the Criminal Tribes in the Punjab for the Year Ending 31st December, 1936. 1938. Lahore: Superintendent Government Printing, Punjab.
Annual Report on the Administration of the Criminal Tribes in the Punjab for the Year Ending 31st December, 1938. 1940. Lahore: Superintendent, Government Printing, Punjab.
Arnold, David. 1985. 'Crime and Crime Control in Madras 1858–1947', in A. Yang (ed.), *Crime and Criminality in British India*. Tucson: University of Arizona Press.
ASER.(*Annual Survey of Education Report 2005*). 2007. New Delhi: Pratham.
ASER. 2015. img.asercentre.org/docsPublications/ASER%20Reports/ASER%202015: %20Punjab/aser2015punjabfindings.pdf (accessed 19 January 2018).
Bachrach, P. and M. Baratz. 1970. *Power and Poverty: Theory and Practice*. London and New York: Oxford University Press.
Baines, J.A. 1893. *Census of India, 1891, General Report*. London: Eyre and Spottiswoode.
Bains, A.S. 1982. 'Judgement', in *Civil Writ Petition No. 132 of 1975*. Chandigarh: Punjab and Haryana High Court.
Banaji, Jairus. 1970. 'The Crisis of British Anthropology', *New Left Review*, Vol. I, No. 64, November–December, pp. 71–85.
Banga, Indu. 1978. *Agrarian System of the Sikhs: Late Eighteenth and Early Nineteenth Century*. New Delhi: Manohar.
Barik, Satyasundar. 2019. 'The Guardians of Niyamgiri', *The Hindu*, March 17.
Bauman, Zygmunt. 2004. *Wasted Lives: Modernity and Its Outcasts*. Cambridge: Polity Press.
Baviskar, Amita. 1995/2004. *In the Belly of the River: Tribal Conflicts Over Development in the Narmada Valley*, 2nd edn. New Delhi: Oxford University Press.
Bayley, D.H. 1976. *The Police and Political Development in India*. Berkeley: University of California Press.
Bhalla, G.S. and G.K. Chadha. 1982. 'Green Revolution and the Small Peasant: A Study of Income Distribution in Punjab Agriculture', Vol. II, *Economic and Political Weekly*, Vol. XVII, No. 21, May 22, pp. 870–77.
Bird-David, Nurit. 1992. 'Beyond "The Original Affluent Society": A Culturalist Reformulation', *Current Anthropology*, Vol. 33, No. 1, February, pp. 25–47.

References

Booth-Tucker, F. 1923. 'The Criminal Tribes of India', *Journal of the Royal Society of Arts*, Vol. 70, No. 3061.
Census of India (Punjab). 2011. Chandigarh: Punjab Government.
Chahal, M.S. 2007. *Punjab ka Bawaria Kabila: Parichay, Sanskriti evam Bhasha* (Hindi). Patiala: Twenty First Century Publications.
Chaudhury, Nazmul et al. 2005. 'Missing in Action: Teacher and Health Worker Absence in Developing Countries', *World Bank Report*, May 19.
Damodaran, Vinita. 2011. 'Colonial Construction of the "tribe" in India: The Case of Chotanagpur', pp. 55–87, in Biswamoy Pati (ed.), *Adivasis in Colonial India*. New Delhi: ICHR and Orient Blackswan.
Darya. 1997. *Punjab de Sansi Kabile da Sabhyachar* (Punjabi). Amritsar: Lok Sahit Parkashan.
Das Gupta, P.K. 1982. 'Transformation of Tribal Economy in an Industrial Context: A Case of the Ho in Singhbhum', pp. 355–68, in K.S. Singh (ed.), *Economies of the Tribes and Their Transformation*. New Delhi: Concept Publishing Company.
Deswal, K.R. 1993. 'Ex-Criminal Tribes: Born Criminals?' *The Tribune*, 2 January.
Dhillon, K.S. 1996. 'Servility and Oppression: Twin Legacies of the Police in India', in a Seminar of the Institute of Punjab Studies, Chandigarh, February 26–28.
Diwana, Mohan Singh. 1933/2014. *A History of Punjabi Literature (1100–1932)*. Patiala: Punjabi University.
Dreze, Jean and Amartya Sen. 2002. *India: Development and Participation*, 2 edn. New Delhi: Oxford University Press.
Ellul, Jacques. 1969. *Violence: Reflections from a Christian Perspective*, Trans. C.G. Kings. New York: Seabury Press.
Encyclopaedia of Indian Tribes and Castes. 2004. New Delhi: Cosmo Publications.
Encyclopaedia of Sikhism, Vol. I-IV. 1995–1998. Patiala: Punjabi University.
Fox, R.G. 1987. *Lions of the Punjab: Culture in the Making*. New Delhi: Archives Publishers.
Freitag, Sandra B. 1991. 'Crime in the Social Order of Colonial North India', *Modern Asian Studies*, Vol. 25, No. 2, pp. 227–61.
Furer-Haimendorf, Christoph von. 1989. *Tribes of India: The Struggle for Survival*. New Delhi: Oxford University Press.
Gandhi, M.K. 1908. *Hind Swaraj*. Ahmedabad: Navjivan Press.
Gandhi, Rajmohan. 2013. *Punjab: From Aurangzeb to Mountbatten*. New Delhi: Aleph.
Ghuman, R.S. 2008. 'Growth and Structural Changes in Punjab Since 1960s: A Politico-Economic Analysis', paper presented at National University of Singapore, Singapore. (unpublished).
Giddens, Anthony. 1990. *The Consequences of Modernity*. Cambridge: Polity Press.
Gill, S.S. 2010. 'Viability Crisis of the Small and Marginal Farmers and Response of the Farmers' Movement in Punjab', pp. 231–44, in Birinder Pal Singh (ed.), *Punjab Peasantry in Turmoil*. New Delhi: Manohar.
Goldthorpe, J. 1987. *Social Mobility and Class Structure in Modern Britain*. Oxford: Clarendon Press.
Grann, David. 2017. *Killers of the Flower Moon: Oil, Money, Murder and the Birth of the FBI*. London: Simon & Schuster.
Grewal, J.S. 1990. *History of the Sikhs*. New Delhi: Cambridge University Press.
Guha, Ramchandra. 1994. 'Fighting for the Forest: State Forestry and Social Change in Tribal India', in Oliver Mendelsohn and Upendra Baxi (eds.), *The Rights of the Subordinated Peoples*. New Delhi: Oxford University Press.

Gupta, Dipankar. 1985. 'The Communalising of Punjab, 1980–1985', *Economic and Political Weekly*, Vol. XX, No. 28, July 13.

———.1992. 'Ethnic Images and Their Correlative Spaces: An Essay on Some Aspects of Sikh Identity and Perceptions in Contemporary Punjab', *Contributions to Indian Sociology (n.s.)*, Vol. 26, No. 2, pp. 223–44.

Habib, Irfan. 1976. 'Jatts of the Punjab and Sind', pp. 92–103, in Harbans Singh and N. Gerald Barrier (eds.), *Punjab: Past and Present: Essays in Honour of Dr. Ganda Singh*. Patiala: Punjabi University.

Hardiman, David. 2011. 'Knowledge of the Bhils and their System of Healing', pp. 293–315, in Biswamoy Pati (ed.), *Adivasis in Colonial India*. New Delhi: ICHR and Orient Blackswan.

The Hindu. 2018. 'In Odisha, Government Schools Lose Students', January 7.

Hindustan Times. 2018. 'State Students Off the Mark in Math, Fare Better in Languages', February 5.

Hira, G.S. 2008.'Depleting Groundwater, Causes and Remedial Measures', in A.S. Dhesi and Gurmail Singh (eds.), *Rural Development in Punjab: A Success Story Going Astray*. New Delhi: Routledge.

Ibbetson, Denzil and H.A. Rose. 1883/1970. *A Glossary of the Tribes and Castes of the Punjab and North-West Frontier Province*, Vol. II–III. Patiala: Punjab Languages Department.

India Edunews.net. 2008. '50 Percent Students Cannot Read Punjabi', http://india edunews.net/Punjab(accessed 12 July 2012).

Institute for Development and Communication. 1996. *Status of Depressed Scheduled Castes in Punjab*. Chandigarh: IDC.

Iyer, Raghavan. 1993/2005. *The Essential Writings of Mohandas Gandhi*. New Delhi: Oxford University Press.

Jaggi, Rattan Singh. 2005. *Sikh Panth Vishavkosh* (Punjabi). Patiala: Gur Rattan Publishers.

Jayaraman, Gayatri. 2018. 'The Invisible Nomads of Madurai', *Hindustan Times*, October 8.

Jodhka, Surinder. 2002. 'Caste and Untouchability in Rural Punjab', *Economic and Political Weekly*, May 11, pp. 1813–22.

Joshi, R.S. 1982. 'Impact of Industrialisation on Tribals: A Case Study of Bailadila (Bastar)', pp. 369–80, in K.S. Singh (ed.), *Economies of the Tribes and Their Transformation*. New Delhi: Concept Publishing Company.

Judge, Paramjit Singh. 1992. *Insurrection to Agitation: The Naxalite Movement in Punjab*. Bombay: Popular Parkashan.

Judge, Paramjit Singh and Gurpreet Bal. 2008. 'Understanding the Paradox of Changes Among Dalits in Punjab', *Economic and Political Weekly*, October 11, pp. 49–55.

———. 2009. *Mapping Dalits: Contemporary Reality and Future Prospects in Punjab*. Jaipur: Rawat.

Kaul, Hari Kishan and L.L. Tomkins. 1914. *Report on Questions Relating to the Administration of Criminal and Wandering Tribes in the Punjab*. Lahore: Superintendent, Government Printing, Punjab.

Kaur, Amanjot. 2014a. *Punjab de Gaadi Loharan de phirtu jivan da samaj vigyanak adhyan*, (Punjabi). M.Phil dissertation (unpublished), Punjabi University, Patiala.

Kaur, Bhupinder. 2010a. *Beet de Gujjaran da Sabhyachar* (Punjabi). Punjabi University, Patiala.

References

Kaur, Harinder. 2010b. 'Bangala', pp. 51–73, in Birinder Pal Singh (ed.), *'Criminal' Tribes of Punjab*. New Delhi: Routledge.

Kaur, Harinder. 2010c. 'Barad', pp. 74–92, in Birinder Pal Singh (ed.), *'Criminal' Tribes of Punjab*. New Delhi: Routledge.

Kaur, Kirandeep. 2016. *Sansi kabile diyan aurtan vich apradh da samaj vigyanak adhyan*, (Punjabi). M.Phil dissertation (unpublished), Punjabi University, Patiala.

Kaur, Malkit. 2010d. 'Gandhila', pp. 93–102, in Birinder Pal Singh (ed.), *'Criminal' Tribes of Punjab*. New Delhi: Routledge.

Kaur, Manpreet. 2018. *Intergenerational Occupational Change: A Sociological Study of the Barad Tribe in Punjab*, Ph.D. thesis submitted to the Punjabi University, Patiala.

Kaur, Manvir. 2014b. *Bazigar aurtan de parampragat kitte da ethnographic adhyan*, (Punjabi). M.Phil dissertation (unpublished), Punjabi University, Patiala.

Kaviraj, Sudipta. 1984. 'On the Crisis of Political Institutions in India', *Contributions to Indian Sociology (ns)*, Vol. 18, No. 2, pp. 223–43.

———(ed.). 1997. *Politics in India*. New Delhi: Oxford University Press.

Kazak, Kirpal. 1990. *Sikligar Kabile da Sabhyachar* (Punjabi). Patiala: Punjabi University.

———. 2005. *Gaadi Lohar Kabile da Sabhyachar* (Punjabi). Patiala: Punjabi University.

Kingdon, G.G. 2007. 'The Progress of School Education in India', *Oxford Review of Economic Policy*, Vol. 23, No. 2, pp. 168–95.

Kohli, Atul. 1997. 'Crisis of Governability', pp. 383–95, in Sudipta Kaviraj (ed.), *Politics in India*. New Delhi: Oxford University Press.

Kulkarni, S.D. 1982. 'Alienation and Restoration of Adivasis' Lands in Maharashtra', pp. 417–29, in K.S. Singh (ed.), *Economies of the Tribes and Their Transformation*. New Delhi: Concept Publishing Company.

Kumar, Deepak. 2010. 'Nat', pp. 103–11, in Birinder Pal Singh (ed.), *'Criminal' Tribes of Punjab*. New Delhi: Routledge.

Lal, Vinay. 'Modernity, Frameworks of Knowledge, and the Ecological Survival of Plurality: An Introduction to the Multiversity', http://vlal.bol.ucla.edu/multiversity/. (accessed 19 August 2018).

Lipset, S.M. and R. Bendix. 1959. *Social Mobility in Industrial Society*. Berkeley and Los Angeles: University of California Press.

Madhopuri, Balbir. 2004. *Chhangia Rukh* (autobiography in Punjabi). Chandigarh: Lokgeet Parkashan.

Major, Andrew J. 1999. 'State and Criminal Tribes in Colonial Punjab: Surveillance, Control and Reclamation of the "Dangerous Classes"', *Modern Asian Studies*, Vol. 33, No. 3, pp. 657–88.

Majumdar, D.N. 1961/1965. *Races and Cultures of India*. Bombay: Asia Publishing House.

Mallick, Md. Ayub. 2016. 'Aspects of Positive Discrimination and Tribal Development in India', *South Asian Survey*, Vol. 20, No. 2, pp. 163–90.

Mathur, K.S. 1972. 'Tribe in India: A Problem of Identification and Integration', pp. 457–61, in K.S. Singh (ed.), *Tribal Situation in India: Proceedings of a Seminar*. Simla: Indian Institute of Advanced Study.

McLuhan, Marshall. 1964. *Understanding Media*. New York: McGraw-Hill.

Misra, P.K. 1982. 'Tribal Economy in Southern Zone,' pp. 82–94, in K.S. Singh (ed.), *Economies of the Tribes and Their Transformation*. New Delhi: Concept Publishing Company.

Motiram, Sripad and Ashish Singh. 2012. 'How Close Does the Apple Fall to the Tree? Some Evidence from India on Intergenerational Occupational Mobility', *Economic and Political Weekly*, Vol. 47, No. 40, pp. 56–65.

Nabha, Bhai Kahn Singh. 1995. *Hum Hindu Nahin* (Punjabi). Amritsar: Singh Brothers.

Nasr, Seyyed Hossein. 1976. *Man and Nature: The Spiritual Crisis of Modern Man*. London: Unwin Paperbacks 1968, Mandala edn.

Nehru, Jawaharlal. 1961/1977. *The Discovery of India*. Bombay: Asia Publishing House.

Oommen, T.K. 2007. *Knowledge and Society: Situating Sociology and Social Anthropology*. New Delhi: Oxford University Press.

Pace, David. 1986. *Claude Levi-Strauss: The Bearer of Ashes*. London: Ark.

Padel, Felix. 2011. 'Mining Projects and Cultural Genocide: Colonial Roots of Present Conflicts', pp. 316–37, in Biswamoy Pati (ed.), *Adivasis in Colonial India*. New Delhi: ICHR and Orient Blackswan.

Pantham, Thomas. 1995. *Political Theories and Social Reconstruction: A Critical Survey of the Literature on India*. New Delhi: Sage.

Parsons, Talcott. 1951. *The Social System*. New York: The Free Press.

Pettigrew, Joyce. 1975. *The Robber Noblemen: A Study of the Political System of the Sikh Jats*. London: Routledge and Kegan Paul.

———. 1995. *The Sikhs of Punjab: Unheard Voices of State and Guerrilla Violence*. London: Zed Books.

Piketty, Thomas. 2014. *Capital in the Twenty First Century*, Trans. Arthur Goldhammer. Cambridge: Harvard University Press.

Polanyi, Karl. 1957. *The Great Transformation: The Political and Economic Origins of Our Time*. Boston: Beacon Press.

Portman, M.V. 1899. *A History of Our Relations with the Andamanese*. Calcutta: Superintendent of Government Printing.

Prasad, Archana. 2011. 'Unravelling the Forms of "Adivasi" Organisation and Resistance in Colonial India', pp. 216–36, in Biswamoy Pati (ed.), *Adivasis in Colonial India*. New Delhi: ICHR and Orient Blackswan.

Punjab Government. 2007. *Statistical Abstract of Punjab 2007*. Chandigarh: Punjab Government.

———. n.d. *Report of the Evaluation Committee on Welfare: Regarding the Welfare of Scheduled Castes, Backward Classes and Denotified Tribes in Punjab State for the Period Commencing from 15 August 1947(December 1965 – August 1966)*. Chandigarh: Department of Welfare.

Radhakrishna, Meena. 2001. *Dishonoured by History: 'Criminal Tribes' and British Colonial Policy*. New Delhi: Orient Longman.

Raghavaiah, V. 1971. *Tribal Revolts*. Nellore: Andhra Rashtra Adimajati Sevak Sangh.

Ram, Ronki. 2010. 'Social Exclusion and Social Resistance: Exploring Jutt-Dalit Conflicts in Punjab', pp. 265–96, in Birinder Pal Singh (ed.), *Punjab Peasantry in Turmoil*. New Delhi: Manohar.

Rani, Sharmila. 2019. *Punjab de Malwa khetar vich Bangala kabile de jivika diyan vangiyan: Ik ethnographic adhyan*, (Punjabi). Ph.D. thesis submitted to Punjabi University, Patiala.

Ray, Niharranjan. 1972. 'Introductory Address', pp. 3–24, in K.S. Singh (ed.), *Tribal Situation in India: Proceedings of a Seminar*. Simla: Indian Institute of Advanced Study.

―――. 1975. *The Sikh Gurus and the Sikh Society: A Study in Social Analysis*. New Delhi: Munshiram Manoharlal.

Report on the Administration of Criminal Tribes in the Punjab For the Year Ending December 1917. 1918. Lahore: Superintendent, Government Printing, Punjab.

Report on the Administration of Criminal Tribes in the Punjab For the Year Ending December 1922. 1923. Lahore: Superintendent, Government Printing, Punjab.

Report on the Administration of Criminal Tribes in the Punjab For the Year Ending December 1926. 1927. Lahore: Superintendent, Government Printing, Punjab.

Report on the Administration of Criminal Tribes in the Punjab For the Year Ending 31st December 1949. 1952. Simla: Controller of Printing and Stationery, Punjab.

Report on the Administration of the Punjab and Its Dependencies For the Years 1905–06. 1907. Lahore: Punjab Government Press.

Report on the Administration of the Punjab and Its Dependencies For the Years 1908–09. 1910. Lahore: Punjab Government Press.

Report on the Working of the Criminal Tribes Act (Act XVII of 1871) For the Year 1901. 1902. Lahore: Punjab Government Press.

Report on the Working of the Criminal Tribes Act (Act XVII of 1871) For the Year Ending 31st December 1902. 1903. Lahore: Punjab Government Press.

Report on the Working of the Criminal Tribes Act (Act XVII of 1871) For the Year 1910. 1911. Simla: Punjab Government Branch Press.

Report on the Working of the Criminal Tribes Act (Act III of 1911) For the Year 1911. 1912. Simla: Punjab Government Branch Press.

Report on the Working of the Criminal Tribes For the Year Ending December 1916. 1917. Simla: Superintendent, Government Printing, Punjab.

Robertson, Ronald. 1992. *Globalisation: Social Theory and Global Culture*. London: Sage.

Sachidananda. 1979. *The Changing Munda*. New Delhi: Concept Publishing Company.

Sahlins, Marshall. 'The Original Affluent Society', www.primitivism.com/original-affluent.htm (accessed 8 September 2018).

Sanave, Vilas. 2005. 'Phanse-Pardhis of Kolhapur: A Tribe in Transition', in Priyaram M. Chacko (ed.), *Tribal Communities and Social Change*. New Delhi: Sage.

Saraswati, Baidyanath. 1993. 'Tribal Lifestyle: The Changing Context', pp. 23–31, in Mrinal Miri (ed.), *Continuity and Change in Tribal Society*. Shimla: Indian Institute of Advanced Study.

Sharma, B.D. 2010. *Unbroken History of Broken Promises: Indian State and the Tribal People*. New Delhi: Sahyog Pustak Kuteer.

Sharma, D.R. 1992. 'A Bridge Bar', *The Tribune*, December 20.

Sharma, Suresh. 1994. *Tribal Identity and the Modern World*. New Delhi: Sage and Tokyo: United Nations University Press.

Shekhar, H.S. 2017. *The Adivasi Will Not Dance*. New Delhi: Speaking Tiger.

Sher, Sher Singh. 1965. *The Sansis of Punjab: A Gypsy and De-Notified Tribe of Rajput Origin*. New Delhi: Munshiram Manoharlal.

―――. 1966. *The Sikligars of Punjab (A Gypsy Tribe)*. New Delhi and Jullundur City: Sterling Publishers.

Shiva, Vandana. 1992. *The Violence of Green Revolution: Third World Agriculture, Ecology and Politics*. Goa: Other India Press.

Simhadri, Y.C. 1991. *Denotified Tribes: A Sociological Analysis*. Delhi: Classical Publishing Co.

Singh, Birinder Pal (ed.). 1996. *Economy and Society in the Himalayas: Social Formation in Pangi Valley*. New Delhi: Ajanta.

―――. 2002. *Violence as Political Discourse: Sikh Militancy Confronts the Indian State*. Shimla: Indian Institute of Advanced Study.

―――. 2005. 'Punjab the "best" State! – Really?' *The Tribune*, September 11.

―――. 2008a. 'An Ethnographic Study of the Denotified, Nomadic and Semi-Nomadic Tribes of Punjab', Report submitted to the Punjab Government, Department of Social Welfare, Chandigarh.

―――. 2008b. 'Ex-Criminal Tribes of Punjab', *Economic and Political Weekly*, Vol. 43, No. 51, pp. 58–65, 20 December.

―――.2010a. 'Bauria', pp. 1–25, in Birinder Pal Singh (ed.),'*Criminal*' *Tribes of Punjab*. New Delhi: Routledge.

―――. 2010b. 'Bazigar Banjara', pp. 26–50, in Birinder Pal Singh (ed.),'*Criminal*' *Tribes of Punjab*. New Delhi: Routledge.

―――. (ed.). 2010c. '*Criminal*' *Tribes of Punjab: A Social-Anthropological Inquiry*. New Delhi: Routledge.

―――. 2010d. 'Denotified Tribes of Punjab: Economic Ethnography and Political Economic Explanation', pp. 409–26, in R.S. Ghuman et al. (eds.), *Globalisation and Change: Perspectives from Punjab*. Jaipur: Rawat.

―――(ed.). 2010e. *Punjab Peasantry in Turmoil*. New Delhi: Manohar.

―――. 2012. 'Gandhian Perspective on Tribal Resources and the Modern State', *Gandhi Marg*, Vol. 34, No. 2–3, July–December, pp. 185–204.

―――. 2018. *Sikhs in the Deccan and North-East India*. London and New York: Routledge.

Singh, Ganda. 1956. *A Brief Account of the Sikhs*. Amritsar: Shiromani Gurdwara Parbandhak Committee.

Singh, Indera P. 1975. 'A Sikh Village', pp. 272–97, in Milton Singer (ed.), *Traditional India: Structures and Change*. Jaipur: Rawat.

Singh, K.S. (ed.). 1982. *Economies of the Tribes and Their Transformation*. New Delhi: Concept Publishing Company.

―――. 1993. 'Tribal Perspectives – 1969–1990', pp. 5–10, in Mrinal Miri (ed.), *Continuity and Change in Tribal Society*. Shimla: Indian Institute of Advanced Study.

―――(ed.). 1994/2001. *People of India, National Series Vol. III: The Scheduled Tribes*. New Delhi: Anthropological Survey of India and Oxford University Press.

――― (ed.). 2003. *People of India: Punjab*, Vol. XXXVII. New Delhi: Anthropological Survey of India and Manohar.

Singh, Lakhwinder and Sukhpal Singh. 2002. 'Deceleration of Economic Growth in Punjab: Evidence, Explanation, and a Way-Out', *Economic and Political Weekly*, Vol. 37, No. 6, February 9.

Singh, Narinder. 2015. *An Ethnographic Study of Tribal Children from 06–15 Years in the Patiala City of Punjab*, Ph.D. thesis (unpublished), Punjabi University, Patiala.

Singh, Randhir. 1999. 'Of Nationalism in India: Yesterday, Today and Tomorrow', *Mainstream*, August 14.

Singh, Sant Parkash. 1961. 'Activities of Notorious Criminals', *The Tribune*, March 3.

Sinha, Dikshit. 1982. 'Economy of the Hill Kharia of Purulia', pp. 159–69, in K.S. Singh (ed.), *Economies of the Tribes and Their Transformation*. New Delhi: Concept Publishing Company.

Srinivas, M.N. 1962. *The Caste in Modern India and Other Essays*. Bombay: Asia Book House.

State of Environment Punjab-2007. Chandigarh: Punjab State Council for Science & Technology and New Delhi: The Energy & Resources Institute (TERI).

Sundar, Nandani. 2007. *Subalterns and Sovereigns: An Anthropological History of Bastar (1854–2006)*, 2 edn. New Delhi: Oxford University Press.

Tyagi, Mohan. 2013. *Bazigar Kabile da Sabhiyachar* (Punjabi). New Delhi: National Book Trust of India.

Valjot, Inder Singh. 2009. *Guar Rajputan/Bazigaran da Itihas* (Punjabi). Chandigarh: Lokgeet Parkashan.

Varady, Robert G. 1979. 'North Indian Banjaras: Their Evolution as Transporters', *South Asia: Journal of South Asian Studies (ns)*, Vol. II, No. 1–2, March and September, pp. 1–18.

Weber, Max. 1992/1930. *The Protestant Ethic and the Spirit of Capitalism*. New Delhi: Routledge.

Xaxa, Virginius. 2008. *State, Society, and Tribes: Issues in Post-Colonial India*. New Delhi: Pearson Longman.

Yang, Anand A. 1985. 'Dangerous Castes and Tribes: The Criminal Tribes Act and the Magahiya Doms of Northeast India', pp. 108–27, in A. Yang (ed.), *Crime and Criminality in British India*. Tucson: University of Arizona Press.

Index

acrobatic(s) 67, 69, 83, 85, 104, 141, 154, 160–1
ancestor(s) ix, 3, 5–6, 66, 79, 82, 90–1, 95, 151, 163, 170
ASER 181–2, 198

Baines, J.A. 31, 68–9, 90
Balmik viii, 3, 22, 136
Bangala 3–4, 6–7, 64–5, 76–7, 79, 82, 104–5, 107–9, 141, 148, 154, 158, 160, 168, 177, 184, 187, 196
Barad 3–4, 6, 31, 33, 49, 64, 79–81, 105, 107–9, 143, 145, 154–9, 160–1, 183–4, 188
baur 67, 73
Bauria ix, 2, 6–7, 28, 30–1, 33, 37–9, 42, 57, 59, 64–7, 72–6, 82, 87–8, 102, 104–5, 107–9, 136, 144, 154, 158, 170, 178, 183, 187, 189, 191, 198
bazi 67, 70–1, 104
Bazigar ix, 3–4, 6, 31, 33, 49, 64–5, 67, 72, 87, 104–5, 107–9, 141, 143–5, 154–7, 160, 178, 183, 187
Bird-David, N. 164–5
broom(s) 3, 49, 71, 81, 83, 104, 150, 154

Chamar viii, 3, 23, 136
colonial viii, 1–3, 8–9, 11, 19–20, 26–7, 31, 37–8, 42, 50–1, 54–60, 64, 76, 99, 140, 148–9, 152–3, 167–8, 170, 172–5, 178, 180, 184, 187–8, 190–1, 201
crime viii, 27, 31, 33–8, 52, 56–7, 66, 75, 77, 89–90, 140, 167–8, 189–92, 200
Criminal Tribes Act (CTA) 1, 4, 8, 25–30, 39, 41–2, 46–7, 60, 65, 140, 149, 163, 167–71, 188, 190

criminal viii–ix, 1–2, 9, 11, 30, 32–3, 37, 39, 59, 83, 88, 99, 148, 163, 191

dacoities 34, 38
dacoits 38, 140, 170, 190, 200
denotified viii–x, 1–2, 4, 6, 8, 28, 38, 56, 64–5, 99, 101–2, 170–1, 178, 193
detribalisation 12, 169, 184
DNT 28, 65, 100–1, 103
Doaba 6, 13, 23, 59, 71, 79, 158, 196

economy 3–4, 10–11, 17, 23, 148–9, 151–2, 155, 162, 164–5, 169, 172, 177–8, 180–1, 195, 200
education 10–11, 24, 30, 40–1, 49–50, 56, 60, 62, 65, 103, 113–14, 139, 150–1, 156–7, 159, 161, 169, 178–9, 181–4, 197–9
ethics 93, 175, 191–2
ethnographic viii–x, 1–2, 5, 11, 64, 67, 72, 99, 104, 136, 163

forest viii, 3–4, 8, 22, 28–9, 41, 43, 58, 63, 66, 68, 76, 86, 119, 126, 140, 149, 153–4, 158, 162–9, 171, 177, 187, 190, 195–6, 199
Furer-Haimendorf, C. 166, 172–3

gaadi 95, 143
Gaadi lohar ix, 4, 64, 67, 94–7, 104–5, 107–9, 136, 140–1, 143, 145, 155–6, 168, 187
Gandhi, M.K. 10, 19, 121, 165–6, 194
Gandhi, Rajmohan 13–14
Gandhila 3, 6–7, 31, 33, 38, 64–5, 77, 82–4, 105, 107–9, 154, 187, 189, 199
globalisation 185–6, 193, 200

Index

Guha, Ramchandra 172–3
Gujjar 4, 64, 97–9, 104, 107–9, 133, 141, 145, 155–6, 168, 187, 191

Habib, Irfan 17–18
hawker 4, 83, 142, 144, 151, 153–7, 159, 160–1

Ibbetson, Denzil ix, 1, 5, 58–9, 64, 67–8, 70, 72, 75, 77, 79, 82, 84–90, 94, 163
Indian Forest Act 4, 8, 119, 140, 169, 171–2, 176
indigenous 65–6, 184–5, 193, 199
industrialisation 4, 11, 106, 139, 149, 154, 162
intergenerational (occupational change) 5, 11, 149–50, 157, 162

Judge, P.S. 21, 23–4, 150

kabad 71, 90, 107, 142, 144–5, 147, 154, 156–7, 160–1
Kaul, Hari Kishan 31–2, 34, 36, 39, 41, 46, 53, 61, 75, 83, 87, 104, 200
Kaur, Harinder 79–80, 104, 183–4
Kazak, Kirpal ix, 91, 93, 96, 105

lohar 73–4, 90–1, 94

Majha 6, 21, 71, 196
Major, Andrew 59, 170, 180
Malwa 6, 14, 22, 56, 71, 158, 196
Mazhabi viii, 18, 22–3, 136, 169–70
modernisation 4–5, 11, 21, 81, 106, 138–40, 149, 162–3, 168, 178, 184–6, 188, 193, 197, 200–1
modern occupation 10–11, 49, 138, 141, 143–4, 152–4, 158–60, 162–3, 169, 178
morality 58, 191

Nat 4, 6, 31, 33, 64–5, 67–8, 73, 83, 85, 87, 104–5, 107–9, 141, 154, 160, 168
nomadic viii–x, 1–4, 8, 25, 29, 31, 40, 43, 53, 57–9, 63–4, 66, 72, 76–8, 82, 86, 90–1, 94–5, 97, 99, 105–7, 136, 140, 143, 153, 162–4, 166–8, 174–5, 188, 190, 193

occupation viii, ix, xi, 8, 11, 24, 27, 30–1, 33, 40–1, 43, 63, 67, 79, 81–3, 89, 90, 95, 97–9, 103–7, 138–63, 167–8, 188
occupation change ix, 4–5, 11, 140, 150, 157, 161–2, 168–9, 178

peddler 68, 157, 160, 168
police 6, 8–9, 21, 27–9, 31, 33–40, 42–3, 45–6, 48, 50–8, 60–1, 69, 73, 75–6, 100, 102, 167, 169–70, 187, 189, 190–2, 194, 197, 200–1
post-colonial 2, 8–9, 51, 58, 63–4, 100, 149, 152–3, 168, 172, 174–5, 178–80, 192, 197
poverty 11, 60, 78, 100, 106, 112, 128, 131, 136, 162, 165–6, 169, 178, 187, 190
Punjab government viii, 2, 7, 30, 41, 46, 49, 52, 61, 63–5, 87, 101, 180, 182, 196
Punjabi community 11, 14, 20, 67, 114, 136, 141, 148, 171, 177, 180
Punjabi language ix, xi, 14–16, 20–1, 148, 175, 181, 198

Radhakrishna, Meena 28, 53, 59
rag-picking 4, 8, 10, 147–8, 159–60
Ray, Niharranjan 17, 24
reformatory 29–30, 41, 44–7, 60, 171
robbery 34, 36, 86, 170
Rose, H.A. ix, 1, 5, 58–9, 64, 67–8, 70, 72, 77, 79, 82, 84–90, 94, 163

Sahlins, Marshall 162–5, 167, 194
Salvation Army 26–7, 30, 43, 47, 54, 60, 190, 200
Sansi viii–x, 2–3, 6–7, 28, 30–3, 36–8, 42, 46–8, 50, 52–3, 55–61, 64–5, 75, 77, 83, 86–90, 101, 104–5, 107–9, 143, 148, 154, 156, 170, 178, 187–91, 198
Scheduled Castes viii–ix, 1, 3, 7–8, 12, 22, 63–4, 80, 103, 106, 136, 150, 171, 179, 183
Scheduled Tribes ix, 2–3, 61, 63, 100–1, 103, 105–6, 150, 171, 193
scrap 8, 71, 90, 93, 107, 144–5, 147–8, 151, 153–4, 156–7, 160–2, 168
semi-nomadic viii, x, 2, 4, 25, 97, 140, 193
settlement 6–7, 27–30, 38–50, 52, 59, 61, 66, 83, 87, 89, 95, 106, 116, 153, 170–1, 175
Sher, S.S. viii, 6, 28, 43, 54, 87–9, 91–2, 170, 190–1, 200

Sikligar viii, ix, 64–5, 67, 90–4, 104, 107–9, 133, 137, 140, 143, 145, 153, 155, 168, 187, 192

Singh, Birinder Pal 2, 5–7, 11, 21, 39, 64, 66–7, 69, 72, 83, 91, 93, 104, 136–7, 140, 145, 151, 160, 163, 168, 172, 174, 180–1, 183, 195–7, 200

Singh, K.S. 2, 66, 76–7, 80–3, 85, 90, 94, 97–9, 105, 149, 177, 191, 199

Sundar, Nandani 9, 195

thief 35, 93, 192

Tomkins, L.L. 31–2, 34, 36, 39, 41, 46, 53, 61, 75, 83, 87, 104, 200

traditional occupation ix, 3–5, 7–8, 10–11, 24, 30, 49, 69, 71–2, 76, 78, 81–5, 93, 96, 138–41, 147–63, 168–9, 178, 180, 184, 187–8

urbanisation 154, 157, 172, 177

vimukt 1–2, 6, 64, 100–1, 105, 170–1

wage labour 4, 10, 81, 83, 85, 90, 107, 140, 143, 151, 154, 156–60, 162, 168

Xaxa, Virginius 100, 103, 106

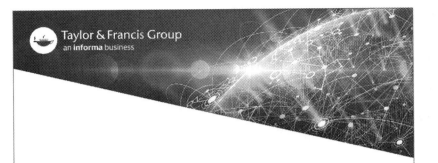

Printed in the United States
By Bookmasters